Human Rights and Drug Control

This book uses a human rights perspective – developed philosophically, politically and legally – to change the way in which we think about drug control issues.

The prohibitionist approach towards tackling the 'drugs problem' is not working. The laws and mentality that see drugs as the problem and tries to fight them makes the 'drugs problem' worse. While the law is the best-placed mechanism to regulate our actions in relation to particular drugs, this book argues against the stranglehold of the criminal law, and instead presents a human rights perspective to change the way we think about drug control issues. Part I develops a conceptual framework for human rights in the context of drug control – philosophically, politically and legally – and applies this to the domestic (UK) and international drug control system. Part II focuses on case law to illustrate both the potential and the limitations of successfully applying this unique perspective in practice. The conclusion points towards a bottom-up process for drug policy which is capable of reconfiguring the mentality of prohibition.

This book will be of interest to students and scholars of human rights, criminal law, criminology, politics and socio-legal studies.

Melissa L. Bone teaches Criminal Law and Law Justice and Society at the University of Leicester.

Human Rights and Drug Control

A New Perspective

Melissa L. Bone

Routledge
Taylor & Francis Group
LONDON AND NEW YORK

First published 2020
by Routledge
2 Park Square, Milton Park, Abingdon, Oxon OX14 4RN

and by Routledge
605 Third Avenue, New York, NY 10017

First issued in paperback 2021

Routledge is an imprint of the Taylor & Francis Group, an informa business

A GlassHouse Book

British Library Cataloguing-in-Publication Data
A catalogue record for this book is available from the British Library

Library of Congress Cataloging-in-Publication Data
Names: Bone, Melissa L. author.
Title: Human rights and drug control: a new perspective / Melissa L. Bone
Description: Abingdon, Oxon; New York, NY Routledge, 2020. |
Based on author's thesis (doctoral – University of Manchester, 2015), issued under title: How can the lens of human rights provide a new perspective on drug control and point to different ways of regulating drug consumption? |
Includes bibliographical references and index.
Identifiers: LCCN 2019029107 (print) | LCCN 2019029108 (ebook) |
ISBN 9781138224025 (hardback) | ISBN 9781315310213 (ebook)
Subjects: LCSH: Drugs of abuse—Law and legislation. | Human rights. |
Drugs of abuse—Law and legislation—Great Britain. |
Civil rights—Great Britain.
Classification: LCC K3641.B66 2020 (print) | LCC K3641 (ebook) |
DDC 344.04/4—dc23
LC record available at https://lccn.loc.gov/2019029107
LC ebook record available at https://lccn.loc.gov/2019029108

ISBN 13: 978-1-03-208717-7 (pbk)
ISBN 13: 978-1-138-22402-5 (hbk)

Typeset in Galliard
by codeMantra

For my Grandad – Stanley J. Quest

Contents

Table of international instruments

Drug control instruments

Human rights instruments

Other international instruments

Table of international documents

Council of Europe

Economic and Social Council of the United Nations

International Narcotics Control Board

Office of the United Nations High Commissioner for Human Rights

United Nations Committee on Economic, Social and Cultural Rights

United Nations Commission on Narcotic Drugs

United Nations General Assembly

United Nations Human Rights Committee

United Nations Human Rights Council

United Nations Official Commentaries

United Nations Office on Drugs and Crime

World Health Organization

Other sources

Table of national legislation and documents

Brazil

Canada

France

New Zealand

South Africa

The United Kingdom

The United States of America

Table of cases

Canada

European Court of Human Rights

Human Rights Committee

Italy

Mexico

South Africa

United Kingdom

United States

Acknowledgments

I owe a huge debt of gratitude to many people during the compilation of this book. First, thank you to Routledge and to Colin Perrin for initially considering my proposal, and thank you to the anonymous reviewers who have helped to improve my work. Thank you to Nicola Sharpe, a fantastic editorial assistant at Routledge, for helping me to see this book over the finish line.

I would like to thank the University of Leicester for supporting a period of study leave from September 2018 to January 2019, this period really helped me to develop my ideas further. I would also like to thank the head of Leicester Law School, Professor Francois du Bois for his support during the writing process.

A special thank you is earmarked for my research mentor, Professor Elizabeth Wicks – your support, advice and feedback on the draft manuscript has been invaluable, thank you so much.

I would like to thank Dr Ed Bates, Dr Joe Wills, Professor Peter Cumper and Dr Rebecca Askew for reading drafts of earlier chapters and for offering very useful feedback.

A profound thank you also to Charlotte Walsh at the University of Leicester for first inspiring a dedication to this area of research.

While this book was written during my time at the University of Leicester, it is a development of my PhD thesis which was generously funded by the Arts and Humanities Research Council at the University of Manchester. I am very grateful to everyone involved in my PhD journey, especially my supervisors – Professor Toby Seddon and Dr Javier Oliva, and Professor's Judith Aldridge and Julia Buxton – my PhD examiners.

This book would not have been possible without the support of my friends and family. Louise, Ewa, Maribel, Marie, Ad, Jess, Tom, Lisa, Katherine, Aunty Val and Uncle Dave thank you for your encouragement throughout this lengthy process!

Mum, Dad, Jess, Luigi and Andy – thank you always for the unwavering support you give me and the belief that I can do whatever I set my mind to!

Will – my deepest thanks are reserved for you. Your love, support and patience over the last 18 months has been immeasurable – thank you so much for helping me see this book through to completion.

Abbreviations

1971 Convention	United Nations Convention on Psychotropic Substances (1971)
1988 Convention	United Nations Convention Against Illicit Traffic in Narcotic Drugs and Psychotropic Substances (1988)
2018 Regulations	Misuse of Drugs (Amendments) (Cannabis and Licence Fees) (England, Wales and Scotland) Regulations (2018)
2-CB	4-Bromo-2,5-dimethoxyphenethylamine
ACMD	Advisory Council on the Misuse of Drugs
AIDS	Acquired Immune Deficiency Syndrome
APPG	All-Party Parliamentary Group
BBR	British Bill of Rights
BPNA	British Paediatric Neurology Association
Charter	Charter of the United Nations (1945)
CBD	Cannabidiol
CBPMU	Cannabis-based product for medicinal use
CESCR	Committee on Economic, Social and Cultural Rights
CHR	Commission on Human Rights
CMO	Chief Medical Officer
CND	Commission on Narcotic Drugs
COP	Conference of Parties
CONAD	Conselho Nacional de Politicas sobre Drogas
CSA	Controlled Substances Act (1970)
CSC	Cannabis Social Club
CSR	Corporate Social Responsibility
DMT	N,N-Dimethyltryptamine
EBP	Evidence-based policy
ECDD	WHO's Expert Committee on Drug Dependence
ECHR	European Convention on Human Rights (1950)
ECtHR	European Court of Human Rights
ECOSOC	Economic and Social Council
ENCOD	European coalition for just and effective drug policies
EU	European Union

EU Charter	Charter of Fundamental Rights of the European Union (2000)
FAAAT	For Alternative Approaches to Addiction Think and Do Tank
FCTC	Framework Convention on Tobacco Control
GA	General Assembly
HIV	Human Immunodeficiency Virus
HRA	Human Rights Act (1998)
HRCa	Human Rights Committee
HRCb	Human Rights Council
ICCPR	International Covenant on Civil and Political Rights (1966)
ICEERS	International Center for Ethnobotanical Education, Research and Service
ICESCR	International Covenant on Economic, Social and Cultural Rights (1966)
IDPC	International Drug Policy Consortium
INCB	International Narcotics Control Board
INPUD	International Network of People Who Use Drugs
LSD	Lysergic acid diethylamide
MA	Medicines Act (1968)
MCCS	Medical Cannabis Clinicians Society
MDMA	3,4-Methylenedioxymethamphetamine
MDA	Misuse of Drugs Act (1971)
MDR	Misuse of Drugs Regulations (2001)
MMAR	Marihuana Medical Access Regulations
NAC	Native American Church
NGO	Non-Governmental Organisation
NHS	National Health Service
NICE	National Institute for Clinical Excellence
NPS	New Psychoactive Substances
OHCHR	Office of the United Nations High Commissioner for Human Rights
PSA	Psychoactive Substances Act (2016)
RCP	Royal College of Physicians
RCT	Randomised Control Trial
Single Convention	Single Convention on Narcotic Drugs (1961)
THC	Tetrahydrocannabinol
Transform	Transform Drug Policy Foundation
UDHR	Universal Declaration of Human Rights (1948)
UDV	União do Vegetal
UK	United Kingdom of Great Britain and Northern Ireland
UN	United Nations
UNAIDS	Joint United Nations Programme on HIV/AIDS

UNESCO	United Nations Educational, Scientific and Cultural Organization
UNDP	United Nations Development Programme
UNGASS	United Nations General Assembly Special Session
UNODC	United Nations Office on Drugs and Crime
UNPF	United Nations Population Fund
UPR	Universal Periodic Review
US	United States
USAID	United States Agency for International Development
WHO	World Health Organization

Introduction

> The human condition is not pre-empted by its past. Human history is not predetermined by its past stages. The fact that something has been the case, even for a long time, is not proof that it will continue to be so. Each moment of history is a junction of tracks leading towards a number of futures. Being at the crossroads is the way human society exists. What appears in retrospect an 'inevitable' development began in its time as stepping onto one road among many stretching ahead. (Bauman, 1988: 89)

The global system of drug prohibition began at the start of the 20th century, as political leaders and governments around the world constructed a regime which criminalised some actions in relation to certain psychoactive substances, excepting for medical and research purposes. Fast forward to the 21st century and the system as a global regime is at a crossroads and is beginning to fragment. This book uses a human rights perspective to step 'onto one road among many…' (Bauman, 1988: 89) and challenge the existing paradigm of 'drug prohibition'.

Background and context

Harry G. Levine: the 'uses' and 'crises' of global drug prohibition

In 2003, Harry G. Levine observed the predominant 'crises' which pose a threat to the global system of drug prohibition and the 'uses' to understand why the system still perseveres. Almost two decades later, Levine's observations are just as relevant as an introduction to the global drug prohibitionist framework, and to illuminate the transformations which are taking place in this field. Levine's (2003: 148–151) three 'crises' which threaten global drug prohibition are: 'the growing opposition to punitive drug policies', 'the cannabis crisis' and 'the emergence and development of the harm reduction movement'. All three crises pose a threat to a moral ideology which promotes 'drugs' as particularly dangerous and destructive (ibid).

Some states are recognising that punitive, criminalised drug policies are ineffective at reducing drug use, they are expensive and they take scarce resources away from other policing and health activities (ibid). Nearly every country in the world is signed up to at least one of the three United Nations drug conventions: The Single Convention on Narcotic Drugs (1961), the Convention on Psychotropic Substances (1971) and the United Nations Convention Against Illicit Traffic in Narcotic Drugs and Psychotropic Substances (1988). Together the three treaties establish the current system of global drug prohibition, a system which has spiralling enforcement costs of approximately $100 billion per year, despite the fact that drug supply and use is increasing, and drugs are becoming cheaper and stronger (Werb et al, 2013; Rolles et al, 2016). The drugs trade has been conservatively valued at $320 billion and it is considered one of the most lucrative illicit markets, constituting around 1 per cent of global GDP (UNODC, 2005; Rolles, 2017). It is estimated that approximately 275 million people have used drugs worldwide at least once in 2016 (UNODC, 2018). Even the United Nations Office on Drugs and Crime (UNODC, 2008: 216), the very agency responsible for enforcing global drug prohibition, have recognised several 'unintended consequences' resulting from this approach.

Three of these 'unintended consequences' specifically relate to enforcement issues, since this strategy does not eliminate drug use, rather people who use drugs move on to using another substance (substance displacement), and enforcement does not eliminate production, transit and supply, instead it simply shifts it elsewhere ('the balloon effect'). In further support of Levine's (2003) statement, the UNODC (2008) also recognise that redirecting scarce resources from health to enforcement (policy displacement) is another unintended consequence of prohibition. These 'unintended consequences' have facilitated alternative policies worldwide, as some decriminalisation policies redirect enforcement funds, which would have been spent on prosecuting the individual, to the public health sphere (Hughes and Stevens, 2010). Under a decriminalisation model, the possession of small amounts of drugs could still be unlawful and could incur an administrative sanction or a treatment requirement, but there is a diversion away from the criminal justice system (see Eastwood, Fox and Rosmarin, 2016). Portugal is especially held up as the standard for this regulatory model, as the country decriminalised the personal possession of all drugs in 2001. More recently, the Chief Executives Board of the UN, which represents the leadership of 31 UN agencies including the UNODC, has adopted a common position on drug policy; recommending the decriminalisation of drug possession for personal use (Chief Executives Board for Coordination, 2019: CEB/2018/2).

Decriminalisation policies are becoming increasingly prevalent across the globe (Eastwood, Fox and Rosmarin, 2016), especially in relation to cannabis. Diverging cannabis policies are identified by Levine (2003) as another 'crisis' for drug prohibition, since cannabis is the most widely used illicit drug worldwide, with conservative estimates of 192 million people using it at least once in 2018 (UNODC, 2018). Regulatory systems for medicinal cannabis have become increasingly widespread (Aguilar et al, 2018) and at the time of writing Canada, Uruguay, 10 US states and the District of Colombia have created legal regulatory systems for recreational use; in direct opposition to international drug control law. Since the Levine article, the phenomenon of New Psychoactive Substances (NPS) has also evolved (UNODC, 2018), which could pave the way for other alternative legal regulatory markets as well. NPS are psychoactives which fall outside of the laws relating to the international drug control regime but mimic the effects of currently prohibited drugs. The increasing discourse surrounding these substances in the 21st century, combined with the fact that we are living in the internet age, pose distinct challenges to the overarching goal of prohibition, to reduce the supply and use of certain psychoactives; thereby seriously undermining the current global system.

Besides, in relation to cannabis at least, the international drug control system is beginning to dismantle from within. The World Health Organization (WHO, 2019a), the body responsible for the scheduling status of cannabis under international law, has recommended that cannabis and cannabis resin is removed from Schedule IV of the Single Convention (a category reserved for the most dangerous substances with extremely limited or no medical value). Similarly, the UK government rescheduled cannabis in 2018 to recognise its medical efficacy, despite decades of perpetuating the prohibitionist ideology that this plant has no medical use and a high potential for abuse (Bone and Seddon, 2015). Interestingly, comparable arguments are now being made about psychedelic drugs, as scientists are re-discovering the therapeutic potential of these controlled substances which include: MDMA, LSD, psilocybin, ibogaine and ayahuasca (Sessa, 2017, 2018). This so-called ‘psychedelic renaissance’ has gained significant momentum over the last decade (Sessa, 2017: title; Sessa, 2018: 551). This is likely to pave the way for diverging psychedelic policies as well, culminating in a separate psychedelic ‘crisis’ to threaten the global system of drug prohibition.

The emergence and development of the harm reduction movement is considered to be a further ‘crisis’ posing a threat to the international system of drug prohibition (Levine, 2003). The harm reduction movement is a pragmatic health movement, which serves to mitigate against the harmful effects from drug use and prohibitionist policies themselves. The movement was borne in response to the growing AIDS epidemic in the 1980s, and this is still a key concern. Excluding sub-Saharan Africa, 30 per cent of all global HIV infections are due to unsafe injecting drug use (UNAIDS, 2014). The United Nations Office on Drugs and Crime (UNODC), the World Health Organization (WHO) the Joint Nations Programme on HIV/AIDS (UNAIDS), and other relevant UN bodies and stakeholders devote substantial resources towards reducing the threat posed by this epidemic (UNODC, INPUD, UNAIDS, UNDP, UNPF, WHO, USAID, 2017).

This pragmatic response, when combined with the increasing prevalence of other programmes across the globe such as: ‘syringe distribution and exchange, methadone maintenance, injection rooms, prescription heroin, medical use of cannabis, drug education for users, and pill testing at raves’ unintentionally serve to undermine the global prohibitionist regime (Levine, 2003: 149). Such initiatives have become increasingly prominent since 2003 and encourage policy makers to shift policies away from criminalised, coercive and repressive drug control regimes, towards ones which promote tolerance, regulation and public health. Thus, by default, the harshness and the punitive effects of the global prohibitionist system are better illuminated (ibid). The harm reductionist approach is also strongly rooted in humanist values (Goode, 1997). Harm reduction initiatives within this area seek to respect the human rights of users, and actively work to alleviate any human rights violations – both in relation to drug use itself and the harms associated with disproportionate criminal sanctions. Given the subject matter of this book, existing research which studies the interplay between the human rights and drug control systems will be explored in more detail below.

All the same, global drug prohibition has its 'uses' (Levine, 2003: 145), which helps to explain why the system still stands globally. Levine (ibid) observes that a state's police and military can be endowed with additional powers to enforce prohibitionist policies, many of which are able to legitimately infringe civil liberties. Throughout the 20th century, political opponents were also united under this system, since a negative view of psychoactives further legitimised an increase in state power (ibid). However, it should be acknowledged that in more recent times, politicians are becoming more divided on this issue.

In a similar vein, this global system is thought to have enjoyed widespread support from the United Nations (ibid), an eminent intergovernmental organisation, who at the end of the 20th century advocated that the overarching, Sisyphean goal of drug prohibition was to create 'a drug free world' (Arlacchi, 1998: n.p.). Twenty years later, the situation is markedly different. The most recent UN General Assembly Special Session on Drugs (UNGASS, 2016) promised to constitute a more open and wide-ranging debate, to develop more effective responses rooted in public health, human rights and harm reduction. Although, the extent to which UNGASS 2016 achieved these goals, given the ideological constraints imposed by this regime is somewhat questionable.

The global system of drug control adopts a discriminatory discourse to articulate a moral ideology which promotes 'drugs' as particularly dangerous and destructive (Levine, 2003). While the discourse used in this area will be unpacked in more detail throughout this book, it is worth noting that the ideological commitment to global drug prohibition, promulgated by anti-drug discourses and legal instruments which adopt a dogmatic terminology, serve an important purpose (see Cohen, 2003). Levine (2003) observes that moralising discourses allow states to manipulate individuals to conform to a certain moral and ethical outlook, which can be used to divert attention away from other issues, and to justify state infiltration into an individual's private sphere (Levine, 2003).

Levine (ibid) additionally observes that a commitment to this hegemonic narrative is beneficial for the media since it is an economic fact that sensationalist, moralist drug reporting increases profits. Yet, the ideological commitment to drug prohibition has economic 'uses' which extend far beyond media profits.

It will be illustrated throughout this book that the drivers for this global regime largely centred on the economic interests of powerful nations, such as the UK and the US. 'Power politics and trade' are at the heart of drug prohibition (Seddon, 2013: 5). Identifying the criteria believed to be at the crux of this global paradigm, should necessitate questions concerning what the goals of drug policy should be.

Human rights and drug control: integrating the parallel universes

When promoting human rights as a goal for drug policy the majority of commentators centre their research in the harm reduction sphere. When exploring the interplay between the two global regimes the research largely stresses the vast amount of human right violations carried out in the name of drug control. For instance, Harm Reduction International has produced extensive reports on the use of the death penalty, the use of corporal punishment and the use of disproportionate sentencing practices for drug offences committed throughout the world (Iakobishvili, 2011, 2012; Girelli, 2019).

Barrett and Nowak (2009), Barrett et al. (2008), Transform Drug Policy Foundation (2012) and the IDPC (2019) also provide an extensive list of the human right abuses committed within this sphere. These non-exhaustive lists additionally highlight: the denial of basic health care in this field, the use of arbitrary detention and forced labour, the denial of a fair trial and due process standards, the infliction of torture and ill treatment by authorities, the prevalence of systemic discrimination against users which is often exacerbated further depending upon the individual's race and/or sex, and the effect of crop eradication programmes which detrimentally impact upon the health, social security and livelihoods of those involved. It is little wonder then that Professor Paul Hunt (2008: 9), the then UN Special Rapporteur on the Right to Health, acknowledged both the UN drug control and human rights systems to inhabit 'parallel universes', since the UN drug control system can evidently operate free from human right constraints, and hence contrary to the basic, fundamental principles of international law.

For most academics and practitioners examining the interplay between these two systems, a more integrative and human rights orientated approach is essential. Though there are of course exceptions, Takahashi (2016) for instance provides a useful exception to the broader literature, as he perceives there to be no fundamental incompatibility between the drug control and human rights frameworks. Takahashi (2016: 9) argues that lots of the arguments employed to show that drug control violates human rights are actually 'standard issues of human rights in criminal justice matters'. He notes that while human rights must be protected in the administration of justice and any abuses must be stopped – this is hardly unique to drug control. However, the criminalising underpinnings of the global system of prohibition is exactly why this book would argue that a fundamental incompatibility between drug control and human rights exists in the first place. Lines (2017: 9) cites a useful example where the legal context underpinning and justifying executions carried out in the name of drug control is highly relevant:

> [A] 2001 report by the UN Secretary General recorded a 50% increase in the number of countries prescribing the death penalty for drugs into domestic law between 1985 and 2000, the exact period during which the 1988 drug treaty was being drafted, adopted and ratified at state level.

In an effort to resolve the impasse, the broader literature focusses on ways in which the international bodies regulating the two regimes can co-operate. Barrett et al. (2008) believe that through joint-working practices the international drug agencies can: seek to reject the stigmatising language they employ, increase meaningful civil society engagement, abolish any punishment practices which are contrary to human rights, ensure access to treatment and care for problematic users, and improve donor accountability, so that a few powerful western states can no longer influence the operation of oppressive drug control practices (ibid).

Given the level of detail now devoted to securing a more rights-orientated approach, it is fair to suggest that in many ways Gilmore's (1996: 356) assertion from the mid-1990s stipulating 'little has been written about drug use and human rights' is no longer accurate. Various UN bodies now recognise the need to incorporate human rights. The UN's Chief Executives Board for Coordination, the highest level coordination forum of the UN system has stipulated a 'call for changes in laws, policies and practices that threaten the health and human rights of people' (Chief Executives Board for Coordination, 2019: CEB/2018/2, 14). These calls for reform come as part of a wider move to more effective and humane drug policies, rooted in evidence, human rights and public health, which also contribute to the sustainable development goals envisaged in the UNGASS 2016 outcome document (UNODC, 2016).

While the aims of these bodies, academics and practitioners are clearly laudable, it is important to note that the tensions between drug control and human rights can often be viewed from a similar, rather fixed perspective. A harm reductionist approach is regularly recommended to rectify any core human rights violations. Yet, researching the interplay between human rights and the drug prohibitionist framework could be unduly restrictive; since a harm reductionist approach could ultimately be compatible with the philosophy of drug prohibition; a global system which seeks to limit the usage of all psychoactives. Though Hunt (2008: 9) stipulates that the two regimes inhabit 'parallel universes', by seeking largely to reduce the harms which stem from this system, this conception of human rights could help to legitimise the global system of drug prohibition. While harm reduction is a crucial lynchpin of drug policy reform – since harm reduction initiatives are presented as a *pragmatic* response to flagrant human rights abuses – the success of this approach often rests on its presumed ideological neutrality.

This means that harm reduction initiatives could ultimately be compatible with a prohibitionist regime by failing to question the overarching goal or ideology of prohibition; to reduce or eliminate drug use. Thus, a human rights approach informed from a harm reductionist perspective could perpetuate the current regime, even if it ameliorates some of the worst effects resulting from this system. However, human rights are thought to constitute a revolutionary discourse designed to: 'change entrenched political behaviour, as well as entrenched social behaviour', hence they are capable of extending beyond the paradigms currently imposed (Brems, 2009: 366). This book strives to move past the 'parallel universes' the human rights and drug control systems are thought to inhabit, to generate new thinking – which is unconstrained by the logic of prohibition. Weil (1983: 22–31) observes:

> I often have the suspicion that everything we do in the name of the drug problem is the drug problem. It's not just the laws but the whole mentality that sees drugs as the problem and tries to fight them. By doing that I think we've made it all worse.

Offering a new perspective

To challenge ideology of prohibition, alternative human rights dialogues are moving increasingly into the fray. Academics and other legal commentators have explored case law where an individual's human rights conflict with our drug control laws; to challenge the legal framework of drug prohibition and ultimately change our mentality and our approach to drug control. In his authoritative monograph 'Drug control and human rights in international law', Lines (2017) details how drug control laws can be interpreted dynamically within the context of human rights law. To explore the potential future of drug control, Lines proposes the development of a human rights-based approach to treaty interpretation, and reviews case law where a dynamic, human rights-based approach has been used by courts and international bodies. He successfully highlights the potential of such an approach to 'mitigate the negative human rights impacts of drug control efforts' (ibid: 15).

For the most part, reviews of case law which challenge drug control laws have historically centred upon human rights to 'health' 'religion' and a few related rights, as more protective power is perceived to exist here. The UN's drug control framework accords particular significance to health and religious rights, since the global prohibitionist regime is expressly concerned with limiting psychoactives for medical and scientific uses (see the preamble, Single Convention), and any latitude afforded to states on a human rights basis is predominately concerned with reservations relating to 'traditional' or 'religious' rights (Article 32(4) the 1971 Convention; Article 14(2) the 1988 Convention). Some case law examples this book explores (non-exhaustively) include the health rights of individuals to consume cannabis for medicinal purposes, the right to use ayahuasca and cannabis for religious and spiritual purposes, and the right to expand one's own consciousness by consuming certain psychoactives.

It is an interesting time to explore case law where drug control and human rights laws conflict, since broader, autonomy-based human rights are becoming increasingly prominent as well. Individuals in South Africa and Mexico successfully challenged the constitutionality of their respective states' cannabis prohibition laws on rights to privacy and free development of personality grounds in 2018 – grounds which traditionally have not been so readily relied upon.

Notwithstanding these significant developments, this book argues that the legal judicial method is limited in its application to specific drugs, jurisdictions and drug-using contexts. In order to delve deeper and profoundly challenge 'the whole mentality that sees drugs as a problem and tries to fight them', this book develops a broader human rights perspective, philosophically and politically, as well as legally. This book not only examines the architectural framework of human rights and drug control systems, to reveal where the legal room for manoeuvre exists, but it scrutinises the very idea of human rights, as applied to drug control. In doing so, Chapters 1–3 develop key conceptual arguments to fundamentally change the way in which we think about drug control issues. In sum, these arguments are:

- Human rights are broad living instruments capable of reflecting and understanding human drug use (Chapter 1);
- Human rights can better address the state/individual binary which is identified to be at the crux of drug policies (Chapter 2); and
- For the most part, human rights and drug control frameworks are legally compatible (Chapter 3).

When this conceptual framework is applied to the case law in Chapters 4 and 5, it can be seen how human rights provide a new perspective on drug control issues. A human rights lens can challenge the ideology of prohibition if we are to accept human rights as broad living instruments, capable of understanding and reflecting the multitude of reasons as to why we use drugs, and the significance that can be accorded to their use. A human rights lens could also help us to develop an alternative moral policy response to prohibition, by addressing a fundamental conflict between state interests in restricting certain drugs to protect *perceived* societal interests, and an individual's freedom to consume. This book challenges dominant state narratives on the 'morality' of drug use, and questions the interests a state actually represents, by engaging with more normative ways of thinking about drugs and drug policy.

Engaging in both deontological and consequentialist reasoning in a human rights adjudication process allows judges to move beyond prohibitionist logic – focusing solely on the harms and risks caused by drugs – towards acknowledging the benefits psychoactives can have for the individual and for society more broadly as well. While the human rights and drug control frameworks can be legally compatible, this book also recognises that both systems have been politicised. Accordingly, the limitations of applying the legal judicial method to change our approach to drug control is highlighted, and the conclusion chapter points towards a drug policy making process capable of reconfiguring prohibitionist mentality from the bottom up. By contextualising human rights philosophically and politically as well as legally when applied to drug policy, this book opens up a dialogue to think about drug control issues in a more thoroughgoing and far-reaching way.

To further challenge prohibitionist logic and the moral hegemony of the global regime, it is also important to note from the outset that the very concept of 'drugs' is premised on the basis of moral and political evaluations (Derrida, 1995). One of the identifiable 'uses' of the system is the moral hegemony used to justify certain measures for social control (Cohen, 2003; Levine, 2003). As well as being an 'evaluative' concept, carrying with it a set of moral judgments, Seddon (2010, 2016) also observes that the concept is a regulatory construct, invented at the start of the 20th century. The creation of the international prohibitionist regime generated a division between 'licit' and 'illicit' psychoactives; thereby producing a new categorisation of illicit substances considered to be 'drugs'. Hence, the question as to what actually is a 'drug' – is an ontological one – and the answer produced affects all consequent investigative, philosophical and policy considerations on the matter (Seddon, 2010).

Tupper (2012: 475, 477) identifies two dominant metaphors which continue to inform the prohibitionist regime: 'drugs as malevolent agents' and 'drugs and pathogens'; individuals who consume drugs are bad, sick or both. The global system of drug prohibition thereby glosses over the complexities of the human lived experience in a simplistic pharmacological reductionism. An awareness of the regulatory and moralistic construction of 'drugs' pervades throughout this book. The terms: 'drugs' 'psychoactives' and 'substances' will be used throughout to ameliorate the licit/illicit divide and in full awareness of the socio-political ontologies. In fact, these terms are used interchangeably so that any normative distinctions cannot be drawn.

The incapacity of the global system of drug prohibition to fully appreciate drug use as a complex human phenomenon, with both benefits and risks attached, is the reason why 'everything we do in the name of the drugs problem is the drugs problem' (Weil, 1983: 22–31). We are locked in a prohibitionist legal paradigm which perceives the law as the key framework to regulate psychoactive use (Seddon, 2013). This book does not disagree. Rather, it contends that the predominant legal framework should not be the criminal law, but the remit of human rights. The following chapters comprehensively explore the value of 'human rights' on a philosophical, political, and legal basis, to thoroughly appreciate the capacity of human rights to challenge prohibitionist logic.

Clarifying expectations

The scope

Throughout this book, no attempt is made to cover a vast array of controlled psychoactives or legal jurisdictions. Such an approach would be superficial, given the sheer number of psychoactives, and it would add little to the existing literature. An analysis of existing case law primarily focuses on health rights, religious rights and autonomy-based human rights arguments to consume cannabis and certain psychedelics, such as peyote and ayahuasca. It is these substances which dominate the case law when the drug control and human rights frameworks conflict. It could be argued then, that this book is constrained to a certain extent by focusing on the drugs which typically expose the conflict between the two systems. In fact, Chapter 4 exclusively focuses on cannabis case law, but this sole focus can allow for helpful comparisons to be drawn, given the variety of cannabis policies in comparable jurisdictions.

In addition, both health and autonomy rights have been employed when challenging the legality of cannabis prohibition, therefore, any overlaps or distinctions can be more easily highlighted.

Regulatory regimes for licit psychoactives, such as sugar, alcohol, tobacco are also explored for comparison purposes, most notably in Chapters 1 and 3. Chapter 4 also alludes to how the case law might develop in the future for other psychoactives. Discussions pertaining to the medical use of cannabis could apply to psychedelic substances such as MDMA, LSD and psilocybin, given the increasing recognition of their therapeutic potential (Sessa, 2017). In any event, the dominant focus on certain psychoactives (i.e. cannabis) over others should not restrict the significance of the book's findings, which are applicable to the drug policy field more broadly.

This book is primarily focused on drug control and human rights issues in the UK, to comprehensively contextualise the research by limiting the geographical scope. Since drug control laws and human rights can be politicised, focusing on how the two systems conflict in the UK is especially pertinent given the rise of partisan politics, the growing resistance to transnational forms of governance and increasing calls to withdraw from the European Convention of Human Rights (1950) and/or repeal the Human Rights Act (1998) after we leave the European Union. The UK general public are becoming increasingly hostile to the idea of human rights (see Chapters 1 and 3). What is more, the UK government have further politicised our drug laws by enacting a thoroughly illiberal statute, the Psychoactive Substances Act (2016) – which imposes a blanket ban on any non-exempted psychoactive substance. Taken together, this state of affairs provides a fertile breeding ground to explore, in-depth, an escalating conflict between the human rights and drug control frameworks.

Of course drug policy issues are transnational and this book draws on case law from other jurisdictions (including Canada, Italy, Mexico and South Africa) but most notably the United States, where relevant. The US has a rich history in the juridification of human rights claims (especially in the religious liberties field). Most importantly, the US was the main driving force behind the global system of drug prohibition (see Chapter 3). Other states largely deferred to them given the rise of their global political power throughout the 20th century. It is interesting then, that despite such a partisan approach, the US judiciary will be shown to have (at times) upheld the health, religious and related rights of people who use drugs, to a far greater extent than in the UK; further highlighting the potential compatibility of both the drug control and human rights frameworks. More thorough comparisons can also be drawn here since the jurisdictions cited constitute western pluralist democracies and are concerned with maintaining drug prohibition and respecting human rights.

Though, it is worth noting that human rights themselves are considered to be rooted in western traditional thought and polity, and they have a distinctly liberal bias (for more detail, see Chapter 1). A human rights perspective could therefore be accused of being individualistic, state-centred and legalistic, neglecting the fact that different societies may prioritise different values. To go some way towards countering this shortcoming, Chapter 1 recognises the limitations of a western conception of human rights and the importance of stimulating a cross-cultural dialogue. In addition, the definitions subsections in Chapters 4 and 5 challenge the orthodox way in which health and religious rights have typically been defined in practice. Chapter 5 in particular moves away from divisive health and religious categorisations – recognising shamanic drug-using practices which fully integrate health, religion and spirituality.

The synopses

This book is split into two parts: Part I develops a human rights perspective philosophically and politically as well as legally (see Chapters 1–3), while Part II applies this perspective to the case law to provide a new perspective on drug control issues (see Chapters 4 and 5), and to improve our approach to the drug policy making process (see the Conclusion chapter).

Chapter 1 contextualises the origin and value of human rights and human drug use to show how human rights can provide a good lens through which to view and understand human drug use. This chapter involves a philosophical exploration of what human rights are and from where they have originated, to legitimise them as a valid concept. It also justifies their application to human drug use by tying the idea that human rights are rooted in our common humanity *and* are culturally diverse to the commonality and diversity of human psychoactive use. Chapter 2 advances the idea that human rights can embrace normative thinking by addressing a key conflict in this field: the interests of the state in restricting psychoactives versus the interests of the individual striving to consume them. This chapter argues that the dominant philosophical arguments, which underpin reformist or prohibitionist positions on drug control, all advocate either increases in individual empowerment or in state control. At its core, drug policy concerns the relationship between the state and the individual. Discussions on Levine's 'uses' of prohibition largely centre upon enhancing state power and diminishing individual control. This chapter shows how a human rights perspective could reconfigure the binary to focus on the individual consumer; this could alter existing power struggles and point to more innovate policy proposals which could benefit both the individual and broader societal interests. Chapter 3 explores the legal nature, function and purpose of the drug control and human rights regimes (internationally and domestically). For the most part, the two frameworks are legally compatible, but they are not immune from political pressures and both systems can be politicised.

Part II builds on the conceptual arguments developed in Part I and applies these to the case law, revealing where there is domestic (UK) and international legal room for manoeuvre, and it highlights the potential and the limitations of using human rights law in the courts to challenge the legal framework of drug prohibition. Chapters 4 and 5 demonstrate that health rights, religious rights and related human rights can be broadly construed (capable of responding to the often enmeshed contexts of drug use), but in practice, a narrow, westernised state conception of health and religion is adopted when human rights and drug control laws conflict. Both chapters explore key normative questions which draw attention to the power dynamic between the state and the individual. These include how much/little responsibility the state has to: provide treatment – or at the very least to ensure procedural proprietary when making health care decisions – while simultaneously respecting an individual's own health choices, uphold their rights to freedom of religion, belief, thought and/or their rights to be left alone. The UK case law[1], in particular, builds on Chapter 3, by alluding to the politicisation of drug control issues, as judges are reluctant to engage with relevant human rights questions and defer instead to parliament. Though it will be shown that the UK courts are more constrained legally than comparable jurisdictions in light of the UK's procedural human rights framework.

While human rights to health and religious exemptions can be accommodated within the drug prohibitionist framework, Chapters 4 and 5 additionally explore related autonomy-based human rights which fully challenge the ideology of prohibition. Autonomy-based arguments threaten the idea of global drug prohibition because they apply to everyone, as opposed to a select few; taking the conflict between the state and the individual to its zenith. Autonomy-based grounds such as the right to privacy, the free development of personality and the

1 Although the United Kingdom has three legal jurisdictions: England and Wales, Scotland and Northern Ireland, the phrase 'UK case law' and 'UK courts' will be used throughout this book as the domestic drug control and human rights legislation applies to the whole of the UK. This shorthand is also used so that the reader can more easily draw comparisons between the UK and other jurisdictions which operate within different legal, socio-political, economic and cultural contexts when judges consider the conflict between human rights and drug control laws.

right to freedom of thought will be shown to place the onus on the state to justify its prohibitionist drug laws (thereby reversing the burden which is typically placed on the individual to justify their use on health or religious grounds). Broader autonomy-based arguments also give credence to the multi-faceted ways in which humans use drugs, reflecting the complexity of lived experience. Most defendants have been reluctant to place such arguments before the court, given the short thrift which has historically been afforded to them. Though this is beginning to change in some jurisdictions, Chapters 3–5 reveal that the legal room to deviate away from the UN drug conventions only applies to personal consumption, and not to more serious offences. To transcend such limitations, this book's concluding chapter considers ways to improve our approach to the drug policy making process, employing the key conceptual arguments developed and applied throughout Parts I and II – which provide a new perspective on drug control.

Part I

Developing a human rights perspective

Chapter 1

The origin and value of human rights and human drug use

To fully gauge whether human rights can provide a new perspective on drug control, it is important to first consider what human rights actually are, the history of human rights and the key debates pertaining to whether they even truly exist, why they are perceived as being so important, and how they are grounded. This exploration of the idea of human rights is justifiable, in order to frame how human rights can provide a new perspective on drug control through a philosophical lens. Examining the conceptual foundation of human rights and looking critically at their content and justification is particularly weighty, since the vast majority of academic engagement on this topic has debated our right to drugs from other moral and ideological standpoints (see Mill, 1859/2001; Husak, 1992; Van Ree, 1999).

The notion of human rights is often commandeered to support an author's own moral theory, as opposed to exploring the intention and meaning of the term (Griffin, 2008 citing Kant, Mill and Rawls). Hutson (1991) further explains how a societal fondness for asserting our rights has effectively outrun our ability to analyse them and reach a consensus on their scope and meaning. Accordingly, human rights are being increasingly rendered 'indeterminate' or 'criterionless', since the runaway growth of the extension of the term has made its intention particularly thin (Griffin, 2008: 17). Therefore, Chapter 1 initially explores the historical legal origins of human rights, before recognising that this history drives debates which critique their foundations, importance, relevance and place in society. A particular emphasis will be placed on the UK context.

The chapter then explores how human rights are grounded, and presents an overview of the debate as to whether human rights are universal or relativist. Making the case that human rights can be pluralistically universal will feed into the final section which focuses on the origin and value of drug consumption. Chapter 1 ties the idea that human rights are rooted in our common humanity *and* are culturally diverse to the commonality and diversity of human psychoactive use, to justify why a focus on human rights offers a good lens through which to view human drug use. The chapter devotes more attention to the origin and value of human rights, to thoroughly elucidate that human rights strive to understand, reflect and respond to the human condition. They are thereby better placed to put forth a new paradigm for regulating drugs, one which is not constrained by a narrow cultural, historical, political and economic narrative.

Chapter 1 is an exploratory and investigatory endeavour. By contextualising the legal history, the validity and the key philosophical debates relating to the idea of human rights, this chapter provides a useful introduction to some of the key human rights ideas to be expanded upon in later chapters. Chapter 1 ultimately explores how the idea of human rights can provide a useful lens through which to re-conceptualise and understand the phenomena of human drug use.

The history of human rights: Where have they come from?

The idea of human rights is arguably one of the most pervasive features of present-day international relations. Certainly, the most basic idea of the human rights movement does not relate to the rights themselves but relates to the regulation of governmental behaviour through international norms (Pogge, 2000; Nickel, 2010). We have burgeoning global, regional and domestic lists of rights which states are required to protect and enforce. Yet, despite their political prominence, the ontological status of a human right remains questionable, since for many there is a common belief that we do not have a clear enough conception of what human rights actually are (Griffin, 2008).

Most academics subscribe to the philosophical notion that human rights are something every person possesses simply by virtue of being human (Donnelly, 2003; Edmunson, 2004; Hunt, 2007; Griffin, 2008; Nickel, 2010). While the increased political standing of human rights in the international and domestic sphere is relatively new, tracing the history of human rights is a controversial matter and any attempt to credit any one region of the world, religion or culture with the origins of human rights would be 'politically charged' (Ishay, 2004: xxii). According to Bates (2018: 4):

> [T]here are many different threads to the human rights idea as it exists today, and it is invidious to locate any one specific thread as the beginning.

One could go back thousands of years and uncover ideas related to human rights in ancient civilisations across the world. The Law Code of Hammurabi, created by the Babylonian king Hammurabi in the 8th century BC, stoic philosophies in ancient Greece, or other religious codes throughout history could be drawn from to trace the origins of the human rights idea (ibid).

Ishay (2004: xxii) offers a much broader perspective on the history of human rights to avoid privileging 'a particular world view' of the concept or otherwise defending a certain 'status quo or value system against possible challenges'. However, for the purposes of this book, the focus will be on how human rights, as a legal concept, can be used to challenge drug control laws, particularly within a UK context. Therefore, this history of human rights will be limited to focusing on the origins of legal measures in the human rights field. The following account has a distinctly liberal, western bias when tracing key human rights documents and developments. It is important to be aware of this from the outset, since Chapter 5 highlights both the limitations of applying a westernised human rights framework to issues of drug control, and the potential of human rights to transcend their occidental legal origins and respond to the complex phenomena that is human drug use (see 'A third way: pluralist universalism', 'The history and origins of human drug use' and Chapter 5).

The middle ages

The earliest modern conception of human rights in a legalistic sense is thought to have originated in the 12th or the 13th century under papal rule, where it was determined that property rights, no matter how small, were natural God-given rights conferred upon us all as human beings (Edmunson, 2004). The ensuing dialogue surrounding this decision further developed the idea that human beings were created in God's own image, and thus were endowed with an inherent sense of dignity and worth, from which a comprehensive rights system could flow (Griffin, 2008). Debates at this time additionally made the distinction between objective and subjective rights: the former referring to a sense of rectitude in relation to being right, whereas the latter was subjective, referring to a sense of entitlement that the right-holder has, placing the individual firmly in the foreground (Donnelly, 2003). The Magna Carta (1215) was a crucial turning point in articulating the concept of human rights at this time. This British document enumerates property rights, as well as due process rights and equality before the law.

The enlightenment

During the enlightenment, the idea of human rights attained greater prominence, since the construction of human rights as natural rights coincided with questioning the order of the natural world (Griffin, 2008). While the idea remained that human rights were natural, rooted in a person's moral nature, and centred on the dignity of the human person (Donnelly, 2003); philosophers began to sever the conception away from its theistic origins (Griffin, 2008). For instance, Hugo Grotius (1646), a Dutch lawyer, regarded humans as inherently social beings imbued with sociability and understanding, which when combined created justice. For Grotius, the development of such concepts was sufficiently determinate to have 'some degree of validity even if we should concede that which cannot be conceded without utmost wickedness, that there is no God...' (ibid: 13).

Grotius further expanded the subjective sphere of rights by acknowledging that the sphere was not just limited to property, but could extend to cover a whole range of an individual's actions, so that they may enjoy a natural liberty (Edmunson, 2004). This extension expanded the secular vision further, since the notion that individuals could freely enjoy different actions and form their own conceptions of a worthwhile life lends itself to pluralist values.

In further accordance with such values, it was later conceived by Purfendorf (1673/1991) that rights could not arise without another subsequently coming under obligation to the putative right-holder. This notion was characterised as the correlativity of rights and duties, and coincides with the renowned enlightenment thinker John Locke's philosophy on the relationship between individuals and the state. For Locke (1690), a man's natural right to life, liberty and estate could operate to control governments, as they are duty-bound to respect a man's natural rights; given that the consent of the governed should be the only legitimate basis for forming a government. The English Bill of Rights (1689) reflects Locke's ideas and sets out the rights of parliament, certain rights of individuals and the limits of the powers of the monarch.

The American and French Revolutions

Such political concerns about the relationships between people and their governments and between people and each other prevailed throughout the 18th century. The American and French Revolutions, in particular, sought to overthrow the hierarchical power structures of British colonial rule and an absolute monarchy. Both Revolutions were informed by enlightenment ideals and culminated in the formulation of two human rights instruments: the American Declaration of Independence (1776) and the French Declaration of the Rights of Man and Citizen (1789). The preamble to the American Declaration (1776) explicitly acknowledges that governments derive their power 'from the consent of the governed', and the French Declaration (1789) contains several provisions designed to protect citizens from their own government (see Articles 9, 25 27, 33, 34, 35).

Political concerns pertaining to both the rights and duties of the individual and the state were now contained within two more legal human rights documents. Yet, although the American Declaration was considered successful in providing the foundation and justification for an American government, the French Declaration proved incapable of preventing the so-called reign of terror; the revolutionary governments' violent response against those suspected of opposing the French Revolution (Edmunson, 2004: 41). As such, the practical value of making the concept of human rights pivotal to the understanding of political arrangements led to 'decidedly mixed' results (ibid). Of course, it is worth noting that the 18th-century formations of natural rights were the antecedents of modern human rights, not human rights themselves. They were linked to nation-state building, rather than the universal notion that we now have (see Moyn, 2012).

The 19th century

Though the French Revolution sparked scepticism about rights and threw the notion into some disarray, influencing philosophers who questioned the validity of the concept (see Bentham's critique below), the idea of human rights was further consolidated and retrenched during the 19th century (Edmunson, 2004).

Philosophers at this time were concerned about furthering their own ethical, moral and/or political theories and they utilised the term in order to do so (Griffin, 2008). These writers were therefore unconcerned with exploring the historical notion of human rights (ibid). While the moral theories derived here, such as utilitarianism appear somewhat superfluous to the historical notion of rights, such theories were nevertheless driven by the history of human rights, just as the history drives the moral theories (see 'Contextualising the history and validity of human rights' for more detail).

Moreover, moral theories inform key debates on human rights which have considerable relevance during later discussions where the balance between the maintenance of social order and respect for individual rights will be explored (see Chapter 2 for more detail). In any event, for Edmunson (2004) and Griffin (2008), this period, the late 18th century and the enlightenment period were exploratory, provocative and concerned with finding sense for the term – 'human rights'.

Responding to World War II

The aftermath of the Second World War facilitated a further expansionary period for human rights. Although the Magna Carta (1215), the Bill of Rights (1689), The American Declaration (1776) and the French Declaration (1789) are important examples of written precursors to many human rights documents today, in practice these documents were exclusionary for women, people of colour and members of certain political, economic, religious and social groups. However, there was a concerted effort to rectify this position in the early 20th century. The League of Nations, an intergovernmental organisation established after the First World War to maintain world peace, made some attempt to protect minority rights (see Article 23, the Covenant of the League of Nations, 1924). Nonetheless, the onset of World War II led to the League's demise.

After World War II, the League was replaced with the United Nations, as governments from around the world wanted to prevent the atrocities from World War II from reoccurring. The international community were especially outraged by the holocaust and they adopted the Universal Declaration of Human Rights (UDHR) (1948) in recognition of: 'the inherent dignity and of the equal and inalienable rights of *all members* of the *human family*' (preamble, emphasis added). Though the UDHR is not legally binding, it strengthened the concept of human rights, and it has achieved the status of customary international law, since it is regarded as 'a common standard of achievement for *all* people and *all* nations' (ibid).

The UDHR provided a foundation for two legally binding human rights covenants: the International Covenant on Civil and Political Rights (ICCPR) (1966) and the International Covenant on Economic Social and Cultural Rights (ICESCR) (1966). UDHR principles are further elaborated on in other human rights treaties, and the existence of the UDHR helped to justify the creation of regional human rights instruments, such as the European Convention on

Human Rights (ECHR) (1950). The ECHR is legally binding on state parties, and it has been directly incorporated into British law via the Human Rights Act (HRA) (1998) (see 'Losing sense of the term'; see also Chapter 3 for more detail on the evolution of human rights in international and UK law).

As Perry (1998: 13) notes, the inclusive discourse articulated in the UDHR can be found in several international human right documents which consistently refer to 'the inherent dignity of human beings' and the notion that we are all members of one 'family'. For Perry (ibid), the similarities between this discourse and the original theistic conviction that every human being is sacred, means the idea of human rights is 'ineliminably religious' and still firmly attached to its theistic origins; as the notion of sacredness and familial ties are embedded in religious cosmology.

This could suggest that human rights are foundational; rooted in our human nature, and our status as human beings. On the other hand, the UDHR's broad influence and inclusive discourse could have more directly resulted from the need to respond to the 'barbarous acts which have outraged the conscience of mankind' (preamble, UDHR). Therefore, it could be argued that while the devastation wreaked by two world wars at the beginning of the 20th century strengthened the idea of human rights, the concept is nevertheless socially constructed and is reflective of its time.

Contextualising the history and validity of human rights

Questions pertaining to the foundations of human rights, i.e. whether they are rooted in our human nature and our status as human beings, or are a social construction dreamed up by the west, has meant that the concept of human rights has been subject to much penetrating criticism and debate. As demonstrated, the idea that human rights are natural or inalienable has a history dating back to the middle ages, through to the enlightenment, and up to and including the present day, with modern human rights instruments drawing upon 'ineliminably religious' theistic discourse (Perry, 1998: 13). The idea that human rights are only possible if they are based on metaphysical or theological assumptions about human nature will be contrasted with the notion that they are socially construed; deriving their validity from humankind's decision to act as though they exist. This section deliberately refrains from choosing which philosophical narrative is more compelling, since it will later be shown that both justifications for the validity of human rights (be they foundationalist or constructionist), provide a good lens through which to understand drug use as a complex, human phenomena.

Critiquing human rights foundationalism

One of the most cutting criticisms of natural rights theory was formulated by Jeremy Bentham in response to the revolutionary government's French Declaration. He famously declared natural rights to be no more than 'rhetorical nonsense – nonsense upon stilts' (Bentham, 1843: 501). Bentham was unwilling to assign any sense to the idea of a natural right outside of a legal setting, highlighting the inconsistency and instability within the construct, and a distinct lack of any strong foundations. Rorty (1999: 69) too has asserted that we should stop trying to defend the idea of human rights and abandon 'human rights foundationalism'. This phrase refers to the attempts to trace human rights and natural rights theory back to their original source – an 'outmoded' endeavour for Rorty (ibid: 73):

> Such events as the French Revolution and the ending of the trans-Atlantic slave trade prompted nineteenth-century intellectuals in the rich democracies to say: It is enough for us to know that we live in an age in which human beings can make things much better for ourselves. We do not need to dig behind this historical fact to non-historical facts about what we really are.

For human rights foundationalists, the 'non-historical' facts refer to the normative idea that a person derives human rights by virtue of her humanity, her human nature or her status as a human being. Hence, the term posits 'a deep moral foundation on which legal recognition of human rights ought to be based' (Sangiuliano, 2014: 223), and that a person possesses these rights irrespective:

> [O]f her membership in any legal, political or social association. Instead, the grounds of human rights are found in a more foundational pre-political substratum of moral thought in terms of which positive institutions may be criticised. (ibid: 219)

Sangiuliano (ibid) observes that the term 'human rights foundationalism' has also been called 'the orthodox conception of human rights', 'naturalism' or 'traditionalism' (ibid: 219). In keeping with this idea, both Edmunson (2004) and Griffin (2008) have observed that the only way to reconcile any conflicting opinions about the idea of human rights is to trace the history of rights discourse. Contrastingly, for Rorty (1999 as cited in Perry, 1998: 37–38) this attempt at rationality is 'futile', since the premise that human beings have certain inalienable rights through virtue of their humanity alone is nothing more than 'a moral point of view', and an 'acquired taste' of the west.

Perhaps such arguments are why the idea of human rights are the subject of such controversy. Brown (1999) observes how even the notion that only human beings or homo-sapiens should have rights is in itself contentious, since throughout history some have failed to draw sharp distinctions between humans and other creatures (ibid; Donnelly, 2003). For example, Kant (1798) contemplated the potential rights of extra-terrestrials during the enlightenment, and today questions arise as to whether great apes, elephants, dolphins, and whales are sufficiently sentient to be afforded rights or recognition as a legal 'persons' (BBC, 2012a; Nonhuman Rights Project, 2019: n.p.). Griffin (2008: 32) puts forth a foundationalist counter-argument, to justify speciesism in the human rights sphere, acknowledging that humans are normatively distinct from non-human animals, since we are agents: 'deliberating, assessing, choosing, and acting to make what we see as a good life for ourselves'.

Though speciesism – while contested – has been permitted to justify the validity of human rights, there are nevertheless compelling arguments which frame human rights as historically and culturally contingent, and not applicable to all of humanity. This argument holds particular relevance for civilisations outside of Europe and America, as they did not have a hand in the conception of rights. Rorty (1999) notes how societies that have been untouched by the European enlightenment fail to construe all humans as human beings per se. Rather, these civilisations distinguish themselves as 'good' or as 'true humans' from their foes who are rendered 'bad' or 'pseudo-humans', and who thereby fail to satisfy the necessary criteria to be afforded human rights status (ibid: 67).

At the time of writing, Rorty (ibid) employed the then-current Bosnian genocide as an example to demonstrate how the Serb's ethnic cleansing of the Bosnian Muslims was not viewed as a human rights violation, as the Muslims were not perceived to be fellow human beings. As well as recognising the cultural contingency present, Rorty (ibid: 68) also acknowledges the notion of rights to be historically contingent, since natural rights theory focused on the rights of 'man' to the exclusion of women, slaves and people who were deemed to be 'not like us'. Hence, moral choices relating to rights are merely historically or culturally contingent facts of the world (ibid). Accordingly, why should membership in a biological species suffice for membership in a moral community, particularly since many civilisations would deem it too risky to allow their sense of community to extend beyond their immediate family/clan/tribe? (ibid). While there is easy no way to reconcile these competing philosophical narratives, it has also been argued that the contentious foundations upon which rights rest are ultimately irrelevant anyway.

Critiquing human rights as a social construction

Academics have recognised that problems of circularity and vulnerability are applicable to all moral concepts and practices and are not just limited to human rights (Donnelly, 2003). As such, Donnelly (2003) observes human rights to ultimately rest upon the social decision to act as though such 'things' existed, and then through the social action directed by these rights, to create the world they envision. Gregg (2012) similarly views human rights as a social construction, as something made – and made by us – as a product of our human agency. Gregg (ibid: 38, 234) considers the idea that 'we humans *can* pull ourselves up morally by our own normative bootstraps', actively producing our own fate, as preferable to perceiving ourselves as 'passive "consumers" of otherworldly givens'.

These views are anti-foundationalist since 'to embrace the idea of human rights ... one need not ground it' (ibid: 14). Though this view appears to directly contrast with Perry's (1998) proposal that for human rights to be coherent they must have a religious foundation, Perry nevertheless recognises the concept of human rights to represent a utopian ideal, with both moral ideas and political practice being fused together. Perry (ibid) further asserts that it was this ideal that attributed to the creation of the UDHR in the first place, providing the foundations for legally enforceable human rights treaties; to prevent the genocidal atrocities of World War II from ever reoccurring. Although such atrocities have occurred to varying degrees, it is possibly fair to suggest that the foundationalist concept of human rights has acted as an important safeguard.

Indeed, even if human rights foundationalism, and with it the idea that every human being is sacred, is an imaginary, socially constructed concept, it is arguably an essential one, serving an important function, since it prevents a situation where every culture acts in their own self-interest. In his book's concluding sentence, Edmunson (2004) also recognises the importance of rights as a safeguard, noting that rights can make it possible for people to experiment with their lives, without making mere experiments of others, and to that extent, they are to be cherished. Accordingly, a total dismissal of human rights foundationalism, from a constructionist perspective, could be unwarranted, since it is on the premise that every human is sacred that rights can legitimately act as a safeguard for humankind.

Griffin (2008) and Edmunson (2004) have additionally found human rights constructionism with a foundationalist veneer to serve other practical purposes. They believe the concept of human rights helps empower individuals, with Edmunson (ibid) noting that when aspirations are expressed as entitlements people are psychologically readier to fight for what they perceive to be theirs. Donnelly (2003) too reaffirms that human rights claims are not merely aspirations, but rights-based demands for change. It has been posited that such empowerment could extend beyond an individual level, as Hunt (2007) observes that it is individual minds that help shape and reshape entire social and cultural contexts via rights discourse.

At the risk of going full circle, and moving away from accepting (if at all) human rights foundationalism exclusively as a practical, social construction, Hunt (ibid) acknowledges that such deep moral and social shifts via individual minds are facilitated by the *self-evident nature* of human rights. Hunt (ibid) considers that human beings understand and act on their meaning simply because they are distressed if their rights are violated. Arguably then, a foundational account is necessary to trace the alteration of individual minds and to gleam where and when new kinds of understandings and feelings arise. Moreover, to believe that such rights are self-evident by human nature alone could suggest that the concept of rights is not merely a social construction of the west and that it is grounded in natural law.

This corresponds with the view expressed by Donnelly (2003) that human rights have humanity at their source, as they are rooted in a substantive vision of a person's moral nature, wherever the person may have originated. Therefore, in contrast with a social constructionist perspective, it has been suggested that foundationalism and natural rights theory can go a long way towards preserving the essential universality of a human right, since the idea of rights is regarded as entrenched in human nature itself (Donnelly, 1982).

The malleability of human beings

Yet, as discussed above, it can also be asserted that 'human nature is a social project more than a pre social given' (Donnelly, 2003: 14). From the 18th century to the present, we have been able to view the extension of rights and appreciate how they are now applicable to persons without regard to sex, race or resources (see Article 2 UDHR). Rorty (1999) attributes such changes to our developing sentiments and sympathies. He considers that a human rights culture concerned with sentimental education and persuasion, trumps moral, rational philosophising relating to 'theories of human nature' (ibid: 69). There is an increasing willingness to replace the *foundationalist* question, 'what is our nature?' with the *social constructionist* question 'what can we make of ourselves?' (ibid). Rorty regards human beings as extraordinarily *malleable*, and calls for us to recreate ourselves, as opposed to questioning our nature:

> If we can work together, we can make ourselves into whatever we are clever and courageous enough to imagine ourselves becoming. (ibid: 73)

We are continuously developing our own idea of human rights and such developments may well have led to the explosion of rights discourse present now and throughout the latter decades of the 20th century; further evidencing our malleability. In spite of this, as will be discussed in later chapters, our developing sentiments and sympathies are beginning to stall. Human rights are facing a legitimacy crisis (see Chapters 2 and 3 for more detail), and the concept is failing to achieve Rorty's (ibid: 74) goal to manipulate our sentiments, in order to expand the reference of the terms 'our kind of people' and 'people like us'.

A rise in particularistic positions operates in direct contrast with Rorty's aims. It will be demonstrated – especially within a UK context – that some people are becoming more likely to think of those different from themselves as less deserving or as 'quasi-humans' (ibid). While regrettable, this attitude nonetheless is still demonstrative of our *malleability* and our capacity to change (see 'Losing sense of the term' subsection). Moreover, due to the continuing prevalence of rights discourse, human rights are becoming subjected to extravagant formulations and impractical demands, as citizens are increasingly asserting individual or egotistical claims without considering the possibility of burdening others with any corresponding obligations (Glendon, 1991; O'Neill, 1996; Griffin, 2008).

Losing sense of the term

It has been suggested that the original sense of the term human rights has been lost, since an all-encompassing focus on persons as right-holders steers rights away from traditional questions concerning what one ought to do and how one ought to live (O'Neill, 1996). Glendon (1991; 14), who helped pioneer this argument, acknowledges how such an insular focus on our individual rights could impede social progress, since abandoning these traditional questions has promoted 'mere assertion over reason giving', inhibiting the possibility of finding common ground.

Yet, Glendon's critique of 'rights talk' does not extend beyond American rights discourse, which could suggest that individualistic rights-based saturation has not occurred at an international level (Perry, 1998). Perry (ibid) cites numerous international human rights documents that are explicit about individual responsibilities and duties, and notes that from a communitarian perspective, it is for the common good of the community that diverse individual beliefs are upheld (ibid citing Hollenbach, 1994). It could also be argued that rights talk is not inherently individualistic or bourgeois-liberal or androcentric; rather, it takes on those properties only when society establishes the wrong rights (Fraser, 1989).

Perhaps then, it is worth considering whether or not the UK is guilty of establishing the wrong rights, since the public perception on the importance of human rights is now more questionable than ever before. The British Conservative Party planned to scrap the HRA (1998), a statute which incorporates the ECHR directly into domestic law, and replace it with a British Bill of Rights, in order to: 'break the formal link between British courts and the European Court of human rights' (The Conservative Party Manifesto, 2015: 60). The effect of this would make the UK Supreme Court 'the ultimate arbiter of human rights matters in the country' (ibid). The aim was to distance the UK from the 'mission creep' of the European Court of Human Rights (hereafter the ECtHR) in Strasbourg (see the Conservative Policy Paper, 2014). However, in light of the political upheaval generated by the Brexit vote, whereby UK citizens voted to leave the European Union, these plans have been put on hold.

The Conservative Party Manifesto (2017: 37) stated: 'We will not repeal or replace the Human Rights Act while the process of Brexit is underway but we will consider our human rights legal framework when the process of leaving the EU concludes'. Though the operation of this legal architecture and the implications of Brexit will be explored in Chapter 3, it is sufficient to argue here that proposals to replace or repeal the HRA are a populist response to concerns in the UK relating to how human rights are being interpreted. According to Gies (2015), a key objection to human rights in the UK is that they protect the wrong people, and that the media in particular selectively portray who is considered to be deserving of human rights protection. An 'us' versus 'them', 'deserving' versus 'underserving' mentality has become increasingly prevalent in the UK over the last decade.

In the BBC (2012b) documentary 'Rights Gone Wrong', the TV presenter Andrew Neil observed that segments of the UK public are becoming increasingly hostile to the whole idea of human rights, as many believe the concept has extended too far and is now more offender orientated than victim orientated. A UK human rights enquiry conducted in 2009 by Britain's national equality body, the Equality and Human Rights Commission further reinforces this perception. The commission found that 42 per cent of the public agreed with the proposition that the 'only people to benefit from human rights in the UK are criminals and terrorists', while 40 per cent disagreed (Equality and Human Rights Commission, 2009).

It has been asserted that the tabloid press, in particular, are responsible for utilising the HRA as a vehicle to demonise certain communities and minority groups, and it is thus used only in terms of sensationalist journalism (ibid). In light of such negativity, topical human right issues such as giving prisoners the right to vote, and granting asylum to known terrorists have sparked much debate and disagreement from the UK public (Gies, 2015). It is precisely these issues which are exemplified in a Conservative Policy Paper (2014) to justify the Manifesto's proposals.

Yet, it is arguably unsurprising that most human rights cases involve the least popular members of society (immigrants, prisoners, mental health patients and suspected terrorists) (Wicks, Ziegler and Hodson, 2015), and when combined with the claim that human rights are being expanded, further objections can often arise (ibid). For instance, newspaper headlines stating: '[I]t's your human right to take drugs: *Junkies* could use privacy law to avoid jail say MPs' are deliberately provocative and evoke further criticism of human rights from the UK public (Slack, 2015: n.p., emphasis added). Such hostility towards rights demonstrates a lack of understanding as to how human rights operate.

Human rights are evolutive 'living' instruments, and it is thought that courts ought to respond to scientific advances and social changes (Wicks, Ziegler and Hodson, 2015). Human rights are also concerned with the political relationship between people and their governments and they are designed to protect individuals from their governments (see 'The American and French Revolutions' subsection). It is important to recognise their function and significance and that human rights law does not prioritise individuals' rights, rather it simply requires that any limitation of a human right is non-arbitrary, pursues a legitimate aim and is proportionate.

Human rights have their strongest appeal when they are understood as benefitting individuals against the exercise of public power (Wicks, Ziegler and Hodson, 2015; Chapter 2 will explore how this can be achieved). Conversely, changing a system of human rights to suit a political party's priorities deprecates their position, function and significance (ibid). According to Wicks, Ziegler and Hodson (ibid), one way to address any misunderstandings is to develop a human rights culture of constructive and substantive debate, and build an informed, educated approach in relation to the concept of human rights. With that in mind then, combined with the evolutive organic nature of human rights, and in light of our malleable response to the concept of rights, it is prudent to explore which rights can be classified as human rights. Hence, the following section is concerned with how the concept is grounded.

The grounds for human rights

When deciding which rights ought to be classified as human rights, it is possible to make too much or too little of international human rights documents such as the UDHR or the ECHR. According to Nickel (2010), one could make too much of such documents if one assumed that by being on an official list a right automatically has its status affirmed as a human right, as this could potentially lead to a fundamentalist position. Yet, one could also easily make too little of such documents by drawing up a new list of important rights, and by believing that such an action is a novel idea, thereby dismissing the detailed thought processes and practical wisdom which is found in the choices of rights that went into such official documents (ibid). In order to successfully navigate between these two positions, it is necessary to explore the general criteria deemed necessary for a right to be classified as a human right.

The defining features of human rights that most commentators subscribe to are as follows: rights should have governments as their primary addressees; they should ensure that people can have minimally good lives; they should be universal and have high priority, and they should be supported by strong reasons that make plausible their universality and high priority (Nickel, ibid). Additionally, it remains debatable as to whether human rights are absolute, as such this criterion is also explored. While it is possible for human rights to have a horizontal effect in impacting the legal relations between private juristic persons, the subject matter of this book dictates that a vertical relationship between the state and its citizenry will be the primary focal point.

Governments as primary addressees

Since human rights concern political arrangements between people and their governments, it is accepted that they mainly deal with how states should treat their people. As Pogge (2000: 47) asserts, 'to engage human rights, conduct must be in some sense official'. Donnelly (2003: 12) similarly observes the significance of the relationship between governments and the individual here since it is this relationship that has led human rights claims, unlike other claims, to be endowed with a unique 'last resort' status, as no higher appeal is available. In light of this human rights are often viewed as a standard for political legitimacy, the UDHR (preamble) for example presents itself as 'a common standard of achievement for all people and all nations'.

Thus, to be afforded human right status a right should operate as an important safeguard in ensuring that a state acts legitimately and protects its people.

Additionally, given that human rights should have governments as their primary addressees, a human right should also operate to address the power imbalance between the government and the individual. It is this unique set up which, as previously noted, empowers and enables individuals to vindicate their rights (Edmunson, 2004; Griffin, 2008); this, in turn, secures a government's legitimacy under the enlightenment correlativity of rights and duties doctrine. This doctrine will be more thoroughly explored in Chapter 2 when looking at the capacity of human rights to address a fundamental issue at the core of drug policy; the conflict between the interests of the state and the interests of the individual.

Are human rights absolute?

Likewise, the debate as to whether any human rights are absolute, and which if any take precedence in case of a conflict will be more thoroughly illuminated in Chapters 4 and 5, when exploring how human rights and drug policy regimes operate in practice. Although it is largely accepted that human rights can never be completely unconditional, since there exist (largely theoretical) utilitarian considerations which prevent such recognition (Perry, 1998), from a practical viewpoint, there is good sense in ensuring that some legal human rights are absolute. Both Perry (1998) and Brems (2009) recognise the right not to be subjected to torture as a core human right obligation for governments, with Perry (ibid) recognising its legally absolute status to be a necessity here. This absolute status operates as a safeguard to prevent any potential 'escape clauses' for political authorities (ibid: 106). However, the vast majority of rights are not legally absolute, even if they are considered to be core rights (i.e. the right to life), and they can often be subject to reasonable restrictions in the public interest.

For instance, Articles 8–11 ECHR are qualified rights and they allow for government interference providing it is in accordance with the law, necessary in a democratic society and the interference must pursue a legitimate aim such as: protecting the public order, health, morals, public safety, and/or to protect the rights or freedoms of others. The imposition of such restrictions corresponds with a key 'feature of the human predicament', as we are incapable of foreseeing or identifying all possible situations involving human right provisions (Hart, 1994: 128), thus it makes sense to allow for open-ended, limited and qualified rights. Moreover, human rights are generally accepted as being incommensurable, a concept which means that where clashes of value exist, it is not possible to rank and rationally compare competing accommodations (Alder, 2006). Since rights encompass human nature, which in itself comprises of competing and irreconcilable impulses (ibid), it logically follows that human rights themselves will clash.

Supported by strong reasons

Therefore, although Nickel (2010) highlights that human rights should be supported by strong reasons, these reasons can often conflict, particularly where any intrinsic values for an individual are weighed against consequentialist concerns in the public interest. What is more, academics acknowledge that when this conflict occurs, a consequentialist perspective tends to dominate the judicial balancing exercise; hence, restrictions justified in the public interest largely tend to override individual rights (Alder, 2006; Beck, 2009; see Chapters 4 and 5 for more detail). Additionally, any legal mechanisms in place to aid the judiciary in balancing competing values, such as a proportionality test, are not always successful in maximising human rights protection for the individual (Brems, 2009). In later chapters, this book demonstrates that such safeguards can be arbitrarily applied, which arguably conforms to the notion that human rights should be minimalist, and should go no further than strictly necessary to achieve their aims.

Ensuring a minimally good life

Commentators who subscribe to human rights foundationalism and the traditional account that rights are rooted in human nature itself, usually favour a minimalist approach (Raz, 2010). This is because the traditional doctrine is so conceptually broad it is generally thought that boundaries have to be imposed to guard against human rights inflation (ibid). Therefore, for traditionalists, the aim of human rights is to protect minimally good lives for all people, as they are 'much more concerned with avoiding the terrible than with achieving the best' (Nickel, 2010: n.p.).

Edmunson (2004) is a particularly strong advocate of the minimalist approach, observing that the proliferation of rights has served to debase rights discourse, has enfeebled the protection offered to core human rights and has facilitated a situation where the general consensus on human rights is becoming less and less clear. Therefore, to potentially avoid the rights revolution from overplaying its hand, Edmunson (ibid) advocates restricting internationally enforceable rights to a minimal list, to ensure that an international consensus on the values to be cherished can be reached and enforced.

However, some commentators oppose the idea that human rights should offer mere minimalist protection (Brems, 2009; Raz, 2010). Raz (ibid) recognises that rights are continuously expanding and evolving, citing a recent human right to sexual pleasure to evidence his claims. Indeed, if human rights are to represent a truly utopian ideal, as envisaged by Donnelly (2003) where both morality and political practice are fused together, then surely rights should be concerned with achieving the very best? Certainly, for Brems (2009), human rights should strive for the horizon as opposed to having governments fixated with the bottom line.

Brems (ibid) observes that human rights at present undergo borderline control monitoring, where the sole concern is to minimise rights violations as opposed to recognising areas of best practice as well. The technique of progressive realisation, which is employed to maximise economically centred rights depending upon when states have various financial resources, should perhaps be extended and applicable to rights in other contexts as well (ibid). Brems (2009: 366) believes rights to be a revolutionary discourse aimed to 'change entrenched political behaviour, as well as entrenched social behaviour', therefore, they are capable of extending beyond the boundaries currently imposed.

Digging deeper: universalism v relativism

While the grounds for human rights which centre upon questions of their absoluteness, incommensurability and the need for governments as primary addressee's will be explored in later chapters, the notion that human rights constitute a revolutionary political discourse holds distinct relevance for this chapter, as it links back to the idea that human rights are a social construction, responding to and reflecting our malleability, and our capacity to recreate ourselves. Yet, the idea that human rights are *universal* (one of Nickel's key grounds) predates the social constructionist conception of the term, since this notion carries remnants of theism. Hence, the universalist ground for human rights could be linked to human rights foundationalism, if it centres on the assumption that there exists a common humanity, where all human beings are essentially alike and should be entitled to the same rights.

Since human beings belong to the same species, it is generally accepted that they share a set of basic capacities, appetites and needs which can only be meaningfully fulfilled under certain conditions (Parekh, 2005). These conditions which define human well-being and constitute common fundamental interests (ibid) have been legislated for within the human rights sphere, as it is *legally* accepted at least that human rights are universal. However, on a metaphysical level, there remains much debate about whether human rights can ever truly be universal in a *foundationalist* sense, or whether their universality is *socially constructed*, since there are diverse ways to interpret human rights, in light of national, regional and cultural particularities. A more extreme relativist position would argue that there is no such thing as universal human rights, since all values and beliefs are culturally relative, and accordingly only apply within certain cultures (Good, 2010).

There is no room in this book to explore the prevailing conflicts between universality and relativity in depth (see Perry, 1998: 58 for more detail on this debate which he presents as the 'the relativist challenge'). Suffice to say, those defending the concepts today can appreciate that both ideals represent incoherent extremes, and that a more sophisticated analysis can acknowledge the value in their opponents position (Donnelly, 2007). Perhaps the best way to give effect to the universality of human rights, then, is to accept the notion of pluralist universalism, an idea introduced by the prominent political theorist, Bhikhu Parekh. The following section explores this concept, to further investigate the validity and the grounds for human rights. The conclusion that human rights can be pluralistically universal, helps to justify why a focus on human rights offers a good lens through which to view human drug use.

A third way: pluralist universalism

In his book, 'Rethinking multiculturalism: Cultural diversity and political theory', Parekh devotes a chapter towards '[c]onceptualising human beings' (Parekh, 2006: Chapter 4). Parekh acknowledges that human beings belong to a common species and share a set of universal capacities, needs and dispositions, which can help them to lead a good life under certain conditions. The common conditions required for human beings to grow and flourish include (but are not limited to): good health, a stable, loving environment, access to the cultural resources of their community, a measure of privacy and control over their lives, freedom from the arbitrary exercise of power and opportunities for self-expression (ibid: 132). When considered altogether, Parekh calls this 'the fact of common humanity' (Parekh, 2005: 285).

At the same time, humans understand themselves and their world under different circumstances, they face different challenges, have varied histories and make sense of a variety of contingencies in their own ways (ibid). As a result, humans develop different cultures based on diverse ideas of human life, since humans respond to the common conditions of existence in different ways (Parekh, 2006). Parekh (2005: 285) calls this 'the fact of cultural diversity'. Accepting both the facts of common humanity and cultural diversity can allow one to reconcile the two competing concepts of universalism and relativism. Both concepts could be said to capture a vital truth about human life, especially in light of the recurrent competing theoretical debates around foundationalism and social constructionism. However, we ought to combine the two to appreciate the 'dialectical interplay of universality and diversity' and avoid misinterpretation, exaggeration or distortion by advancing one incoherent extreme over the other (ibid: 285).

For Parekh (ibid: 286), a pluralist universalist conception of human rights can merge these competing narratives:

> Qua universalist, the pluralist universalist champions human rights, considers them an indispensable feature of the good society and judges all societies and cultures in terms of them. Qua pluralist [s]he values moral and cultural diversity and appreciates that different societies interpret and prioritise human rights differently and resolve their unavoidable conflicts in their own different ways.

Pluralist universalism recognises that humans can belong to both a common species and a distinct culture and that one only exists because of the other:

> Humans belong to a common species not directly but in a culturally mediated manner and they belong to a cultural community by virtue of belonging to a common species. (Parekh, 2006: 124)

Thus, cultures do not exist in vacuity, rather they are limited by and entrenched in universally shared features of our human nature (ibid). A pluralist universalist conception of human rights can therefore appreciate that what is good or bad for human beings, in general, is not inconsistent with there being diversity and different preferences for how best to live a human life. Parekh (2005: 286) acutely surmises this position as the 'relativisation or contextualisation of universal values' (as opposed to absolutising the values of a particular culture, as seen in relativism).

When we conceive of human beings in this way we can appreciate that they are neither 'basically like us' which a universalist account of human rights requires, nor 'totally different' which a relativist account of human rights requires (Parekh, 2006: 124). Rather, a pluralist universalist conception of human rights can promote an intercultural dialogue, since it promotes the idea that there is no one way of conceiving human values, including through the lens of human rights. Instead, the stimulation of an intercultural dialogue, through the milieu of human rights is constructive, since it offers an essential opportunity to delve greater insights into the nature and complexity of universal values (Parekh, 2005).

Therefore, pluralist universalism facilitates openness and debate within the human rights field, as well as respect for the shared humanity and cultural differences of other human beings, which is arguably important when considering human drug use through a human rights lens. Human rights themselves are considered to have a distinctly liberal bias, to the extent that they are rooted in western traditional thought and polity (see 'The history of human rights' section). In providing a mechanism to realise universal values, human rights are thus accused of being individualistic, legalistic and state-centred, unmindful of the fact that different societies may prioritise different values; rooted in the language of duty, social solidarity, social conditioning and moral pressure (Parekh, 2006).

Pluralist universalism appreciates that we need a cross-cultural dialogue to avoid universalising our own values, to better understand and respond to the human condition. Though this book does have a liberal bias (see Introduction for more detail), it will consider where an intercultural dialogue can take place, the limitations of a western conception of human rights and the potential to redefine human rights. Where possible I consider how to move away from exclusivist, proprietary terms thought to be common in liberal societies (ibid) when defining human rights to health and religion (see Chapters 4 and 5), and the potential for human rights to better unpack societal values (see Chapter 2).

Most importantly, a pluralist universalist idea of human rights also provides a useful way to understand human drug use, since this will be shown to be rooted in our *common humanity*, while simultaneously constituting a *culturally diverse* activity. By concluding that the universality of human rights does not negate their cultural diversity, this section provides the groundwork to unearth how human rights are well suited to understanding drug use as a complex human phenomena.

The history and value of human drug use

Moving on from contextualising and grounding the idea of human rights, this section demonstrates how key debates within human rights theory are well suited to catering to the complexities of drug use, since it is hoped that this chapter will provide the initial footing for how the lens of human rights can provide a new perspective on drug control. This section looks at the history of human drug use, and applies concepts discussed above such as human rights 'foundationalism', 'social constructionism', 'the malleability of rights' and 'pluralist universalism' to justify how a philosophical exploration of the idea of human rights can offer a useful lens through which to understand human drug use.

The history of human drug use

There are approximately 4,000 plants containing psychoactive substances (Buxton, 2006). Around 60 of these have been consumed throughout history, as humans have ingested naturally occurring drugs since the beginning of civilisation (ibid). Smail (2008) also notes that human beings have consumed psychoactives for millennia. This practice stretches far back into the deep history of human beings, and it is found in most cultures and societies worldwide (ibid). Out of 237 cultures across the globe, Blum (1969) found only four which had no record of intoxicating substance use, since these societies were regarded as so isolated that they were incapable of cultivating psychoactive plants. Weil and Rosen (1983) reiterate this through observing that Inuit's were unable to grow plant drugs, and thus had to wait for other humans to bring them alcohol.

Such observations reinforce the prevalence of human drug use throughout time and geographical space. Smail (ibid) takes a deep historical perspective towards understanding human psychoactive use, since he argues that we can only understand our brain/body behaviour, and ultimately the human condition itself, through delving into the deep history of the brain; a history which extends beyond written texts. For Smail (ibid: 8 citing Geertz, 1973: 68), there is 'a reciprocally creative relationship between biology and culture', and he argues that the brain is an obvious device for making the deep past intelligible.

In order to truly account for the origin of human drug use and ascribe a value to this phenomenon, it is necessary to adopt a long historical narrative. According to Smail (ibid: 202):

> [T]here is a grandeur in this view of history ... We need not dig only in the dusty top soil of the strata that forms the history of humanity. The deep past is also our present and our future.

To free ourselves from the constraints of the existing paradigms of the present, and with that the system of drug prohibition, a deep historical perspective facilitates an unconstrained narrative. This narrative can apply key aspects of human rights theory to begin to think about how a human rights perspective can help to re-conceptualise and respond to human psychoactive use.

The fact of common humanity and human drug use

Smail (ibid) observes that the human brain has a history that could be older than humanity itself, since non-human animals, after all, engage in mood-altering activities. He notes that they nibble cat-nip, consume fermented fruit, and like us, some primates such as bonobos engage in the bonding experience and pleasures of recreational sex (ibid). Siegel (2005) writes far more extensively on this topic as he asserts that intoxication with plant drugs and other psychoactives has consistently occurred across time in almost every species throughout history. He substantiates his rather broad claims through devoting several chapters of his book – 'Intoxication the Universal Drive for Mind Altering Substances' – to scientifically documenting patterns of intoxication and the drug-seeking behaviour of a variety of animal species including goats, birds, cats, pumas, koalas, mongooses and apes.

Siegel (2005: vii) argues that this demonstrates that intoxication is a natural part of our biology, much like the drives for thirst, hunger and sex; he considers that the pursuit of psychoactives functions as a 'fourth drive'. This notion corresponds with human rights foundationalism and the idea that human rights are entrenched in human nature itself (Donnelly, 1982). This perspective acknowledges that human rights have humanity at their source as there are certain appetites, social senses and needs which are shared across all cultures, thus some needs are not local, but human (Perry, 1998). Though human rights foundationalism is subject to criticism, the consideration that human rights derive from our human nature is worth considering. Indeed, if human rights respond to the human condition by design, and human drug use is a naturalistic phenomenon rooted in our common humanity, then human rights could be utilised to respond to human drug use as a universal need; in a way that could help human beings grow and flourish.

What is more, prior to the agricultural revolution, Palaeolithic societies acquired a range of mood-altering practices including dance, song and mood-altering substances which were often used in a ritualistic context (Smail, 2008). Psychedelic philosophers such as Terrance McKenna (1992), perceived plant-based hallucinogens as having a pivotal role in the development of anthropoid awareness. While this subscribes to the idea that human psychoactive use is a naturalistic, foundational phenomenon, McKenna (ibid: 13) additionally links the way in which humans ingested drugs in those eras with more recent psychedelic movements in the 20th century, observing there to be an 'archaic revival'. Tupper (2002: 499) confirms McKenna's (1992) view that plant psychedelics were historically utilised as 'cognitive tools' to help humans make sense of the world, and facilitated different types of intelligence.

He suggests that ancient shamanic practices brought experiential, existential and spiritual intelligence to the fore through the use of these psychoactives (ibid); a view which Moore (2007) and Siegel (2005) confirm to have occurred across human history. Siegel (ibid) refers to the high regard ancient Greeks had for certain psychoactive plants, and Moore (2007: 357) establishes that the Romantics (an 18th-century forerunner to the psychedelic movement in the 1960s), accorded drugs a valuable position, observing: '[d]rugs could take one closer to truth, could reveal, through hedonistic self-exploration, the real, authentic self, buried beneath capitalism and social convention'.

The revival of these ancient wisdoms introduces an element of circularity towards understanding the history and the value humans ascribe to the use of psychoactives. Most importantly, it gives credence to the idea that human drug use could constitute a *fact of our common humanity*, and that human rights could be utilised as a tool to respond to human drug use as a foundationalist, naturalistic phenomena. Indeed, Part II (Chapters 4 and 5) of this book will discuss in far greater detail how certain psychoactives like cannabis, ayahuasca and peyote have been revered and utilised for pleasure, health, spiritual, religious and for thought expanding purposes on a global scale. Chapters 4 and 5 consider both the limitations and the potential of the human rights framework to respond to this.

The fact of cultural diversity and human drug use

However, the idea that psychoactive use can be solely attributed to our nature as chemical beings is too simplistic a concept for Smail (2008). In keeping with the social constructionist conception of human rights, and the ideas expressed by Parekh (2005, 2006) such as *the fact of cultural diversity* and a pluralist universalist conception of human rights, Smail (ibid) posits that culture is a biological phenomenon wired in the brain, and that our neurophysiology adapts to changes in behaviour and customs. Parekh (ibid: 123) similarly accepts that human nature is largely a product of human self-creation, and that while it may have a degree of permanence, it can be altered over a lengthy period of time:

> As beings who constantly push against their inherited limits and sometimes succeed in stretching them, [our] nature is not static and finished but subject to further development.

Notwithstanding the exceptions detailed above, the plant psychoactives which humans ingested in the Neolithic and Palaeolithic eras largely occurred in a remarkably different setting to the way in which most human cultures ingest psychoactives today. Post the agricultural revolution, the advent of 'civilisation' and sedentism is thought to have altered our body chemistry, given an evolving economy and political systems which were increasingly organised around the delivery of institutions, sets of practices and goods (Smail, 2008). Smail (ibid) observes that the 17th and 18th centuries, in particular, constitute distinctive time periods in the neuro-history of human beings. According to the historian August Ludwig Schözer (1809 as cited by Burke, 1990: 36):

> [t]he discovery of spirits, the arrival of tobacco, sugar, coffee and tea in Europe have brought about revolutions just as great as, if not greater than, the defeat of the Invincible Armada, the wars of the Spanish Succession, the Paris Peace, etc.

In fact, in these centuries economies became orientated in large part around the production and circulation of psychoactive substances. According to Smail (2008) advances in the 17th and 18th centuries expose psychotropic profiles which were no longer linked with worldwide geographical regions, rather psychoactives became linked to class or status identities, given their increasing availability and cultural integration. What is more, traditional boundaries between using substances as medicines, using them recreationally and abusing them were breaking down (ibid). While our human ancestors are thought to have ingested plant psychedelics, largely to enhance different knowledge bases and to make sense of the world, the development of an increasingly consumerist economy altered the way in which we consume psychoactives, and the way in which they are socially construed.

Consumption is now regarded as being a consequence of society as well as being constitutive of it (Burnett, 1999). Substances such as tea and coffee and even alcohol have undergone many civilising processes, are thought to be ingrained in the collective consciousness, and can be perceived as useful and beneficial; facilitating a common element of sociability and hospitality. Other psychoactives such as sugar are subject to very little restriction since sugar is exploited commercially to fulfil our innate, hedonistic drives in an increasingly global capitalist world (Courtwright, 2002). The reasons why certain psychoactives are prohibited and others are not are socially constructed, due to cultural, political and economic reasons, and this will be explored more thoroughly in Chapter 3. For now, it is enough to observe that the essence of modern culture allows: 'sovereign individuals to ransack the world store house, casting aside traditional restraints in the pursuit of self-fulfilment' (ibid: 206).

The malleability of human drug use

Our evolving political and economic systems altering the way in which we consume and construe certain psychoactives could be demonstrative of us actively producing our own fate. This fits well with the social constructionist conception of human rights, which perceives rights as malleable concepts – which are made and made by us – since 'human nature is more of a social project than a pre-social given' (Donnelly, 2003: 14). The idea that our human nature is subject to further development, as opposed to being static or finished (Parekh, 2006), demonstrates the utility of human rights here. As malleable concepts, capable of responding to changing political, cultural, social and economic paradigms, human rights could respond to our malleable drug-using behaviours.

This is particularly pertinent since human technology is evolving faster than our neurophysiology allows (Smail, 2008). The invention of the hypodermic syringe and the safety match have altered our drug-using patterns and behaviours (Siegel, 2005). We can now have instantaneous more powerful ‘hits’ or ‘highs’ from psychoactives, a situation which conforms to the consumerist capitalist narrative, but one which Siegel (2005) cautions against. The age of the internet and the advent of new psychoactive substances (NPS) have also completely reconfigured humankind’s relationship with psychoactives, and more recently, the hegemonic narrative of prohibition (Walsh, 2011).

Such technological advances, i.e. mass communication via the internet, further challenge the simplistic view garnered by the prohibitionist regime that all drugs are the same and are equally dangerous (Babor et al., 2010). It is only by understanding human drug use as a complex phenomenon occurring in a vast array of changing social, political, cultural, economic and technological contexts throughout history, that meaningful policy responses can be developed.

Reframing the idea of human rights to respond to human drug use

Although human psychoactive use occurs in a multitude of contexts, the pluralist universalist approach, developed within the milieu of human rights, appreciates this diversity, yet simultaneously recognises that some appetites and behaviours are distinctly human. Even though our ancient ancestors may have used psychoactives as cognitive, evolutionary tools, the fact that such use predates humanity, as substances are used by non-human animals for pleasure, substantiates the more westernised hedonistic, pleasure-seeking and consumeristic drug behaviours today.

Moreover, the drug-using purposes for humankind in the 20th and 21st century are remarkably similar to the purposes expressed by our ancestors. Buxton (2008) expands on Inglis’s (1975) six primary drivers for drug use in ancient and modern societies, some of which are discussed above. She notes that psychoactives are used in human societies for pain relief, for physical stimulation, for their cultural, spiritual and religious significance, as a food source, for bartering and financial purposes and for relaxation, recreation and experimentation (ibid).

These broad uses coincide with Chapters 4 and 5 which use health rights and religious rights as conceptual starting points for how human rights law applies to the drug control framework in practice. It is revealed in the case law sections of these chapters that humankind additionally use drugs for pleasure, to escape pain, for well-being, for their spiritual and cultural as well as religious import, and for thought expansion purposes to name but a few. Chapters 4 and 5 illustrate the orthodox way in which health rights, religious rights and related human rights are currently defined in the case law, and how they ought to be defined to better reflect our drug-using purposes.

Such purposes reveal a commonality amongst human beings occurring across time and throughout most cultures. As Smail (2008: 199) remarks:

> [W]e celebrate the diversity of human civilisations, but it is the similarities that are the most startling, the thing that continually reminds us of our common humanity.

It is hoped then that a philosophical exploration of the concept of human rights can be applied to help to understand, reflect, and respond to the complex phenomena that is human psychoactive use.

Conclusion

This chapter sought to understand the origin and value of human rights and human drug use to justify why a human rights lens can provide a new perspective on the drug control framework. The majority of the chapter was justifiably devoted towards contextualising human rights and legitimising them as a valid concept. Since they have been subject to much criticism, I thought it necessary to explore the legal origins of human rights, question key human rights theories, concepts and debates and establish that human rights can be pluralistically universal – capable of viewing drug use as rooted in our common humanity and as constituting a culturally diverse, evolving activity.

A foundationalist conception of human rights could also be employed to reframe human drug use as a universal need, while a socially constructed conception of human rights, adapting to changing political, social, cultural, historical and economic narratives – could be utilised to respond to our malleable drug-using behaviours. Chapters 4 and 5 will explore the potential and limitations of the human rights framework, when viewed this way, to respond to human drug use as a complex human phenomenon; with a particular focus on how drug use is defined in law.

This chapter also considers the broader value of human rights and recognises that human rights are architecturally designed to address the binary between the state and the individual – a binary which will be identified to be at the crux of drug policies. Although this chapter only hinted at the conflicts between the state and the individual in relation to human psychoactive use, and the legal architectural frameworks of the human rights and drug control regimes, Chapters 2 and 3 will more thoroughly explore these issues, to advance the argument that human rights can provide a new perspective on drug control issues.

This chapter ultimately introduced the idea of human rights and applied key philosophical debates pertaining to their origin and value to human drug use. The naturalistic origins of drug consumption, and the commonality of use, combined with evolving malleable contexts for use and cultural contexts of use, confirms that a human rights perspective is capable of understanding and appreciating the complex realities of this phenomena.

Chapter 2

Human rights and the drug policy binary

As highlighted in Chapter 1, the consumption of psychoactive substances is a practice which has existed for millennia; it is found in most cultures and societies across the globe (Weil and Rosen, 1983) and stretches far back into the deep history of human beings (Smail, 2008). As a result of this phenomenon, a conflict has emerged, one which according to Siegel (2005) pits individual needs in pursuing a strong biological drive for intoxication, against those of societies in striving to maintain order. Siegel (ibid) draws on biological and cultural evidence throughout history to suggest that human beings have an instinctive and universal drive for intoxication, one which operates in a similar fashion to other biological drivers such as thirst, hunger and sex. He calls this pursuit for intoxication the 'fourth drive' (ibid).

Chapter 2 demonstrates the inherent arbitrariness in the way the conflict between an individual's 'fourth drive' and the state is presented within the drug policy sphere, as the failure to overtly unpack the moral questions raised when pitting a state's interest against an individual has led to the restrictive policy regime of prohibition. Initially, Chapter 2 recognises the conceptual difficulties involved in defining what constitutes the 'state'. The term is contested both across and within a variety of academic disciplines, it is important to recognise its contestability, and to unpack the key questions raised when formulating a definition, particularly questions pertaining to the interests a state represents.

The chapter then identifies the dominant philosophical arguments which shape the drug control paradigm, as it is these foundations upon which the current paradigm and the resulting conflict between the state and the individual rests. A thorough understanding of the normative – deontological and consequentialist – positions arguing for and against the use of psychoactives is essential to appreciate how the binary was constructed, and continues to be maintained through the employment of standard drug policy proposals: prohibition, decriminalisation, harm reduction, legal regulation and an unregulated legal market.

The central premise of Chapter 2 is to advance the idea that human rights are a conceptually useful tool to embrace normative thinking, by explicitly addressing the core conflict within this field: the interests of the state in restricting certain psychoactives versus the drives of individuals striving to consume them. The language of human rights is fundamentally normative, emerging out of the political liberalism of the enlightenment as alluded to in Chapter 1, and rights are concerned with preserving the liberties of individuals and groups against the powers of the state (Langlois, 2013). It is in this vein then that Chapter 2 recognises the utility of a human rights perspective, as rights are actually designed to address tensions between the state, societies and individuals through the correlativity of the rights and duties doctrine.

Moreover, a human rights lens can reconfigure the binary to focus on the individual drug consumer, this could alter existing power struggles and point to more innovate policy proposals which could benefit both the individual and broader societal interests. While an explicit focus on the human rights of an individual consumer serves to question the morality of drug use, this chapter illustrates how a human rights perspective could go even further and be used to openly unpack shared societal values, in order to develop an alternative moral policy response to the reality of drug use as it currently exists.

Defining 'the state'

In the realms of political theory, the idea of the 'state' has been notoriously difficult to define (Robinson, 2013). While the 'state' has been studied from many perspectives, according to Jessop (2008: 111) 'no single theory can completely capture and explain its complexities'. As a leading state theorist, Jessop (ibid: 111–112) articulates some of the key conceptual questions when identifying the remit and the definition of the state:

> Is the state best defined by its legal form, coercive capacities, institutional composition and boundaries, internal operations and modes of calculation, declared aims, functions for the broader society, or sovereign place in the international system? Is it a thing, a subject, a social relation, or a construct that helps to orient political action? Is stateness a variable and, if so, what are its central dimensions? What is the relationship between the state and law, the state and politics, the state and civil society, the public and the private, state power and micro power relations? Is the state best studied in isolation; only as part of the political system; or, indeed, in terms of a more general social theory? Do states have institutional, decisional, or operational autonomy and, if so, what are its sources and limits?

It is clearly difficult, if not impossible to effectively capture all perspectives which theorise and analyse states. This section broadly introduces the key themes, ideas and theories on what constitutes the 'state', and focuses on why it is necessary to gauge a working definition of the state for this chapter, and throughout the rest of this book. The analytical purchase offered through the concept of the state is in its ability to contextualise political behaviour both structurally and institutionally since, almost without exception, the concept is deployed in these terms (Hay and Lister, 2006). Therefore, this section begins with the renowned Weberian definition of the state and ends with an appreciation of the changing role of the state, the concept of multi-level governance, the nature of the relationships between states and the broader field of international relations; so far as this relates to the UK and the UK's relationship with other state-bodies – given the international nature of the global drug prohibitionist paradigm.

Challenging the Weberian definition

Weber's (1946: 78) celebrated definition defines the modern state as 'a human community that (successfully) claims the monopoly of the legitimate use of physical force within a given territory'. Though this definition has stood the test of time and continues to be used in state theorist literature (see Brenner et al., 2003; Dunleavy, 2007; Jessop, 2008), it perpetuates the 'container' metaphor, which perceives states as spatial entities separated by territorial boundaries (Brenner et al., 2003: 1). For Brenner et al. (ibid), the role of the state is changing, and territorially demarcated forms of state power are being restructured in response to a transformed global setting. When considering the controversies in defining the state, Dunleavy (2007: 802) similarly recognises a progressive shift of policy making from national to transnational institutions and concludes that:

> [T]he age of the unitary nation state commanding strategic resources and acting in a realist mode in international relations may yet prove to be a transitory period in human affairs.

Any challenges posed to the notion of national statehood will be considered in greater detail (particularly in relation to the UK) below. For now, it is sufficient to note that the spatial and temporal horizons of what constitutes a 'state' are changing. It is arguably an oversimplification to offer the conservative legalistic or geographical definition favoured by Robinson (2013), which distinguishes states from governments; noting that the former are non-physical juridical entities of the international legal system, distinct from governments; who are the legally coercive organisations of people through which state power is employed (ibid). However, if one accepts the emerging structure of 'multi-level governance' as the dispersion of authoritative decision-making across multiple territorial levels (Hooghe and Marks, 2001), the conceptual boundaries between a state and a government is blurred.

Along with changing spatial and territorial boundaries, state theorists point to an array of institutions believed to constitute the state. According to Morris (2011), the state is thought to comprise of an increasingly diverse array of institutions and organisations including, but not limited to: central governments, the judiciary, the police, the military, schools and universities, state bureaucracies, the mass media and agencies charged with controlling information. Morris (ibid) observes that 'state' can be used interchangeably with 'government' and that the growth of private corporations and interest groups have increasingly blurred boundaries as to what constitutes the state. Moreover (as already alluded to), the expansion of institutions and organisations within the global political order such as the United Nations, the European Union and the Council of Europe, has led to a system of states; further increasing the difficulty in its characterisation (ibid).

A wider theory of society

Such a wide conception conveys that the 'state' cannot be defined by reference to either its institutions or its territorial dimensions alone. Rather, in keeping with the key conceptual questions Jessop (2008) poses, the state cannot be reified as standing outside and above society. Instead, the complexities of the state can be more fully understood through recognising 'there can be no adequate theory of the state without a wider theory of society' (ibid: 111). For Jessop (ibid), the political system and the state constitute a broader ensemble of social relations, and the state can only be understood through its embedding within this ensemble. However, appreciating the state as part of a wider theory of society presents an unfortunate paradox:

> [O]n the one hand, it is just one institutional ensemble among others within a social formation; on the other, it is peculiarly charged with overall responsibility for maintaining the cohesion of which it is part. (ibid: 129)

Thus, the state is continuously called upon to resolve society's problems, and the concept is thereby doomed for failure, since many problems lie well beyond its control. Lister and Marsh (2006) likewise point to the false dichotomy produced when pitting the state against the individual, particularly in light of arguments that the state has been hollowed out with powers shifting; upwards to supranational bodies, sideways to the private sector and downwards, due to devolution and increasing demands for localism. Hence, there are calls to reject the dualism and to focus more directly on the relationship *between* the state and civil society (ibid).

Although the binary presented under a prohibitionist paradigm pitting the interests of the state against the interests of the individual, runs the risk of oversimplifying the notion, this binary will nevertheless be employed, since it relates to the fundamental conflict identified to be at the crux of drug policies. Moreover, in full appreciation that the state cannot be understood without a wider theory of society, this chapter centres its rationale for defining the state upon the fundamental conflict which pits the individual against the state. This conflict could be construed in a multitude of ways: as pitting individual needs in pursuing a strong biological drive for intoxication, against those of *societies* in striving to maintain order (Siegel, 2005: emphasis added), or else as pitting individual free choice against *societal/state* concerns about public health, morality or public order. Hence, this increases the focus on the relationship *between* the state and society, through recognising the 'state' within Jessop's (2008: 111) 'wider theory of society' context.

What is more, key state-centred theories such as Marxism and feminism adopt a political identity through which to understand society, and to 'portray the kind of society they believe *ought*, *should* and even *must* be brought about' (Heywood, 1992: 2). Accordingly, these key ideas will be discussed in turn, alongside Foucauldian perspectives, since concerns for a moral, fair or good society link back to the state's responsibility for maintaining social cohesion (Jessop, 2008), and questions relating to state morality more generally. For instance, can a state derive its authority from particular sets of cultural and shared values? While it may be unrealistic to charge the state with an overall responsibility for maintaining social cohesion (ibid), it is necessary to have transparency and to question the assumed cultural shared values a state may have. This chapter later demonstrates that a human rights lens illuminates this need for transparency.

Furthermore, unpacking the notion of shared values has relevance for part II of the book, as it exposes the homogenising nature of both the drug policy and human rights frameworks, as they largely protect arbitrary notions of religion, health, etc. within the conceptual boundaries of a state. It is therefore essential to question whether the 'state' can ever follow and represent society, or given its position of power, does the state represent distinct interests within society, as opposed to representing society as a whole?

State-centred theories and beyond

A Marxist perspective perceives the state as either a direct reflection of economic structures and interests or as a vehicle for political class rule, as directed by those in charge. Unsurprisingly then, the state remains a key factor in class domination (Engels, 1875/1975). For Marxists, the state is thought to represent distinct interests within society, given its position of power, as opposed to representing society as a whole. According to Dunleavy (2007), Marxist state theories generally adopt an organic view of the state, and construe it has having a social function, or some moral purpose which requires its coming into existence. He posits that Marxist influenced work seems to reify the state, and produces a unitary social actor, whose precise inner workings or identification are obscure, but yet massive social influence is often assigned to it.

Feminist perspectives, on the other hand, focus on the structuring of state power in ways that reproduce patriarchy. This perspective tends to adopt a more methodological, individualist view of the state as a set of publically organised, designated institutions (ibid). Radical feminist perspectives, in particular, centre their analysis upon state institutions and operations such as the gender bias of welfare rules, laws and the courts (MacKinnon, 1989). Again then, the state is thought to represent distinct interests, as opposed to representing society as a whole.

Foucauldian perspectives are interesting in that they perceive that the state has no essence on its own (Foucault, 1991). Foucault (ibid: 103) postulates: 'maybe the state is no more than a composite reality and a mythologized abstraction'. Foucault (ibid) undermines the analytical centrality of the state as he failed to perceive power as concentrated within the state, rather he advocated a bottom up approach – concerned with where power is actually exercised – 'it is ubiquitous, immanent in every social relation' (Jessop, 2008: 120). For Foucault (1980), state power is dispersed, and involves the actual mobilisation of individuals from a microphysics of power perspective, as opposed to primarily focusing on macro politics and the passive targeting of individuals.

Thus, state power is part of a wider theory of society, whereby individuals are constitutive of this abstract notion. In his seminal work on 'governmentality', Foucault (1991) proposes an alternative analysis of political power through arguing that the state has neither the functionality nor the unity ascribed to it. Rather, what is important 'is not so much the state-domination of society, but the "governmentalization" of the state' (Rose and Miller, 1992: 175 citing Foucault, 1979: 20). Rose and Miller (1992) draw upon Foucault's (1979) idea of 'governmentality' – as the art of government – and argue that Foucault's analysis of power moves away from a traditional 'critical' approach (typified by Marxism), which thinks in terms of state power exercised over individuals and groups.

The idea of governmentality is that power over individuals is exercised in multiple sites, in multiple ways, by multiple actors, and cannot be reduced to the state or state agencies (ibid). Thus, Foucauldian perspectives serve as an example of critical analysis which goes well beyond state-centric theories of power. Though Foucault adopts a broad, overarching analysis, by drawing attention to the ubiquity of power, Foucauldian approaches have nevertheless been criticised for ignoring how class/patriarchal relations shape a state's deployment of power (Jessop, 2008).

Regardless, academic engagement with how power is exercised, as opposed to focusing on whom or what exercises it, when considering the significance we bestow on the idea of the state, is persuasive. When considering any points of convergence between key state theories, Lister and Marsh (2006) acknowledge that most embrace a normative commitment to the diffusion of power. However, we are told that the state is being hollowed out and is losing its power upwards, sideways and downwards (ibid). The nature of the 'state' is changing, hence state theorists may be unwilling to define it by reference to territorial boundaries or institutions alone.

The changing nature of the state

The globalisation age sees transnational, supranational, regional and national negotiations of power, and other factors, such as the amalgamation of corporations and the private sector into conceptions of the 'state' (Bache and Flinders, 2004; see also Bremmer, 2010). Literature on 'multi-level governance' exemplifies the changing spatial and territorial dimensions of the state (Hooghe and Marks, 2001; Bache and Flinders, 2004), and Bache and Flinders (ibid), in particular, highlight the value of governance in relation to the British state. Though the authors recognise that the British government is central to policy making, decision-making competencies are shared increasingly at varied territorial levels. While multi-level governance focuses on one aspect of the state – the process of government – the concept nevertheless highlights the changing conception of state(s) more generally.

Although the primacy of the state as a locus of power has been questioned in more recent times, Lister and Marsh (2006) caution against viewing the state as a victim of structural processes which serve to reduce its power. They regard the state as a 'calculating agent', and 'heavily implicated in these processes, sometimes for deeply political reasons' (ibid: 259). Moreover, in a similar vein to Foucauldian perspectives, international relations literature recognises that how we perceive power to be exercised is ultimately what matters. For instance, Scott (1994: 325) perceives international law as an ideology, which states reinforce to maintain their position within the international order, in order to legitimise the wielding of international power:

> ...the idea of international law is integral to the international distribution of power and it actually sustains the structure of the international political order. In political terms it does not matter whether or not the ideology is true; it is not the verity of an ideology that matters but its acceptance by international actors as a basis for interaction.

Since drug policy is a transnational issue, and the UK is party to various legislative instruments and institutions which seek to address this issue (for more detail, see Chapter 3), it is important that conceptualisations of the 'state' account for international relations literature, and with it the notion that ideas have power, alongside analysing key theorists and themes. Indeed, while the function and form of the state may have changed, the *idea* of the state and from where it derives its legitimacy has not. Despite its changing nature, the 'state', as a distinct concept, maintains legitimacy because it is representative of the people; claiming to represent the public good (Lister and Marsh, 2006). Still, this point is open to dispute. For instance, a Eurosceptic may suggest that the EU is not (or is not perceived to be) representative, thus its power can be criticised as illegitimate. Similar arguments could be made of other international/transnational organisations such as the UN.

Regardless, for the most part, Weber's 'container metaphor' will be applied throughout the book; pitting the state against the individual (particularly) when analysing case law, since legal judiciaries have territorial dimensions (Robinson, 2013). However, this section broadly introduces some of the key literature concerned with the nature of the state, to demonstrate a broad awareness of the complexities involved, to contextualise any definition in line with wider society, to appreciate the relationship between the state and society and to identify the key questions raised when formulating a definition. Questions relating to the interests the 'state' represents and the notion of shared societal values, will be unpacked throughout this chapter.

Four philosophical positions and the binary which underpins them

While philosophical perspectives are not always explicit in contemporary debates which argue for or against the use of psychoactives, MacCoun and Reuter (2001) appreciate that such underlying perspectives nevertheless shape the formation of the standard drug policy options we use today. The philosophical positions and the resulting policy options reveal a rather rigid, inflexible binary existing between perceived state interests and individual interests. To show how a human rights perspective can reconfigure the binary to focus more on individual and broader societal interests, it is necessary to initially present the philosophical foundations which guide the current framework and our resulting perceptions of the conflict. Getting to the heart of our normative values through understanding the philosophical positions could thereby facilitate more innovative policy ideas.

With this in mind, I have chosen to amalgamate MacCoun and Reuter's (2001) discussion on the various philosophical underpinnings in the debate, with Transform Drug Policy Foundation's (Rolles, 2009a, 2009b, 2017) standard policy options: prohibition, an unregulated legal market, legal regulation, decriminalisation, harm reduction (see Table 2.1). Though terminologies may vary (see also Goode, 1997; Husak and de Marneffe, 2005), drug policy reformers tend to employ the same, if not similar, drug policy terms.

It is important to acknowledge that the amalgamated table offers an overly simplified picture, since values and political outlooks cannot be easily categorised. Askew and Bone (2019) found that people who use drugs can draw from a combination of deontological and consequentialist perspectives when discussing drug policy and drug law reform, and that their views can both internalise and challenge prohibition ideology.

Nevertheless, this section broadly catalogues MacCoun and Reuter's (2001) four 'typical' philosophical foundations, since these categories offer a common understanding as to how the current drug policy framework and the resulting dualistic conflict between the state and the individual are constructed. The generality of these positions also lends itself easily to the works of other authors who have attempted to detail the underlying values which are present when arguing

Table 2.1 Amalgamating MacCoun and Reuter's philosophical positions with Transform Drug Policy Foundation's policy options

Philosophical position	*Perspective*	*Policy options*
Legal moralism	Deontological	Prohibition
Strict libertarianism	Deontological	Unregulated legal market
Millian liberalism	Consequentialist	Legal regulation/ decriminalisation
Legal paternalism (soft and hard)	Consequentialist	Harm reduction/ prohibition

for or against the use of psychoactives (Richards, 1986; Goode, 1997; Ruggiero, 1999). MacCoun and Reuter (2001) acknowledge the following positions: legal moralism, strict libertarianism, Millian liberalism and legal paternalism (soft and hard), and for clarity they categorise them into normative – deontological and consequentialist – perspectives. To ensure a degree of precision and transparency, this section does the same.

Legal moralism: a deontological perspective

Deontological arguments claim that certain moral judgments hold regardless of any empirical effects (Alexander and Moore, 2012). Such arguments accord with conventional notions of our morality and are thought to be impervious to policy analysis or research evidence (MacCoun and Reuter, 2001). Legal moralism is considered to be a deontological position as it is prepared to criminalise conduct on the ground that it is widely believed to be immoral, even though there may be no evidence to suggest such conduct causes harm to the individual or to other members of society (Feinberg, 1984). Of course, there is bound to be much disagreement about the requirements of morality, but according to Stewart (2010), most legal moralists accept the notion that whoever holds political power at that moment may impose the requirements of their morality upon everyone else. It is arguable then that this philosophy is heavily weighted towards the interests of the state in achieving social stability, cohesion and control.

Staunch advocates of drug prohibition are often cited to demonstrate this position (see MacCoun and Reuter, 2001: 65–66 citing James Q. Wilson and William Bennett), since such people articulate what anthropologists and psychologists have identified as the *ethic of community* code (the term was first coined by Shweder (1990); see also Haidt, Koller and Dias, 1993; Shweder et al., 1997; Haidt, 2012). This code dictates ones duties in society and one's social roles (ibid), and in this sphere, it is regarded as being infringed upon when individuals consume illicit psychoactives. A previous US drug czar William Bennett articulates this typical stance through proclaiming (without substantiating) that drug users make inattentive parents, poor students, unreliable employees, etc. – and that they are often involved in criminal activity (Office of National Drug Control Policy, 1989).

Goode (1997: 57) recognises that broadly speaking those who hold this viewpoint subscribe to what he terms a 'legalistic definition of drugs'. A sharp distinction is often drawn on legal grounds as to what constitutes a 'drug'. Tobacco, alcohol, and other licit psychoactives would not generally be expected to receive the same level of moral condemnation attached to the illicit. The former US political authority James Q. Wilson (1995: 160) famously articulated this position stating: '[t]obacco shortens one's life, cocaine debases it. Nicotine alters one's habits, cocaine alters one's soul'. More recently, President Donald Trump and the then US Attorney General Jeff Sessions adopted similar moralistic terminology, and they advocated the use of the death penalty against big drug dealers (Ingold, 2018). Such observations serve to reinforce the idea espoused by Stewart (2010) that moralists attach their values to the law, and following Scott's (1994) reasoning; to the ideology of its power, as wielded by the state.

However, moral views on psychoactive use have varied across all cultures and time periods, and prior to the legally constructed drug control framework, civilisations, communities and even certain ideologies held vested interests in exerting some/total control over the use of psychoactives (Courtwright, 2005; Siegel, 2005; Smail, 2008). Again psychologists and anthropologists have identified this form of legal moralism to be consistent with an *ethic of divinity*, which involves drug takers adhering to a moral code in order to maintain their spiritual integrity (Shweder, 1990; Shweder et al., 1997; Haidt, Koller and Dias, 1993; Haidt, 2012). Smail (2008) and McKenna (1992) recognise that even prior to the establishment of organised religion; small communities were known to restrict the use of psychoactives to ritualistic and/or functional purposes. Hence, it could be argued that even prior to the modern construction of legal moralism, which necessitates agreement with the law and the prevailing political authority, i.e. the state, there existed an interest in maintaining social cohesion and spiritual/bodily integrity for the collective.

While the current global drug control framework presents far more stringent legal controls via the UN drug conventions (for more detail, see Chapter 3), its rather dogmatic outlook, which favours total prohibition, has been regarded in a rather circular fashion as being akin to religious texts (Cohen, 2003). The preamble to the Single Convention on Narcotic Drugs (1961) (the Single Convention) articulates that all *illicit* psychoactive use outside of a medical/research setting constitutes 'a serious evil for the individual' and is 'fraught with economic and social danger to mankind'. This hyperbolic rhetoric accurately surmises the legal moralist position here as constituting a heavy moralising philosophy, which derives its authority predominately from the law and a *perceived* need to protect state interests.

Of course, legal moralism is ultimately a deontological position, which means any empirical evidence demonstrating harm for society is not required (MacCoun and Reuter, 2001; Stewart, 2010). There exists a potential circularity here, as the legal moralist position prior to the modern construction of the state would be harder pressed to derive its authority from the law, in line with Stewart's (2010) view. Thus, when taking a deep historical perspective alongside a more recent conception of legal moralism, circular (*mala prohibita* versus *mala in se*) questions arise: does the 'immorality' accrue mainly from the fact that a substance is prohibited by the criminal law (and crime is 'wrong'), or are the 'debasing' substances criminalised/forbidden precisely because it is their consumption which is 'wrong' regardless of legal status? In any event, advocates of legal moralism, within the drug prohibitionist paradigm, are considered content to rely upon moral perceptions of harm attached to the law and the ruling political power – in relation to the ethic of community code – and/or their own ethic of divinity code.

Strict libertarianism: a deontological perspective

The final moral code posited by Shweder (1990) is the *ethic of autonomy* code. Together the three moral codes, *community*, *divinity* and *autonomy*, are thought to encompass all moral systems throughout the world (see Shweder et al., 1997 for the major statement of this theory). The ethic of autonomy is the dominant ethic in individualistic societies and it is based on the idea that people are autonomous individuals and they should be free to satisfy their wants, needs and preferences as they see fit (Haidt, 2012). It corresponds well with the deontological position of strict libertarianism, though it can also be found in the consequentialist position of Millian liberalism as well.

While strict libertarianism is the only other deontological perspective MacCoun and Reuter (2001) identified, it is interesting that this philosophy is located as the exact opposite end of the drug policy spectrum to legal moralism. A strict libertarian's fundamental focus is on the rights of the individual. In direct contrast with the legal moralist approach, strict libertarians believe there should be no controls, restrictions or legislation affecting psychoactives (exceptions for minors), and that the state should adopt a complete *laissez-faire* attitude to regulation and control (Szasz, 1992; Goode, 1997).

Berlin (1969) identifies this stance as negative liberalism, and the leading libertarian in this field Thomas Szasz (1987: 349) clearly expresses this variant: 'the government as our servant rather than our master – does not have the right to meddle in our private dietary and drug affairs'. This approach communicates a division between an individual's interests and the state's, as strict libertarians are typically distrustful of state involvement, and perceive any psychoactive controls to constitute a form of chemical socialism (ibid). Walsh (2014: 218) also eloquently paints the picture of prohibition as: 'the state applying a filter, inducing a kind of psychopharmacological North Korea'. The notion of individual freedom is of paramount concern here, as the strict libertarian would encourage a climate which fosters personal responsibility and accountability over a person's mental and bodily integrity (Fitzpatrick, 2013).

With reference to the current drug policy framework, this philosophy is rooted within the 'unregulated legal market' policy option. According to Goode (1997), this option (which he terms 'full decriminalisation'), would entail a total hands-off approach from the state, where no controls are imposed upon any psychoactives, with the only exception here relating to minors. This has been criticised as an unfeasible and unattainable proposal (ibid). Courtwright (2002), in particular, acknowledges its impracticality in our present global capitalist market, since even the psychoactives regarded as licit are subject to some level of state and/or corporate regulation (see Chapter 3 for more detail on the tobacco and alcohol regulatory regimes). The growth of the legal cannabis market for recreational use in an increasing number of countries including the USA, Uruguay and Canada further substantiates this point (for more detail, see Chapters 3 and 4).

Strict libertarians also promote positive liberalism, the second concept on liberty propounded by Berlin (1969). This concept encourages situations where governments create conditions for its citizenry to achieve self-sufficiency and self-realisation (Carter, 2012). This position again demonstrates an individualistic focus as strict libertarians are critical if they believe the state is encroaching upon an individual's opportunities, abilities or natural freedoms to choose their own pursuits in life. Supporters of this stance believe that individuals have a natural right to consume any substance (Szasz, 1992; Hardison, 2007, 2008) and that every person should be free to determine and act upon their own life plan; what Mill (1859/2001: 74) has termed 'experiments in living'.

There exists a *wealth* of literature demonstrating the benefits altered states of consciousness, via the use of psychoactives, can have for the general human experience (see Chapter 1 and Part II for more detail). Accordingly, prohibitionist drug policies are viewed as an infringement upon the basic constitutional rights of individuals to be and to become what they are (Van Ree, 1999). Locke's (1690/1952) principle of self-ownership which argues that our bodies themselves are property to care for and control as we see fit, is also espoused by some strict libertarians to demonstrate a further infringement upon individual rights within this sphere (Szasz, 1992; Hardison, 2007, 2008).

While these ideas are powerful ones and act as some sort of counterweight to the legal moralistic rhetoric, Berlin (1969) nonetheless recognises the difficulties in attempting to balance state or societal interests with individual ones, given the responsibility endowed upon the state for maintaining social cohesion (see Jessop, 2008). Berlin's well-borrowed statement: 'freedom for the pike is death for the minnows' (ibid: 171 citing Tawney, 1938: 208), acknowledges the core conflict involved in allowing individuals to adopt a life plan which could impede the freedoms of others. Actually, when considering the interdependent nature of human beings, MacCoun and Reuter (2001) find it difficult to imagine many libertarians in the strictest sense of the term; perceiving most to believe that the law should not tolerate acts which cause serious and direct harm to others. Thus, the consequentialist tradition which is rooted in empirical measurements of the status quo, or in predictions about the likely consequences of policy changes, has been strongly prevalent in contemporary drug debates and policy reform reports (see Hughes and Stevens, 2010, 2012; Mungroo, Ping and Bone, 2014; Eastwood, Fox and Rosmarin, 2016; Fielding and Singleton, 2018).

Millian liberalism: a consequentialist perspective

MacCoun and Reuter (2001) discuss two normative consequentialist philosophies, Millian liberalism and legal paternalism. Millian liberalism, a philosophy deriving its name from the prominent utilitarian John Stuart Mill, is largely perceived to encourage the strict libertarian approach of retaining a negative freedom to consume psychoactives: '[o]ver himself, over his own body and mind, the individual is sovereign' (Mill, 1859/2001: 13), corresponding with the *ethic of autonomy*. The only justification for any interference from the state would be to secure its role as preventing harm to others (ibid). This proviso is what makes the philosophy consequentialist, since not causing harm to others necessitates evaluating the empirical consequences of certain acts or rules, i.e. actions relating to drugs or laws pertaining to this.

The focus of this position is largely geared towards the regulated legal market or the decriminalisation policy options. A regulated legal market means the legal governmental regulation of a particular legal or legalised drug (Rolles, 2009a), whereas decriminalisation refers to the removal of criminal sanctions for the possession of small amounts of specified drugs for personal use (Eastwood, Fox and Rosmarin, 2016). However, as mentioned from the outset, it is extremely difficult to compartmentalise political outlooks and their underpinning philosophies. In light of this, Ruggiero (1999) has recognised the inherent flexibility in Mill's harm principle, observing that the principle could be interpreted to justify the prohibition of certain psychoactives, precisely because they have been shown to cause harm to others.

What is of interest here is that despite the contrasting interpretations of the harm principle, when relying upon empirical measurements of harm both factions highlight the state versus the individual binary. Numerous UK government drug strategies which support the prohibitionist construct routinely emphasise the harms individuals can cause the state, communities and societies at large via *illicit* psychoactive use (HM Government, 2008, 2010, 2017). Policy reformers on the other hand tend to reverse the emphasis. They largely stress the harms the state has caused to various individuals/societies/environments by continuing to implement the global prohibitionist paradigm; restricting all illicit psychoactives to medical and research purposes only (see Rolles, 2009b, 2017; Transform, 2012; The Global Commission on Drug Policy, 2019).

Since human rights regimes are predominately individualistic, this chapter's final section – '[h]ow human rights can address the state/individual binary' – will explore whether the binary should be reconfigured by reversing the emphasis from the state to the individual and the implications of this. Under a prohibitionist paradigm, it is suggested that notions of 'harm' are too heavily weighted in favour of the state and *perceived* societal interests. Although evaluations of harm are generalisations, they could potentially support MacCoun and Reuter's (2001) proposition that consequentialist philosophies are rarely free from value judgments. According to them, empirical claims may serve as a means to bolster core value based convictions, since deontological positions could potentially affect all aspects of research findings (ibid). Critiques of the legal paternalist tradition could also support this stance.

Legal paternalism: a consequentialist perspective

Legal paternalism is similarly consequentialist and concerns itself with evaluating the harms individuals cause to themselves as well as to others (ibid). There are varying degrees of paternalism, as with all philosophical outlooks, and these could range from advocating harm reductionist strategies and managing micro level harms to the individual (soft paternalism), to overarching prohibitionist strategies in the interests of reducing macro harms to all (hard paternalism). Liberalists tend to criticise this position as promoting an infantilising culture (Richards, 1986), and Feinberg (1984) and Ruggiero (1999) additionally note that behind a consequentialist condemnation of *illicit* drugs for the harms they cause to others, ultimately lies a condemnation of *illicit* psychoactive use per se.

Even harm reductionist approaches which are largely regarded as pragmatic (Goode, 1997), have been known to include underlying ideals, as they ultimately surrender to the notion of harm elimination espoused by legal moralists (Hathaway, 2001). Therefore, it is important to take normative perspectives seriously, and to use human rights as a tool to weigh up the moral questions involved when balancing the state's interests against an individual's; to illuminate and improve the drug control framework.

However, it would not be fair to suggest that there exist no impartial cost/benefit empirical analyses in this field. Hughes and Stevens (2012: 101) successfully interpreted research evidence detailing whether Portugal's decriminalisation strategy in 2001 was a 'resounding success or a disastrous failure', as they impartially recognised diverging interpretations of evidence depending upon various researchers' policy agendas. MacCoun and Reuter (2011: 62) have similarly produced a guide for 'agnostics' when questioning the merits of legalisation/prohibition, etc., observing the drug policy debate to have 'holy war' like qualities.

Challenging prohibitionist ideology

Yet, even when analysts go deeper and attempt to expose the philosophies or moral values underpinning contemporary debates, it is worth noting that they themselves are often constrained by the overarching prohibitionist narrative. For instance, both of the aforementioned studies readily accept the global legalistic construction of the licit/illicit divide (see Seddon, 2010, 2016), and both evaluations of harm fail to encompass any of the pleasures or benefits that could be derived from using psychoactives (Bancroft, 2009; Bunton and Coveney, 2011; Bone and Seddon, 2015). However, there are an increasing number of researchers who are recognising the value of disengaging with some aspects of the paradigm, particularly when noting the benefits which can be derived from psychoactives, as opposed to solely focusing on the harms. For instance, *the International Journal of Drug Policy* has published two special issues on drugs and pleasure (see Holt and Treloar, 2008; Dennis and Farrugia, 2017) and *Drugs and Alcohol Today* have published one (see Klein and Stothard, 2016).

By overtly unpacking the philosophies underpinning this debate, this chapter exposes how they have helped to perpetuate and construct the state/individual binary, since the standard drug policy positions which result all advocate either increases or decreases in individual empowerment or in state control.

The remainder of this chapter will therefore discuss how reimagining drug policy through the lens of human rights could be useful to reconfigure and question the binary, by reversing the emphasis back to the individual and unpacking the notion of shared values. This could thereby facilitate a more open-minded regime and challenge prohibitionist ideology, by embracing normative thinking and explicitly addressing the binary's existence in the drug policy field.

How human rights can address the state/individual binary

If we are to accept the perpetuating nature of the state/individual binary, it is important to overtly address its existence, as opposed to relying upon the guise of consequentialism, embraced by prohibitors and reformers alike. MacGregor, Singleton and Trautmann (2014) refer to the prevailing view that the increase of evidence in the policy making process would increase the legitimacy of any decisions made and improve outcomes. Although 'evidence-based policy' (EBP) is often hailed as the ultimate aspiration for the drug policy field (see Lancaster, 2014 for a social constructionist critique of EBP), this chapter argues that we should not ignore normative – deontological and consequentialist – arguments. Nor should we de-politicise drug policy, because in and of itself drug policy is inherently political through its predominant focus on the binary between the state and the individual.

Of course, this view does not require human rights to neglect the empirical evidence which informs policy. On the contrary, the correct application of human rights norms requires calling upon relevant, factual and reliable information to guard against parochialism (Buchanan, 2008). Rather, this chapter asserts that human rights can also embrace both deontological and consequentialist perspectives within normative theory. In doing so, human rights can shine a light on the *perceived* conflict between individual and collective interests more effectively to: challenge the policy of prohibition, since a normative perspective facilitates questions including – the interests the state represents, how EBP is constructed and utilised – and it unpacks societal values, to develop an alternative moral policy response to drug consumption.

This section utilises the correlativity of the rights and duties doctrine to demonstrate how human rights can address the state/individual binary, and reconfigure the power dynamics underpinning drug policy design, potentially leading to more innovative regulatory ideas. Most human rights are derogable, qualified or can otherwise be limited, as they strive to protect and respect individual autonomy, but not in ways that allow for the rights of others to be infringed (Perry, 1998). With this in mind, the rise of individualism will be discussed, since states have legal duties to provide environments whereby human beings can flourish, while protecting and respecting the rights of their citizenry to be left alone (Mill, 1859/2001; Bone and Seddon, 2015). The advantages of reversing the emphasis back towards the individual and away from the state in drug policy will be considered, and a human rights lens will be shown to debate the morality of consuming psychoactives.

However, this section goes even further; developing an alternative moral policy response to drug consumption by reflecting on societal values and questioning the interests the state represents. Unpacking the notion of shared values challenges the prohibitionist paradigm, since human rights could alter our moral reasoning process if we approached the conflict with a measure of transparency – particularly if we were to accept the benefits psychoactives could have for the collective as well as for the individual. Finally, this section considers how changing conceptions of the state affects the construction of the binary, and that human rights are dynamic political and legal instruments, with the potential to shape and constitute our social and political realities.

The correlativity of the rights and duties doctrine

According to Wenar (2011), the genesis of the concept of a right presupposes that there will be a conflict. To refer back to the pike analogy popularised by Berlin (1969 citing Tawney, 1938); to afford rights to some often necessitates restricting the rights of others. Van Ree (1999) similarly observes that there is no need to establish any right as a legal human right unless there exists potential for its impediment. Additionally, as established in Chapter 1, human rights encompass human nature. Since this in itself is thought to comprise of competing and irreconcilable impulses, it logically follows then that human rights will clash (Alder, 2006). The fact that rights by their very nature appear to pit one set of values or interests against another alludes to their relevance in the drug policy sphere.

An important tool which demonstrates how human rights can address the binary between the state and the individual is the correlativity of rights and duties. This doctrine is so termed because the test of whether one has the 'right' to something is often dependent upon whether someone else has a 'duty' to provide it (Hohfeld, 1919). Though there are exceptions (see Lyons, 1970), it is generally accepted that the two elements are inseparable. Hence, the doctrine could prove useful to address the inherent state/individual binary present within drug policy.

While human rights can clash on a more horizontal level between individuals, it is the vertical relationship between the state and its citizenry that is often the focal point for the operation of the doctrine in practice. As highlighted in Chapter 1, from the enlightenment onwards, human rights texts centre upon the vertical relationship and the duty of the state to uphold the rights of individuals, so far as they then do not infringe upon the state's duty to uphold the rights of others. The doctrine thereby supports the notion that human rights should have governments as their primary addressees, as they set the standard for political legitimacy and ensure that the division of power is fairer. If a similar standard were employed within the drug control field, exploring how state comprised drug policies affect individuals, then perhaps the tensions would lessen somewhat; as possible solutions which appreciate the rights and duties of both parties could be employed.

Moreover, human rights foster a climate concerned with finding a solution. Specificationists, for example, believe that even when human rights appear to conflict they are in fact 'compossible' (Steiner, 1994). According to Steiner (ibid), all judgments are solely dependent upon the circumstances of any given situation and thus require a careful balancing act. Hart (1994) also observes that a key feature of the human predicament is our inability to foresee all possible solutions which invoke human rights, hence the doctrine and human rights more generally are necessarily open-ended and rarely absolute.

However, the doctrine has faced criticism as it presently stands. Glendon (1991) observes that human rights are increasingly subject to extravagant formulations and impractical demands, as citizens are increasingly asserting individual or egotistical claims without considering the possibility of burdening others with any corresponding obligations. For Glendon (ibid: 14) such an insular focus on individual human rights could impede social progress, since abandoning the correlativity of duties has promoted 'mere assertion over reason giving', thereby inhibiting the possibility of finding any common ground.

It could be argued that the growth of interventionist welfare states has led to a more infantilising culture, with government agencies seemingly unconcerned with the need to educate citizens about their duties, and to endow them with a sense of personal responsibility. Fitzpatrick (2013), for instance, highlights that this cultural shift is evident within the drug policy realm. He asserts that the increasing reliance placed upon harm reduction policies combined with an often paternalistic stance towards prohibition, could encourage a more infantile and self-centred climate (ibid). Libertarians especially advocate increases in personal responsibility, as they are particularly wary of too much state encroachment in an individual's private affairs (Goode, 1997).

Perhaps then the correlativity of the rights and duties doctrine could be successfully employed within the field of drug control if the more traditional or original version was applied; a version concerning itself equally with a commitment to duties. As demonstrated, anthropologists, scientists and historians have all observed degrees of social control which have been exercised across time periods and cultures in relation to the use of psychoactives (Goodman, Lovejoy and Sherratt, 1995; Siegel, 2005; Smail, 2008; Nutt, 2012). They mainly cite instances of controlled use within ritualistic settings, or cite strictly observed rules on when and how a substance is taken, so as not to impact detrimentally on the social order; corresponding with the ethics of divinity and community codes (ibid). Therefore, while it widely is accepted that rights can operate as empowerment tools for individuals (Donnelly, 2003; Edmunson, 2004; Chapter 1), there is no reason why a renewed commitment to duties towards others cannot engender a similar response.

Innovative regulatory initiatives which encompass this idea could therefore impart a greater sense of personal responsibility and be similarly empowering, as it would mitigate the charge for maintaining social cohesion which is largely placed on the state (Jessop, 2008); hence reconfiguring the binary to some degree. Not only that, imparting a greater sense of personal responsibility could go some way towards meeting elements of all three moral codes – divinity, community and autonomy. A renewed commitment towards duties; advocating psychoactive consumption within certain defined settings, recognising broader community interests and respecting the autonomy of individuals, could help reconcile differing value systems and moral concepts from people around the world.

An example of an innovative regulatory initiative which alters the present culture of drug control is the increasing global presence of cannabis social clubs (CSCs). CSCs are small non-profit collectives where cannabis is produced and distributed among a closed circuit of adult users. The CSC model emerged from the grassroots, via bottom-up initiatives and self-regulation, as opposed to any extensive involvement from governments' or legislators'. Developing the model from the grassroots up devolves regulatory power to local movements by facilitating a greater level of consumer control over cannabis production and distribution processes. This rare level of consumer control poses a challenge to traditional regulatory thought, where cannabis is controlled by the government, the free market and/or the medical establishment. Thus, the CSC model is unique since it resists the dominant political powers in drug policy design.

This initiative aligns with the correlativity of rights and duties doctrine's original purpose, focusing on persons as right-holders and bearers of responsibility. The Code of Conduct for European CSCs exemplifies the level of accountability placed upon individual members (ENCOD, 2011). The Code was established by the European Coalition for Just and Effective Drug Policies (ENCOD), a network of European NGOs, and it is employed by CSCs throughout Europe. The code requires CSCs to be characterised by 'transparency, democracy and non-profitability' (ibid: n.p.). Thus, a renewed focus on duties and personal responsibility in this field, demonstrates how CSCs could facilitate a space for a more open, transparent and innovative cannabis policy; where power is devolved back to the individual consumer (for a more detailed overview of the CSC model in the UK, see Bone, 2017; Bone and de Hoedt, 2018; for a detailed overview of the model in Europe, see Decorte et al., forthcoming). While psychoactive use can undoubtedly cause harm, 'there is such a thing as responsible drug use and it is the norm, not the exception' (Hari, 2015: 148 citing Gillespie, n.d.: n.p.). As Gillespie states:

> [F]ar from drugs controlling us, by and large we control our drugs; as with alcohol, the primary motivation is to enjoy ourselves, not to destroy ourselves. (ibid: 148)

The rise of individualism

Besides, the rise of individualism is not necessarily a bad thing. Reversing the emphasis towards individual interests within the drug policy sphere could reconfigure the binary and improve the drug control framework; providing individuals acknowledge their duties in line with the correlativity doctrine. 'Individualism is a belief in the central importance of the individual human being' (Heywood, 1992: 18). Individualism correlates with the growth of natural rights theories during the enlightenment period, to which we attribute the modern conception of human rights (ibid; see also Chapter 1). The belief in the primacy of the individual is a liberal philosophy – desiring a society whereby individuals are capable of flourishing and developing to their full capacity (ibid). MacCoun and Reuter's (2001) strict libertarianism and Millian liberalism categorisations unpack this commitment to individual freedom.

Mill (1859/2001), in particular, demonstrates a primary concern over the limits of power which can be legitimately exercised over the individual. Mill (ibid) perceived the threats to individualism to arise from both society and governments. If we are to accept a definition of the state which embraces a wider theory of society, and the government as forming a key state institution, then in line with the first section – 'Defining the state' – Mill (ibid) considers the 'state' to pose a threat to individual freedom. For Mill (ibid), the pressure to conform within society, and an interventionist government, together forms 'a mass of influences hostile to individuality' (ibid: 68). According to individualists, human progress can only occur if we allow for the diversity, spontaneity and originality of individuals, as it is only through developing our potential as human beings that society is developed and is enriched:

> Human nature is not a machine to be built after a model, and set to do exactly the work prescribed for it, but a tree, which requires to grow and develop itself on all sides, according to the tendency of the inward forces which make it a living thing. (ibid: 55)

Thus, for individualists, respecting the diversity of life is beneficial not just for the individual, but for society as a whole to prevent its stagnation, and to guard against the 'tyranny of the majority' (ibid: 9). Since the enlightenment's conception of human rights increasingly understood society from an individualist viewpoint – affording primacy to individual interests and needs – it follows then that human rights are inherently individualistic. This intrinsic focus facilitates the capacity for human rights to reconfigure the binary, and reverse the emphasis away from perceived state interests, since notions of 'harm' under a prohibitionist paradigm are heavily weighted in favour of the state, and *perceived* societal interests. As will be shown throughout part II of this book, when human rights conflict with the drug control framework they reveal the benefits that psychoactives can have for the individual; whether the individual is asserting a right to consume on health, religious or spiritual grounds or even on the grounds of expanding one's own consciousness.

It is perhaps fair to conclude then, that MacCoun and Reuter's (2001) statement claiming a moral analysis on the benefits of drug use is largely absent from the debate, has lessened somewhat. I have also written about the benefits cannabis holds for the Rastafari religion from a human rights perspective; identifying the beneficial properties of the drug experience within a more deontological and moral remit (see Bone, 2014a). Likewise, I afford the same treatment to discussions concerning the health rights of medicinal cannabis users; since the significance individuals' accord this plant is morally intrinsic to adequately weighing up their rights against a state's interests (see Bone, 2014b; Bone and Seddon, 2015; Chapter 4).

Consequentialist arguments are also moving increasingly to the foray. Empirical literature on the medical benefits of cannabis is increasing, as is evidence pertaining to the medical and therapeutic benefits of psychedelics. This research is also increasingly debunking widely shared views on the risks involved when consuming such strictly controlled drugs. For instance, research by Johansen and Krebs (2015) concludes that psychedelics are not linked to psychosis, contrary to the popularised view.

Though there are of course risks associated with psychoactive consumption, when deontological and consequentialist arguments – exploring the benefits of psychoactives and mitigating the risks – combine, the societal moral reasoning process could be re-construed. Moving beyond a sole focus on the risks psychoactives pose for the individual, through acknowledging the benefits as well, facilitates the possibility that there could be wider benefits for the collective too. To take one specific example, Seddon and I have argued that a broader view of the human right to health, which appreciates internal, social constructionist views alongside external state-orientated perspectives, can induce a public health approach to the medicinal cannabis issue, which could more effectively balance individual and collective interests (Bone and Seddon, 2015).

For example, CSCs and pharmacy regulatory models for cannabis encourage vaporising the plant, as opposed to smoking it with tobacco, as a pleasurable and safer delivery method (ibid). This acknowledges internal views on the importance of pleasure while building upon global public health campaigns which recognise tobacco use as a health hazard (ibid). From a broader perspective, it could also be argued that consuming psychoactives for a variety of purposes linked to rights-based claims such as health, religion, culture, free thought, etc. enhance the richness and diversity of life, in line with individualism, thereby facilitating human progress throughout societies.

From this angle, a human rights lens can debate the morality of consuming certain psychoactives and Chapters 4 and 5 certainly provide a comprehensive overview of UK case law and comparable case law from other jurisdictions, which pit state policies on prohibition against individual human rights to use drugs. However, human rights can go further than questioning the morality of drug use, as they can openly unpack shared societal values, to develop an alternative moral policy response to the reality of drug use.

Developing an alternative moral policy response

It is vital to develop a moral policy response, since what a society believes to be morally right, usually overrides the empirical evidence presented to them

(Haidt, 2012; Rolles, 2017; Bone and de Hoedt, 2018). 'Policy decision making invariably involves questions of values – of questioning how the world "ought to be" as opposed to relying solely on the facts' (Bone, Klein and Potter, 2018: 77). A human rights perspective questions normative standards of behaviour, of what one ought to do and how one ought to live (O'Neill, 1996). While relying on the available evidence is crucial to advance the regulatory process, we should not negate deontological arguments. According to the social psychologist Jonathan Haidt (2012), our minds are hardwired to be moralistic, we are deeply intuitive creatures and our values drive our strategic reasoning processes, leading to a tendency to ignore any evidence that we do not agree with.

Therefore, prohibitionists adopting a legal moralist position, have an advantage at present, by arguing from a position of moral authority. As I have argued elsewhere, one way to make the reform position stronger – integrating deontological and consequentialist perspectives – is to tell the human stories of drug takers, this would facilitate knowledge production by inputting their experiences into the evidence base (Bone, Klein and Potter, 2018). Psychologists, communication scholars, policy scientists and other social scientists are also beginning to recognise the significance of storytelling to appeal to the emotions of policy makers and the general public (Davidson, 2017). As Rolles (2017) notes, telling human stories engages people on an emotive, human level, speaking to their values.

It is crucial to unpack any assumptions about the shared values a society may have, and advocates of policy reform ought to shape and elucidate such values, alongside presenting the empirical evidence. Significantly, states are considered to prohibit acts based upon the shared values a society may have. According to Devlin (1959/1965), states can prohibit acts solely on the basis that they are viewed as morally repugnant by their citizenry, in order to preserve and maintain social cohesion. Yet, when the benefits of drug use are illuminated under a human rights lens, both to the individual and to the collective, Devlin's hypothesis poses a problem. The formation of the global human rights regime alone demonstrates the difficulty in construing societal interests so narrowly so as to protect a specific set of moral principles (see Chapter 1). There is no rigid stasis in the history of human civilisation (MacCoun and Reuter, 2001). Therefore, any construction of the global prohibitionist regime, as being fully representative of a state exemplifying the interests and values of a society, is inevitably a fallacy. Human psychoactive use is a far more common and complex phenomenon than is perceived under a prohibitionist paradigm, with benefits as well as risks attached.

Developing a moral matrix of benefits and harms, alongside empirical matrices of drug harms (see Nutt, Saulsbury and Blakemore, 2007), could help to reconfigure the binary and displace the narrow moralistic approach adopted by the state. One way to test whether the state is truly representing the interests and values of a society through the construction of global prohibition, is to question the 'EBP' paradigm in drug policy – what the concept of 'evidence' even means, and who gets to speak authoritatively (see Lancaster et al., 2017; Ritter, Lancaster and Diprose, 2018). Researchers are beginning to acknowledge that the set of actors at the centre of drug policy making – the medical establishment and law enforcement bodies – are able to legitimise a social control agenda, perceiving individuals who consume drugs to be bad, sick or both (Tupper, 2012; Stevens, 2017). Hence, notions of individual freedom and empowerment are very much on the periphery in the drug policy making sphere (Stevens, 2017).

To rectify this, a human rights perspective, which reconfigures the binary back to the individual, can draw on research which seeks to incorporate drug taker perspectives in the reform process. Along with telling human stories to appeal to people's values and shift public perceptions on drug use, researchers could also adopt participatory methodologies to input drug takers' experiential knowledge into the 'expert' evidence base to help legitimise policy outcomes (Lancaster et al., 2017; Bone and de Hoedt, 2018; Ritter, Lancaster and Diprose, 2018). This would also shift the balance of power, which is well suited to the remit of human rights since 'they articulate the relationship between individuals and groups within a community and their relationship with others, particularly those with power and authority' (Clapham, 2015: 164). Therefore, viewing the state/individual binary through a human rights lens challenges the natural order of things and confronts structures of power and privilege (Goodhart, 2014), through moving beyond the state's monopoly on the 'morality' of drug use and by adopting a more inclusive approach to EBP. When combined, this exemplifies how a human rights perspective can also facilitate a moral policy response to the reality of drug use as it currently exists.

Human rights and the changing nature of the state

Finally, as discussed in Chapter 1, human rights reflect the widely transformative nature of human beings. Therefore, they are arguably capable of altering, evolving and expanding upon our own inner models of reality. This argument corresponds with Brems' (2009) assertion that human rights are a form of revolutionary discourse, adept at changing entrenched political and social behaviours, and as such can extend well beyond the boundaries currently imposed. When human rights are viewed as evolving political practices, as well as abstract legal principles, they could evolve to meet the 21st-century challenges of globalisation and the demise of the nation state.

Human rights are dynamic and could account for the changing conceptions of the state. As will be explored in Chapter 3, there exists an increasing array of institutions, bureaucracies and organisations dedicated to resolving human rights issues, some of which have undergone dramatic legal and political restructuring to afford them a greater international and domestic standing. This increasing presence within the state order could therefore serve to transform the binary between the state and the individual. However, there are also issues associated with the hollowing out of the state and the transference of national political power by global forces, since the distribution of planetary resources and wealth is now largely uncontested by any political mechanism (Dasgupta, 2018). According to Supiot (2007: 156), the withdrawal of the state has had a drastic impact on how society functions. He considers the 'laws of the economy' assumption that rational individuals each maximise their own private interests to be a western myth of society, which ignores basic facts about anthropology:

> [H]uman reason is never an unmediated fact of individual consciousness. Human reason is the product of institutions that allow every person to give meaning to their existence, that grant them a place in society and enable them to express their particular talent within it. Once this process is no longer guaranteed by the state, people attempt to ground their identity in other things: in a religious, ethnic, tribal, sectarian etc. point of reference. (ibid)

It is no coincidence that the retreat to particularistic positions correlates with the waning of national political authority. The fantastical promise of national restoration, of wall building, of 'taking back control' in the Brexit vote leave campaign are all happening in tandem across the world. Barber (1995) was one of the first commentators to argue that rapid change created by globalisation brings with it heightened uncertainty, increasing the appeal of 'traditional' forms of identity and protectionism. To mitigate this uncertainty, it is important to have a more tangible grasp on the institutions which govern us and Chapter 3 will explore the legal architecture behind the human rights and drug control frameworks. Human rights also guard against the retreat to particularistic positions, since their normative, political character is concerned with freedom and equality for all, as they represent a form of emancipatory politics (Goodhart, 2014). Indeed, the resilience of human rights stems from this broad and continuing appeal of challenging hierarchies and power structures by design (Goodhart, 2012).

Conclusion

This chapter identified how human rights address a fundamental issue recognised to be at the core of drug policy: the conflict between the interests of the state in restricting certain psychoactives and the individual's freedom to consume. Prior to exploring the philosophies which underpin the binary, the chapter delved into the conceptual difficulties associated with defining the 'state'. By highlighting key state theorists, ideas, themes and international relations literature, Chapter 2 demonstrates an awareness of the complexities involved here, and flags up fundamental questions pertaining to a state's interests when representing a society.

By contextualising a definition of the state in line with wider society, and in full appreciation of the need to unpack shared societal values, this chapter exposes four typical philosophical positions and the standard policy proposals which result; all of which advocate either increases or decreases in individual empowerment or in state control (see Table 2.1). Only the two deontological philosophies explicitly address the existence of the drug policy binary though, as they are either heavily rooted towards the interests of the state in maintaining order and control (legal moralism), or else they advocate individual rights and freedoms to the exclusion of other prominent concerns (strict libertarianism). Yet, on a more implicit basis, the consequentialist philosophies (Millian liberalism and legal paternalism) are revealed to be rarely free from value judgments. This chapter contends that the failure to overtly unpack the moral questions raised when pitting a state's interests against an individuals has led to restrictive policy regimes and policy-making processes, and that a human rights lens can reconfigure and openly address the binary; facilitating a more open minded approach to drug control.

The correlativity of the rights and duties doctrine embraces normative thinking through its predominant focus on the vertical relationship between the state and the individual. The doctrine can challenge the division of power, creating space for more innovative, bottom-up regulatory ideas such as the CSC model. The rise of individualism also demonstrates how human rights can successfully reconfigure the binary, as a focus on the benefits psychoactives can have for the individual, exemplifies the diversity, richness and progress for societies and the collective more broadly (Mill, 1859/2001). Such considerations could also reconfigure the prohibitionist paradigm, as it is heavily weighted in favour of the state and the perceived 'harms' or 'risks' associated with controlled psychoactives at present. Through the lens of individualism, human rights are able to debate the morality of consuming psychoactives.

However, this chapter goes further and demonstrates how a human rights perspective can develop an alternative moral policy response to drug use and why it is vital to do so. Human beings are hardwired to be moralistic. Therefore, revealing and integrating deontological and consequentialist perspectives explicitly in this policy debate – appealing to societal values and unpacking any shared assumptions about these – is essential to challenge dominant state narratives on the 'morality' of drug use. Additionally, when questioning a state's interests given its position of power, a human rights lens can also help to reconfigure the binary between the state and the individual and shift the balance of power; by challenging the EBP paradigm and adopting a more inclusive approach to the policy making process.

Finally, as dynamic political and legal instruments, human rights could potentially transform the state/individual divide, given their increased legal and political standing internationally. However, the hollowing out of the state and the transference of power upwards, sideways and downwards as a result of globalising forces, has led to considerable uncertainty, the retreat to particularistic positions and the rise of ideological nationalism and protectionism. Domestically, this stoked the partisan politics in the Brexit decision and has led to calls to withdraw from the ECHR. More broadly speaking the effect of the nation state's demise can be felt all across the world (Dasgupta, 2018).

In order to explore this issue from a more practical perspective, Chapter 3 will survey the legal architecture of both the international and domestic human rights and drug control frameworks. The chapter will explore how they relate to each other both institutionally and legally, before Chapters 4 and 5 engage with how the law operates in practice when trying to reconcile the two. For now though, it is enough to identify that there is a state/individual binary at the core of drug policy, and that a human rights perspective can shine a light to address and reconfigure it.

Chapter 3

The legal architecture behind the human rights and drug control frameworks

To thoroughly appreciate the legal tensions and conflicts which exist when looking at drug policy from a human rights perspective, it is important to attain a tangible grasp on the architecture which governs us and consider how the frameworks relate to each other legally, institutionally and increasingly politically. This chapter provides a clear, concise description of the drug control and human rights frameworks. Chapter 3 examines the nature, function and purpose of the international, regional and UK systems. The chapter recognises the influence that international and regional legislation and various institutional bodies have had upon the operation of both systems domestically and if there is any room to deviate from the existing status quo. By exposing the inner workings of the systems at every level, this chapter should facilitate a broader awareness of the international, regional and domestic regimes, and aid a deeper understanding of any subsequent conflicts or tensions between the frameworks, since these will be thoroughly explored throughout the second part of the book.

The international human rights framework

Although the notion of human rights is far older than the prohibitionist concept of drug control (as highlighted in Chapter 1), the international human rights regime as we understand it at present emerged only since 1945 (Bilder, 2004). Prior to World War II, it was generally accepted that human right issues were matters of domestic concern and outside of the parameters of international regulation (ibid). However, the League of Nations, the international forerunner to the United Nations (UN), did consider certain human rights ideas, since they were included in the Covenant of the League of Nations (1919) (Bromley, 2008). Though, it was not until the implications of the holocaust and other Nazi denials of human rights that the promotion of human rights became very central to the mindset of national governments, who decided that they should be a core concern of the new UN organisation.

As such, respect for human rights became one of the three core pillars of the UN, alongside the maintenance of peace and security and the development of economic and social progress, all of which are enshrined within the Charter of the UN (1945) (Charter). While the Charter is legally binding, comprises the foundational basis of UN, and is ratified by virtually every UN member state, its provisions in relation to human rights are not specific (Steiner, Alston and Goodman, 2008). Hence, in 1945, the Commission on Human Rights (CHR) was tasked with drafting the Universal Declaration of Human Rights (1948) (UDHR) to give further effect to the Charter's rights-based aims.

The Universal Declaration of Human Rights

The UDHR is largely considered to be the single most important human rights document in the world, and while it is not legally binding, the declaration is deemed to have exerted a strong moral and political force far beyond the hopes of its drafters (Hannum, 2005). The human rights regime is replete with global treaties, regional conventions and even domestic constitutions that have been inspired by the UDHR; further facilitating the documents status as forming part of customary international law (Rehman, 2010). The UDHR includes an entire gamut of civil, political, economic, social and cultural rights. Although this has raised questions in terms of interpretation and scope, this broad nature was purposely designed to achieve a 'common understanding of what rights could mean for all nations' (see the preamble, UDHR).

Hannum (2005) explains that the UDHR, like other rights-based instruments, was never intended to mandate any particular social order or liberal or democratic ideal within the western hemisphere. Rather, it was created to declare a set of rights and obligations for all nations which does not require them to abandon their own philosophical, moral, religious and/or ethical code (ibid). Although it remains hotly contested as to whether human rights are solely a western construct (for more detail, see Chapter 1), the suggestion is that the UDHR, and all other human right treaties which were later derived from it, did not intend the international community to conform to one particular rights-based paradigm. It is perhaps for this reason that virtual universal acceptance has been achieved.

Despite the UDHR's global significance, the fact remains that it is a 'hortatory', 'aspirational' and 'recommendatory' document as opposed to being binding in any formal sense (Steiner, Alston and Goodman, 2008: 152). Accordingly, the CHR was additionally entrusted to draft a convention to create legally binding human rights obligations on states, and to develop an international supervisory system to monitor state compliance (Nowak, 2005). These latter stages proved slightly more problematic in light of the global political circumstances existing at the time. The cold war divided nations as some states sought to separate civil and political rights and afford them greater prominence than economic, social and cultural rights (ibid). Two separate treaties with separate monitoring systems were adopted in 1966, and it took an additional ten years before they entered into force.

The International Covenant on Civil and Political Rights

In accordance with the desires of western states, the International Covenant on Civil and Political Rights (1966) (ICCPR) was regarded as containing first-generation rights, since states were under a direct and immediate obligation to ensure their fulfilment from the day the ICCPR entered into force (ibid). An example of the rights incorporated within the ICCPR include: the right to life, liberty, privacy, the right to a fair trial, to freedom of thought, conscience and religion, to freedom of expression and the right to freedom of association (see Articles 6, 9, 17, 14, 18, 19 and 22 ICCPR). Ratified by 172 member states including the UK at the time of writing (see the United Nations Treaty Collection, 2019a), the implementation of the ICCPR is monitored by the Human Rights Committee (HRCa).

The HRCa comprises 18 independent experts, who are elected on the basis of their expertise (not their nationality) (OHCHR, n.d.a). These members oblige state parties to submit regular reports (roughly one every four years) on the domestic implementation of the rights contained within the covenant (ibid). Reports are examined in public and in direct confrontation with high-level government representatives, whereby committee members can simultaneously praise and criticise states on the extent to which they are either fulfilling or abandoning their covenant obligations (Nowak, 2005). In relation to drug control, the HRCa have criticised several countries, in their concluding observation reports, including Indonesia and Thailand, as they use the death penalty for drug-related offences (Human Rights Committee, 2013: CCPR/C/IDN/CO/1; Human Rights Committee, 2017a: CCPR/C/THA/CO/2). It is considered that such offences do not meet the threshold of the 'most serious crimes' to which the use of the death penalty should be restricted, in accordance with Article 6(2) of the ICCPR.

In addition, the First Optional Protocol to the ICCPR, entering into force at the same time, allows the HRCa to consider 'communications' from individuals who have alleged to be the victims of human rights abuses (Nowak, 2005). At the time of writing, 116 parties have ratified this protocol (see the United Nations Treaty Collection, 2019b), and Nowak (2005: 195) observes that the HRCa have 'turned it into a surprisingly effective quasi-judicial individual complaints procedure'. While the committee's decisions are not legally binding, they are still argued like judgments, they carry moral and political obligations, and from 1990 onwards, a committee member is designated to oversee and monitor the implementation of the decisions made to encourage state compliance (Rehman, 2010). The moral and political weight the HRCa can carry can also be evidenced in relation to drug control, through an open letter to the Philippines, condemning the *reintroduction* of death penalty for drug offences, since this is contrary to the Second Optional Protocol to the ICCPR (Human Rights Committee, 2017b).

The International Covenant on Economic Social and Cultural Rights

In stark contrast with the ICCPR, the International Covenant on Economic Social and Cultural Rights (1966) (ICESCR), the other treaty drafted by the CHR and adopted in 1966, was regarded as containing programmatic rights which were not immediately applicable and enforceable; rather they could be progressively realised when states had the adequate resources to do so (Rehman, 2010). These second- and third-generation rights include the right to health, social security, an adequate standard of living, the rights to adequate housing, food, and rights to participate in cultural life, education and self-determination (see Articles 12, 9, 11, 15, 13, 1 ICESCR). Unlike the ICCPR, an independent committee of experts tasked with examining state reports and monitoring state compliance was not established until 1985 (ECOSOC, 1985: E/RES/1985/17), as this process was previously (and perhaps unsuitably) undertaken by the Economic and Social Council (ECOSOC); a political body of the UN comprised of state representatives.

Once formed the independent Committee on Economic, Social and Cultural Rights adopted a similar state reporting procedure to the HRCa, however, an Optional Protocol allowing complaints from individuals was only adopted in 2008 (General Assembly, 2008: A/RES/63/117). As of June 2019, there were 45 signatories and 24 parties to this Protocol, none of which include the UK (see the United Nations Treaty Collection, 2019c). Regardless, this amendment could be said to coincide with Rehman's (2010) claim that the international human rights regime is increasingly becoming more transparent, participatory and open to those that it is designed to benefit. One hundred and sixty-nine states including the UK are party to the ICESCR at the time of writing (see the United Nations Treaty Collection, 2019d). Since advancing the recognition at the Vienna world conference in 1993 that human rights are universal, indivisible, interdependent and interrelated (World Conference on Human Rights, 1993), the separation of the two ideological doctrines dividing the ICCPR and the ICESCR, has largely been abandoned; with calls for a move towards a more integrated and holistic understanding of human rights (Marks, 2013).

The core treaties

This section predominately centres on the formulation and operation of the UDHR, ICCPR and the ICESCR since these documents together comprise the International Bill of Rights, the core foundation for the international human rights regime. All other international human right treaties stem from these core documents, as the terms of each new treaty inform and add to the interpretation of others; facilitating a rather unique system whereby all human right treaties can be read as one coherent body (Barrett et al., 2008).

For instance, the International Bill of Rights contains all of the rights found in seven other core human right treaties: the International Convention on the Elimination of All Forms of Racial Discrimination (1966), the Convention on the Elimination of All Forms of Discrimination against Women (1979), the Convention against Torture and Other Cruel, Inhuman or Degrading Treatment or Punishment (1984), the Convention on the Rights of the Child (1989), the International Convention on the Protection of the Rights of All Migrant Workers and Members of Their Families (1990), the International Convention for the Protection of All Persons from Enforced Disappearance (2006) and the

Convention on the Rights of Persons with Disabilities (2006). The UK has ratified the vast majority of these core treaties and they operate in a similar fashion to the ICCPR and the ICESR (see the United Nations Treaty Collection, 2019e). They all have separate, independent committees of experts, a similar state reporting procedure, and with the exception of the committees on enforced disappearances and the rights of the child, they all contain mechanisms to allow complaints to be made from individuals.

The 'high standing' of the international human rights regime

The progression and proliferation of human rights treaties over the past 60 years is also evidenced by a non-exhaustive list of additional human rights instruments featured on the Office of the United Nations High Commissioner for Human Rights (OHCHR) website (OHCHR, n.d.b). These instruments include the United Nations Declaration on the Rights of Indigenous Peoples (2007) and the United Nations Declaration on the Right to Development (1986). While not legally binding, the OHCHR reports such documents to exert an 'undeniable moral force' on states (OHCHR, 2002: xi). This corresponds to the *sui generis* character and the frequently recognised 'high standing' of the international human rights regime (Rehman, 2010). It could be argued that at the start of the 21st century, the regime moved increasingly to the forefront of the UN's legal, institutional and more 'open' ideological agenda, as observed previously by Rehman (ibid).

In 2006, the CHR (initially tasked with drafting the International Bill of Rights) was replaced by the Human Rights Council (HRCb). Previously, the CHR reported to ECOSOC, a principal organ of the UN comprising of 54 state members which are elected by the General Assembly. It is tasked with establishing commissions in economic and social fields and with promoting human rights (Article 68, the Charter). However, the HRCb is now directly elected by and reports to the General Assembly itself; the principal political organ of the UN comprising of all 193 member states. As such, former UN Secretary-General Kofi Annan conceives the rights regime as having a 'more authoritative position corresponding to the primacy of human rights in the Charter' (General Assembly, 2005: A/592005, 183).

At an institutional level at least then, the human rights regime appears to be dominant within the framework of the UN due to the more senior and representative position it has been accorded. There also exists a strong case for the high legal standing afforded to the international human rights regime. Article 103 of the UN Charter (1945) states that 'in the event of a conflict between obligations ... under the present Charter and ... obligations under any other international agreement ... obligations under the Charter shall prevail'. The protection of human rights is mentioned seven times in the Charter, from the preamble, to the purposes of the UN, to the responsibilities of the General Assembly and ECOSOC (see the preamble, Articles 1, 55, 13(1)b 61(2)).

From the outset, human rights have been perceived as one of the key purposes and principles of the UN, which is further confirmed by the creation of the

HRCb. The HRCb has special procedure mechanisms in place which enables independent experts to work closely with governments, victims, civil society and non-governmental organisations (NGOs) on various thematic issues. The HRCb also has a unique Universal Periodic Review (UPR) procedure, which involves it reviewing the human rights records of *all* the UN member states, thereby providing potential for even 'the darkest corners of the world' to be fairly represented (OHCHR, 2008: 1 citing Ban Ki-moon, n.p.). The UPR function, combined with civil societal engagement by the HRCb, and the various human right treaty committees cited above, was designed to ensure that this system is open, transparent and promotes a co-operative working environment; where constructive dialogue can take place with and between states and with individuals themselves (General Assembly, 2006: A/RES/60/251).

Questioning the future of the international human rights regime

Although such procedural mechanisms have the potential to aid broader rights-based discussions, the future of the international human rights regime in practice has been questioned (Douzinas, 2000; Goodhart, 2012; Hopgood, 2013). Despite implementing procedural mechanisms to afford human rights an increased high standing and level of protection internationally, in practice, human rights are considered to be overly reliant on enforcement from western states that have their own political and economic agendas (Hopgood, 2013). Yet, American and European hegemony is declining due to globalising forces (ibid). This could facilitate contestation and challenges from states who have not been as committed to building the international human rights regime in the 20th and early 21st century (ibid).

As alluded to in Chapter 2, there is also a growing national resistance to transnational forms of governance, which includes rights regulation. O'Cinneide (2017: 2) argues that human rights face a legitimacy crisis since regional/ international human rights bodies are accused of:

> [F]ailing to respect the constraints on their authority that should flow from their lack of a clear democratic mandate derived from a specific national demos.

He draws on Habermas' idea of popular 'will formation' to recognise that citizens value democratically approved laws and democratic self-government, which can manifest via a new strain of nationalist populism; as exemplified by the Brexit vote and Trump's electoral success (O'Cinneide, 2017: 6 citing Habermas, 2001: 766). To counteract the recent challenges posed to human rights, it is necessary to build a detailed defence of human rights law:

> [T]o confront some of the ambiguity that exists about its scope, substance and purpose – and in particular to respond to the charges of 'mission creep'

> and counter-democratic overreach. There is a need to provide a substantive justification of how human rights law has expanded its reach over the last few decades, to demonstrate the democratic bona fides of this area of law, and to show how it enhances the functioning, legitimacy and integrity of legal systems at large. (ibid: 5)

It is in this vein then that the following section explores the legal and institutional architecture behind the regional and domestic human rights in the UK and the challenges posed to this system. As highlighted previously, regional and domestic systems have been inspired by, and have developed alongside this regime, with Steiner, Alston and Goodman (2008) noting human rights law to be complexly intertwined, transformative of internal orders and reciprocally influential at every level. The next section acknowledges the influence international, regional and domestic human rights regimes have had upon each other, the potential implications of withdrawing from the European Convention on Human Rights, the implications of Brexit, and the function and operation of human rights in the UK.

The regional and domestic human rights frameworks in the UK

While the international human rights regime will be shown to be consistent with, and influential upon the regional and domestic systems impacting the UK (particularly in light of UPR and treaty committee reporting mechanisms), the fact remains that individual complaints can only be made if the UK has ratified the treaty in question. In addition, any decisions made are not binding domestically. Therefore, regional and domestic human rights regimes have developed across the globe to better assist individuals bringing claims. The following subsections will focus predominately on the operation of the European Convention on Human Rights (1950) (ECHR) and its incorporation into domestic legislation via the Human Rights Act (1998) (HRA). Since the British Conservative Party have also called to repeal the HRA and/or withdraw from the ECHR (Asthana and Mason, 2016; Conservative Party Manifesto, 2017), the legal implications of these actions will be explored, along with the perceived 'legitimacy crisis' facing human rights (O'Cinneide, 2017: 2).

As an important aside, it is worthwhile noting that another human rights text, the Charter of Fundamental Rights of the European Union (2000) also enshrines certain political, social and economic rights for members of the European Union. Yet, under Clause 5(4) of the European (Withdrawal) Bill (2017), the Charter of Fundamental Rights will not be retained in UK law after its exit from the EU. Plans to repeal the HRA and/or withdraw from the ECHR have also been put on hold until the process of leaving the EU is complete (Conservative Party Manifesto, 2017). Additionally, the EU Charter only applies to member states 'when they are interpreting Union law' (Article 51(1)), and EU

Charter rights are not directly enforceable by individuals (in a similar vein to the international human rights regime), in contrast to rights contained in the ECHR (the European Union Committee, 2016). For this reason, the ECHR and its incorporation into domestic law via the HRA have more relevance to individual drug control and human rights cases in the UK. The ECHR and the HRA have more power to reconfigure the drug policy binary; though the continued relevance of these documents is in question, in light of the uncertain political and legal climate in more recent times.

The European Convention on Human Rights

The ECHR was drafted in 1950 by the then newly established Council of Europe, and it entered into force in 1953. The Council of Europe was formed by 10 founding states including the UK, and was created out of a desire to prevent a repetition of the atrocities of World War II (Kerrigan, 2005), in a similar vein to the UN organisation. The Equality and Human Rights Commission (2011) report Winston Churchill to have been instrumental in the creation of the ECHR. In his opening speech to the congress of Europe in 1948, he proclaimed that the new Europe 'must be a positive force, deriving its strength from our sense of common spiritual values', with the idea of a Charter of Human Rights standing at the very centre of the movement (James, 1974: 7635–7639).

Along with Churchill, the Equality and Human Rights Commission (ibid) recognises the British lawyer and politician David Maxwell Fyfe's significant contribution to drafting the ECHR. They note the UK to be the first country in the Council of Europe to ratify the convention in 1951 (ibid), counteracting common misconceptions that the ECHR is somehow a foreign construction and should not be applicable in the UK (for more detail, see Chapter 1). There are now 47 member states in the Council of Europe, all new members are required to ratify the ECHR at the earliest available opportunity (Parliamentary Assembly, 1994). This means that the ECHR is now capable of providing protection to well over 800 million people and according to Dembour (2005: 113), it is 'often heralded as the greatest achievement of the Council of Europe'.

The ECHR (see the preamble) was inspired by the UDHR, which had been proclaimed two years previously. Yet, the Convention possesses a distinct advantage over the Declaration as it created a substantial mechanism of enforcement for individuals, unsurprisingly therefore it does not protect as many rights as its global counterpart (ibid). While there are a few exceptions, the ECHR's predominant focus is on civil and political human rights. This leaves the EU Charter (until the Brexit process is complete) and the European Social Charter (1961), to guarantee the remaining economic and social human rights and establish any relevant enforcement mechanisms. The European Social Charter is another Council of Europe Treaty, but it has not been incorporated into domestic legislation in contrast with the ECHR.

Articles 2–14 of the ECHR set out the rights which are protected by the Convention, and over the years this has been supplemented by a number of protocols which have been agreed by the Council of Europe. The rights contained in the ECHR include (but are not limited to): the right to life, the prohibition of torture, the right to a fair trial, the right to respect for family and private life, the right to freedom of thought conscience and religion and the right to marry (see Articles 2, 3, 6, 8, 9, 12).

Many of these rights are qualified rights, and some contain a subsection 2 which allows the UK to restrict the right in question if it is deemed to be necessary in a democratic society to protect public order, health, morals, safety, to prevent crime, and/or to protect the rights and freedoms of others (see Articles 8, 9, 10, 11). Of course, striking the balance between protecting the public interest in restricting a human right and facilitating an individual's interest in asserting the right has always been a difficult and elusive task (see Chapters 4 and 5 for more detail). Since 1959, the European Court of Human Rights (ECtHR) has had to manage this role (Bonello, 2005).

The ECtHR was established by virtue of Article 19 of the ECHR. It rules on state or individual applications alleging violations of the rights contained within the ECHR. Since 1998, it has sat as a full-time court, individuals can apply to it directly, and its judgments are binding upon the countries concerned (Article 46 ECHR). In relation to the UK, the UK government is bound by Article 46 ECHR to give effect to the final judgment of the ECtHR to which it is a party. This provision has become increasingly contentious, since at the heart of the debate over withdrawal from the ECHR is the sovereignty of the UK; with the conservative party perceiving the present human rights architecture to undermine democratic accountability to the public and the sovereignty of parliament (Conservative Party, 2014). Yet, Dzehtsiarou et al. (2015: 27) acknowledge that 'small changes to the status quo' would suffice for the very limited number of judgments made that the UK government is bound to follow.

The case of *R* v. *Horncastle* (2009) also confirms that the ECtHR takes on board the opinions of domestic courts, and the Joint Committee on Human Rights (2014) notes that the ECtHR is entering a new era, with a focus on the principle of subsidiarity, and the margin of appreciation doctrine. Both doctrines increase the democratic legitimacy of the Convention system, with the former ensuring that respect for Convention rights lies first and foremost with the contracting parties (Jurisconsult, 2010). The latter doctrine allows the various members of the ECHR to interpret ECtHR decisions differently, as the European judges are obliged to take into account any differences in culture, history and philosophy between the European court and the state in question.

In addition, the ECHR system has implemented broader procedural and substantive reforms to better secure access to justice (for more detail, see Gerards and Glas, 2017). Historically however, Bonello (ibid) notes that the ECtHR became a victim of its own success, given the inadequate structures and resources to cope with the daily flood of applications (ibid). Over 20 years ago, in a very different political climate, the New Labour government responded to this and put the promotion of human rights at the forefront of its policy agenda. This government sought to 'bring rights home', to prevent the inordinate delay and cost of necessitating British citizens to go to Strasbourg, where the ECtHR is based (Home Office, 1997).

The Human Rights Act

A UK Labour party consultation paper published in 1996, entitled 'Bringing rights home' acknowledged the need to incorporate the ECHR into domestic legislation, the Human Rights Bill soon followed (ibid). During the second reading of the Human Rights Bill, it was noted that it took approximately five years and £30,000 for a human rights claim to reach the ECtHR, after all other domestic remedies had been exhausted (ibid). Thus, the enactment of the HRA provided a clear means by which people could more easily assert their rights and secure access to justice within the UK's judicial system.

The HRA provides a unique UK model for incorporating the ECHR into domestic law, as it is particularly well adapted to meet the UK's constitutional tradition of maintaining parliamentary sovereignty. Unlike many other jurisdictions, who can strike down any legislation which is incompatible with an often firmly entrenched, codified set of human rights (see the United States Bill of Rights, 1791; the Canadian Charter of Rights and Freedoms, 1982; and the South African Bill of Rights, 1996), the UK has an uncodified constitutional model where the concept of parliamentary sovereignty is paramount (Dicey, 1885/1959).

The celebrated constitutional theorist Dicey recognised that in the UK parliament can alter any law, there is no legal distinction between constitutional and other laws, and no judicial authority can void or strike down an act of parliament, or treat it as unconstitutional (ibid). Hence, it is not possible for the UK courts to declare void any legislation which breaches convention rights. Correspondingly, following, *R. (on the application of Miller)* v. *Secretary of State for Exiting the European Union* (2017) (the *Miller* case), it is thought that there is no prerogative power of the UK government to withdraw the UK from the ECHR. Rather, parliamentary legislation will be needed, since it is a well-established constitutional position that ministers cannot affect fundamental constitutional change (ibid; Peplow, 2017).

In order to adhere to parliamentary sovereignty and simultaneously ensure the effective enforcement of Convention rights, s3 of the HRA requires the courts to interpret all legislation, whenever enacted, in a way which is compatible with Convention rights, 'so far as it is possible to do so'. This legislative power is largely understood to be the principal remedial measure for the UK courts to enforce Convention rights, with s4 of the HRA operating as a last resort. Section 4 of the HRA allows the courts to make a 'declaration of incompatibility' if any legislation is deemed to be incompatible with Convention rights and cannot be interpreted in line with s3. Although any declaration issued has no immediate legal effect, under s10 of the HRA the government then has the power to take remedial action and amend the incompatible legislation if there are 'compelling reasons' for doing so. In practice, the powers created under s4 and s10 are utilised less frequently than s3, and in any event, the individual always has recourse to take their case to the ECtHR as a last resort (for as long as the UK remains a party to the ECHR).

Additionally, s2 of the HRA requires the UK judiciary to 'take into account' any judgment from the ECtHR that is of relevance to the case in question. Despite the fact this provision is not powerful enough to create a doctrine of binding precedent for ECtHR judgments, in order for parliamentary sovereignty to be maintained; it still operates to ensure consistency with any decisions made by the ECtHR. In any event, the requirement under s2 to 'take into account' any judgment from the ECtHR has relaxed considerably in recent years. Lord Neuberger in *Manchester CC* v. *Pinnock* (2010: para 48) acknowledges that:

> The court is not bound to respect every decision of the [ECtHR] ... as it would destroy the ability of the court to engage in constructive dialogue with the European court which is of value to the development of Convention law.

When combined with the margin of appreciation doctrine discussed in the ECHR subsection, the flexibility established in s2 of the HRA affords UK judges an element of freedom to develop their own unique case law and policies pertaining to human rights in the UK. Besides, an initial key aim of the Human Rights Bill was not only to subtly and powerfully interweave human rights more fully into the jurisprudence of UK courts, but to also enable British judges to make 'a distinctively British contribution to the development of the jurisprudence of human rights in Europe' (Home Office, 1997: para 1.14).

However, as stated by Jay (2017: 853):

> Without public awareness and acceptance of the domestic legislation that ties the ECHR to British law, the Convention, Court and HRA are likely to continue to be viewed within the UK as 'foreign' institutions that do not adequately reflect British human rights culture, and thereby foster a reluctance to comply.

Repealing the Human Rights Act

The HRA is viewed as 'politically toxic' and as a foreign construction (Dzehtsiarou et al., 2015: 18). If it is repealed after the Brexit process is complete, then it is likely to be replaced with a British Bill of Rights (BBR) (Conservative Party, 2014), and the procedural requirements under sections 2, 3 and 4, designed to affirm parliamentary sovereignty, will most likely be abandoned (Dzehtsiarou et al., 2015). It is considered that the BBR will have more legitimacy as it is 'home grown' and that it will contain 'a written "catalogue" of rights spelling out their content and the possibilities of limiting them' (ibid: 18–19).

It is, of course, worth noting that there does exist the possibility of human rights in the UK being expanded via the BBR, particularly in relation to due process rights, and the BBR may allow for an enhanced focus on individual freedoms to reflect British liberal values (for more detail on potential areas of rights expansion, see Dzehtsiarou et al., 2015). Though, as will be demonstrated in 'the Psychoactive Substances Act' subsection, recent UK drug policy legislation has curtailed the British tradition of negative liberty. Furthermore, the expert consensus, given the existing political dynamic, is that human rights in the UK will be curtailed in general, through the repeal of the HRA and enactment of the BBR (ibid; the European Union Committee, 2016).

Nevertheless, common law remedies have always existed alongside the HRA and such remedies would continue to exist if it were to be repealed. However, human rights at common law developed in an unsystematic, haphazard fashion prior to the HRA (see Dickson, 2015 for more detail). Human rights scholars have noted that it would be helpful if senior judges were to clarify which of the principles associated with the ECtHR's approach to human rights would be inserted into the common law if the HRA is repealed (ibid; Harris et al., 2014). For instance, the legitimacy, necessity and proportionality tests which the ECtHR applies when assessing whether interferences with rights are justified, are more intrusive than those available at common law, such as the irrationality and unreasonableness tests (Dzehtsiarou et al., 2015; see Chapters 4 and 5 for the application of the ECtHR tests).

Withdrawing from the European Convention on Human Rights

There also exists the possibility that the UK government could go further than repealing the HRA, since the Conservative Party government have – albeit inconsistently – expressed an intention to withdraw from the ECHR as well (Asthana and Mason, 2016; Conservative Party Manifesto, 2017). This would mean that a UK citizen would have no recourse to take their claim to the ECtHR if they have exhausted their options in the UK courts. Not only would this weaken the human rights protections afforded to individuals legally speaking, politically speaking the potential ramifications are substantial. The UK has a strong record of protecting human rights, a withdrawal from the ECHR could therefore have a damaging impact on rights regimes throughout the rest of the world, potentially leading to a disillusionment with the whole system and weaker human rights protections overall.

Even though it is unlikely that the UK will be able to withdraw from the ECHR (following the *Miller* judgment any such withdrawal must be authorised by parliamentary legislation), it is, in any case, a belief in the *idea* of the international political order which is paramount (see Chapter 2 per Scott, 1994). When applying this concept to human rights then, perhaps it does not matter whether or not the *ideology* of human rights is true, what matters is the acceptance of the prevailing human rights architecture by international actors, and increasingly the general public, given the strain of national populism pervading politics at the time of writing.

Presenting the idea of human rights

Accordingly, it is important to think carefully about how best to present the *idea* of human rights to support the existing legal architecture, or at the very least to prevent the curtailment of rights. Arguably, it is no longer enough to solely rely upon the fact the UK played a considerable role in the formulation of the ECHR and the Council of Europe, nor that early British legislation such as the Magna Carta, and the works of British enlightenment thinkers such as John Stuart Mill and John Locke, played an essential role in the formulation of all human rights systems as a whole (Equality and Human Rights Commission, 2011). Instead, 'to demonstrate the democratic bona fides of this area of law' and to enhance the legitimacy of the UK's human rights framework, it is important to show that human rights law has evolved and grown in a similar way to how other common law standards evolve over time:

> [T]hrough judicial interpretation of democratically-approved texts, with courts clarifying the scope and substance of the abstract provisions of human rights instruments through standard procedures of legal reasoning. (O'Cinneide, 2017: 5)

The case law analysed in Chapters 4 and 5 demonstrates the application (or lack thereof) of human rights norms to a variety of drug-taking situations, to show how the UK's system of human rights is consistent with established legal rules in other common law areas. Furthermore, human rights regimes are devised to be organic and to challenge *perceived* embedded moral and societal assumptions about right and wrong (ibid). Hence, they can reflect and shape the will of the public, thereby addressing the legitimacy crises facing human rights law, and the idea that there is a perceived lack of democratic accountability to the public (ibid). A notable example of the UK's human rights regime facilitating a great social change within a short space of time is in relation to LGBT+ rights. The ECHR has been integral to help build gay and lesbian rights over the last three decades (Dzehtsiarou et al., 2015), but the UK has gone further by introducing same-sex marriage via the Marriage (Same Sex) Couples Act (2013). While this Act corresponds well to Articles 12 and 14 of the ECHR, which provides for the right to marry and freedom from discrimination, legislation allowing for homosexual marriage is not (yet) required by the ECtHR.

State legislation across the globe varies to a huge extent in relation to homosexuality, and it was only in 1967 that homosexual activity was decriminalised in England and Wales (The Sexual Offences Act, 1967). If an act that was once criminalised and deemed to offend public morality and affect public order and safety, is now in England and Wales at least, legitimised and protected as an essential human right, then perhaps the same protection and recognition could one day be afforded to other currently criminalised activities? While respect for regional and domestic human rights architecture may be waning in the UK, it is important to outline the architectural mechanisms in place to advance social change, to recognise the ongoing legal and political challenges to human rights regimes (particularly in the UK), and as articulated by Landman (2013: 27) to: 'continue the empirical and normative "conversation" across local, national and international levels'. Such human rights conversations are beginning to happen within in the realm of international drug control, despite the two regimes previously behaving 'as though they exist in parallel universes' (Hunt, 2008: 9).

The international drug control framework

Legal regulatory origins

The drug control system was not always dominated by a mandate which called for either commodity control or penal control; which according to Boister (2001) is the dualistic purpose of this international regime. In fact, prior to 1912, there was only one international document regulating the supply, sale, possession or manufacture of any psychoactive (see the Brussels General Act of 1889–1890 as the first international agreement to limit alcohol consumption). Instead, western countries largely developed their own separate regulatory regimes for different psychoactives in the 19th and early 20th centuries, in light of the mounting regulation imposed upon pharmacies by the growing medical professions at the time (Braithwaite and Drahos, 2000). Increasing regulatory practices favoured the strong in the chemical industry, as larger companies had the resources to impose adequate manufacturing, safety and quality controls (ibid).

As such, large international pharmaceutical companies began to emerge and successfully monopolise and profit from the sale of certain psychoactives (ibid). European pharmaceutical companies commercially manufactured opium, morphine, heroin and cocaine in the 19th century (ibid; McCoy, 1980), and it was this economic control, combined with British economic interests in maintaining their opium trade in China, which led the US to call for the prohibition and suppression of the opium trade in particular (Braithwaite and Drahos, 2000). Moral reformers were also critical of the fact that British colonial powers purveyed opiates to their poorest dependents and lined imperial coffers through these state-run monopolies (McAllister, 2000). In addition, the US wished to strengthen its trading and political relationship with China, and there was also a fear of a potential global 'contagion', as many states considered opium addiction to have contributed substantially to the collapse of the Chinese empire (ibid).

Thus, it was economic, geopolitical and moral reasons that led to an international conference on opium trafficking in Shanghai in 1909, which eventually culminated in the International Opium Convention (1912), the very first international drug convention (Bewley-Taylor and Jelsma, 2011). A vigorous social movement at this time predominately led by the church and women in the US, Australia and the UK also called for the prohibition of alcohol, as well as focussing on other drugs of addiction (Braithwaite and Drahos, 2000). Ultimately though, these efforts failed internationally as alcohol prohibition posed too much of a challenge to entrenched producer interests, to vested state economic interests in taxing this commodity, and because there were too many respectable white drinking men who resented being moralised at by a new women's movement (ibid). Consequently, alcohol regimes are still regulated nationally, though there are increasing calls for international legal strategies for alcohol control (Room, 2006, 2013; Taylor and Dhillon, 2013; Zeigler, 2013; Chapman, 2017).

The licit 'drugs': alcohol and tobacco regulation

Commentators have written extensively on the tension which exists between the alcohol industry wishing to maximise their profits, and the state's interest in promoting and protecting public health (McCambridge, 2012; Miller and Harkins, 2010; Lyness and McCambridge, 2014; Mialon and McCambridge, 2018). This tension becomes increasingly complex when powerful alcohol corporations have the capacity to influence national governments (Lyness and McCambridge, 2014). As noted in Chapter 2, corporations are increasingly perceived as an extension of the 'state'. Lyness and McCambridge (ibid) found in their alcohol industry research that five major UK charities received both alcohol industry funding, and were active in UK alcohol policy processes.

Additionally, a 2018 systemic review on the alcohol industry's corporate social responsibility (CSR) initiatives found no robust evidence that such initiatives reduce harmful drinking (Mialon and McCambridge, 2018). Conversely, the review found good evidence that CSR initiatives are used to influence how alcohol-related issues are framed, i.e. in line with industry interests; thereby impeding the development of evidence-informed policies to reduce harmful drinking (ibid). Perhaps it is of little surprise then that social scientists are increasingly referring to 'the corporate capture' of the alcohol policy environment (Miller and Harkins, 2010: 564). Similar concerns are arising in emerging cannabis policy environments, since researchers have expressed concern over creating for-profit cannabis industries (Lenton, 2014).

Tobacco regimes are similarly subject to national regulation as opposed to global prohibition, since powerful US manufacturers and agricultural producers dominated world markets earlier in the 20th century (Braithwaite and Drahos, 2000). However, this regulatory framework is changing, since tobacco regimes are being increasingly subject to the global public health arena, thereby alleviating state tensions between power, politics, trade and public health; since public health is becoming increasingly paramount (Chan, 2013).

There now exists the World Health Organization's Framework Convention on Tobacco Control (2003) (FCTC), a living document capable of evolving by its governing body; the Conference of the Parties (COP). As of June 2019, the COP is comprised of 181 parties to the FCTC, including the UK (WHO, 2019b). The FCTC strives to control the supply and demand of tobacco products and regulate the marketing and trading of tobacco products in line with public health goals (Chan, 2013). This regulatory framework recognises tobacco use constitutes a transnational threat to health, and that governments should therefore adopt the same regulatory scrutiny they place on the safety of food, air, water, industrial chemicals and medicines (ibid).

For Chan (ibid), the Former Director-General of the World Health Organization (WHO), the enactment of the FCTC 'was a game changing notion. It gave governments the upper hand in a battle against a powerful and highly profitable industry' (ibid: n.p.). According to Nikogosian and Kickbusch (2016), the FCTC is a pioneering legal health instrument which safeguards public health globally, in the face of legal disputes and competing agendas both domestically and internationally. The legal strength of this instrument has also been said to counteract the negative consequences of globalisation (see Puska, 2018). This is because the FCTC places legal responsibilities on governments in both developing and wealthier countries to counteract the fact that 'deadly products are being dumped on the poor' (Chan, 2013: n.p.). Perhaps then the FCTC could be used to spark the development of global public health instruments for cannabis and other psychoactives currently deemed *illicit* at an international level? However, it should be noted that public and professional opinion diverges considerably on cannabis and tobacco regulation (see Arnott, 2017).

The four fundamentals of contemporary drug policy

In any event, for the purposes of this chapter, it is enough to observe that international prohibitory controls were largely reserved for other substances early in the 20th century, as Buxton (2011) notes four core assumptions upon which the modern international system of drug control is based. In coinciding with the differing regulatory approach to alcohol and tobacco, the first assumption is that some psychoactives, but not all, present a danger to public and individual health and morality (ibid). The second assumption is that all states must work within both their national territories and collectively to ensure the continued prohibition of certain substances (ibid). The third is that those who participate in the trade of illicit psychoactives as distributors, producers or users are criminals, and the fourth is that source-focussed approaches are the most effective means to eliminate trade (ibid). The four fundamentals of contemporary drug policy were first set out at the Shanghai conference (ibid), and have prevailed throughout the 20th century and continue to a greater or lesser extent into the 21st century.

The prohibitory controls developed in the early 20th century began with the moral crusade against opium, which continued to gain ground. A racial dimension against the Chinese was incorporated here, where even into the 1960s heroin trafficking was construed by some as a communist Chinese strategy to morally degrade the west (Manderson, 1993). Cocaine was likewise viewed in the US as a vice of prostitutes and African-Americans, and cannabis came to be viewed as a threat from Mexican immigration in the 1920s and 1930s (McAllister, 2000). Although these views were not automatically shared globally, the rise of US hegemony and their global political power during the 20th century facilitated the gradual building of international support for prohibition and criminalisation (Braithwaite and Drahos, 2000).

Various international treaties emerged which distinguished between the licit and illicit psychoactive trades, causing a divide in regulatory systems which created the 'ethical' pharmaceutical industry on the one hand, and the 'illicit' drugs regime on the other (see the Geneva Convention, 1925; the Geneva Narcotics Manufacturing and Distribution Limitation Convention, 1931/Bangkok Opium Smoking Agreement, 1931; the Geneva Trafficking Convention, 1936; the Paris Protocol, 1948; the New York Opium Protocol, 1953). It is worthy of note that the early drug prohibition system was run by the League of Nations; the forerunner to the UN. This offers support to the notion that there is an institutional or structural tie between the historical development of both the international human rights and international drug control regimes. All of the earlier drug control treaties culminated in the Single Convention on Narcotic drugs (1961) (Single Convention), a convention which is still in force today.

The Single Convention on Narcotic Drugs

The Single Convention was designed to consolidate all of the earlier international drug treaties from 1912 onwards, and charts the first time that the cannabis plant (*Cannabis* sp.) was specifically prohibited alongside the opium poppy (*Papaver somniferum*), the coca leaf (*Erythroxylum coca*) and their derivatives, all inventions of which, at that point, were previously controlled (Bewley-Taylor and Jelsma, 2011). The Single Convention introduced more of a dualist approach to drug control (via both commodity and penal control; see Boister, 2001), as earlier treaties, while influenced to some extent by the moral hegemony prevailing in the US, were more concerned with regulating the licit trade of psychoactives, and in ensuring their availability for medical purposes (McAllister, 2000). According to Boister (ibid), the move to an increasingly dualist approach was due to the expansion in the 1950s of illicit drug trafficking, supply, and illicit manufacture in undeveloped regions, alongside the fact that usage patterns of psychoactives were evolving rapidly.

Hence, the preamble of the Single Convention concerned itself with reducing the potential for addiction through drugs in order to 'combat … a serious evil for the individual', while it simultaneously regarded their availability as being 'indispensable for the relief of pain and suffering'. To give effect to these two positions, Article 4(c) requires parties to pursue a single objective in limiting 'exclusively to medical and scientific purposes the production, manufacture, export, import, distribution of, trade in, use and possession of drugs'. As of June

2019, there are 154 parties to the Single Convention (United Nations Treaty Collection, 2019f), and each party is required to provide mutual co-operation and assistance in pursing this overarching objective (Fortson, 2011).

The International Narcotics Control Board

To facilitate this common objective, the International Narcotics Control Board (INCB) was established by Article 9 of the Single Convention. It functions as an independent, quasi-judicial control organ and it is mandated to oversee and support governmental compliance (INCB, n.d.). The INCB has 13 members who are elected by ECOSOC for a period of five years (see Article 9, the Single Convention). Ten of its members are elected from a list of persons nominated by governments, and three are elected from a list nominated by the WHO, for their medical and/or pharmacological expertise (ibid). The INCB is obligated to administer an estimates system, which limits each nation's annual production of controlled substances to the estimated amounts needed for medical and scientific purposes (see Article 12, the Single Convention). These powers are far-reaching as they extend to all nations regardless of whether they have ratified the convention or not (ibid).

Alongside this function, the INCB is mandated to enter into a '*continuing* dialogue' with governments, in a similar manner to the human rights treaty bodies during their periodic review process (see Article 9(5), the Single Convention). Yet, Barratt (2008: 12) observes a distinct difference between the two, as the human rights treaty bodies engage in a '*constructive* dialogue', recognising the need for meaningful engagement with all levels of society, in order to gain an accurate and honest depiction of a situation as it arises. In contrast, the INCB is routinely criticised for failing to engage with civil society, for conducting its negotiations in secret and for only accepting information which is provided by the governments themselves (ibid; Bewley-Taylor and Trace, 2006; Csete, 2012; Harm Reduction International, 2012).

McAllister (2012) notes that these working methods resonate with the era in which INCB was formed along with the biases which were prevalent at this time. The board is often portrayed as the 'guardian' of a more moralistic, prohibitionist approach to drug control (Bewley-Taylor and Trace, 2006: 1):

> [C]hallenging any activity which does not fit with its rigid interpretations of the treaty – and non-responsive to the needs of member states in a world dramatically changed from that in which the INCB was established. (Rolles, 2009a: 169)

However, there are signs that the INCB is beginning to change its working practices. Despite having a previously poor record when addressing human rights concerns, the 2016, 2017 and 2018 Annual Reports (INCB, 2017a, 2018, 2019) evidence a shift towards a health and human rights interpretation of the UN drug conventions. The 2017 report considers drug dependence treatment as a human right, and the 2016 and 2018 reports recommend that states adhere to the principle of proportionality when formulating criminal justice policy, and abolishing capital punishment for drug-related offences (ibid). The latter may seem like an obvious recommendation to some, but the INCB has previously refused to condemn torture and remained neutral on capital punishment for drug-related offences, even when states challenged them on this issue (Barrett, 2012; Human Rights Watch, 2012).

In a similar vein to the human rights treaty committees, the INCB is also required to report on its findings and submit its recommendations to the Commission on Narcotic Drugs (CND) – a functional commission established by ECOSOC in 1946 (see Article 9, the Single Convention). Despite the fact that all of these monitoring bodies have no direct enforcement mechanisms per se, their recommendations or decisions can carry significant political weight. Additionally, it is worth noting that, the CND has remained a functional commission of ECOSOC since 1946, unlike the CHR, which has since been abandoned and replaced by a senior UN council, the HRCb. Thus, the international human rights framework should regardless dominate here institutionally as well as legally (pursuant to Article 103 of the UN Charter).

The Commission on Narcotic Drugs

The CND is the central drug policy making body within the UN system, it reviews and analyses the global drug control situation (UNODC, 2019a). The CND has two distinct segments: a normative segment for discharging treaty-based functions (which includes obtaining regular reports from the INCB, advising ECOSOC on matters pertaining to drug control, drafting UN drug conventions and advising on changes to the UN's drug control framework) and an operational segment, since the CND is also the governing body for the United Nations Office on Drugs and Crime's (UNODC) drug control programme (see ECOSOC, 1999: E/RES/1999/30). The UNODC finances measures (from predominantly donor states) to combat the 'world drug problem' (UNODC, 2019b). Such financial sway, combined with the political influence gained from operating as one of ECOSOC's functional commissions, allows the CND to have extensive influence in the global drug policy arena.

The CND comprises of 53 states (as opposed to individuals), who are elected for a four-year period (ECOSOC, 1991: E/RES/1991/49), and it has previously been criticised for operating on a consensus-based model. At one time, it was believed that this framework resulted in states being nervous about expressing divergent views on drug policy, leading to many so-called decisions to 'retreat into generalities' with states 'abandoning any serious efforts to take action' (General Assembly, 2005: A/592005, 159). In more recent years, profoundly different policy responses have emerged across the globe, which can be loosely characterised as being: 'dominated by law enforcement measures' or as 'accepting the reality of the market and seeking to manage its harmful effects' (Bewley-Taylor and Hallam, 2019: 1). Such policy tensions between member states can be clearly seen in the 62nd session of the CND and its Ministerial Segment which took place in March 2019. One notable example from the 62nd session is the delegation from the Russian Federation who were especially critical of Canada's decision to introduce a legally regulated market for cannabis (ibid).

The increase of diverging viewpoints could also signal that the CND has started to acknowledge its human rights obligations. In 2016, the General Assembly held a Special Session which reviewed the international drug control system (also known as UNGASS, 2016). UNGASS 2016 occurred earlier than originally anticipated because of increased governmental and civil society pressure (particularly from Latin American countries) to consider international drug policy reform (General Assembly, 2013: A/RES/67/193; also see Blickman, 2017). The CND led the preparations for UNGASS 2016, negotiated the outcome document and is working to implement the recommendations that have been made.

UNGASS 2016 was a significant cornerstone in the international drug control arena, since the last General Assembly Special Session on drugs was held in 1998 under the official slogan, 'A drug free world: we can do it!' Although the outcome document from UNGASS 2016 supports maintaining the prohibitionist status quo, in contrast with the unviable aim of UNGASS 1998, it does consider proportional sentencing, health-orientated interventions and access to controlled medicines (UNODC, 2016).

UNGASS 2016 and beyond

UNGASS 2016 provided the first genuine opportunity for UN agencies, international organisations and NGOs focused on human rights, health and development to have their voices heard on the impact that drug control policies have on states worldwide (see Human Rights Council, 2015: A/HRC/RES/28/28 which resulted from broad consultations with relevant stakeholders). This is significant since it brings to light the fragmented approaches to drug control across the international community. The Resolution developed from bottom-up engagement with civil societies and NGOs, and it highlights the existing tensions between a state's human rights and drug control obligations. This fragmented approach to drug control is further evidenced by the CND's failure to reach a consensus on the arrangements needed (i.e. the outcome, agenda, format, etc.), for their 62nd session, which brought the 2009–2019 UN plan of action on drugs to its end (see FAAT, 2018).

It has been surmised that the failure to reach a consensus during their 61st session in March 2018 led the HRCb to take advantage of the situation (ibid). The HRCb swiftly adopted a resolution that called for an appraisal of the prohibitionist era, that mandated the OHCHR to take a proactive approach in defence of human rights, and it broadly increased the role and the involvement of the HRCb in the international drug policy arena (see Human Rights Council, 2018: A/HRC/37/L.41). The Resolution invited the HRCb and the High Commissioner for Human Rights to take a more prominent place at the 62nd extraordinary session of the CND (ibid: 6; see also OHCHR, 2019).

At the 62nd session of the CND, an OHCHR representative specifically addressed the issue of measuring drug policies from a human rights perspective, pointing out a growing realisation 'that traditional indicators regarding arrests, seizures and criminal justice responses are inadequate to show the real impact of drug policies on communities' (OHCHR, 2019: 3). He continued:

> [D]rug control strategies should increasingly be measured through an assessment of the impact of drug control efforts on the enjoyment of human rights and other critical aspects such as security, welfare, health and social-economic development.

The representative also acknowledged that the OHCHR 'values the engagement of civil society organizations and ... people who use drugs, in the development and the implementation of drug policies' (ibid: 2). The 62nd session was in fact 'marked by vibrant civil society engagement', with almost 500 civil society delegates attending (Bewley-Taylor and Hallam, 2019: 1). While UN human rights institutions were historically kept away from global drug policy discussions, this more inclusive approach, encompassing non-traditional (human rights as opposed to punitive) metrics, could potentially signify a shift away from the conventional criminal justice led approach of the CND. At the very least, the consensus-based model is fracturing, given the contradictory policy environment emerging between countries and UN institutional bodies (i.e. the OHCHR) advocating for a human rights approach, and those supporting the status quo.

Constraining conventions

All the same, the fact remains that the CND is required to adhere to the three UN drug conventions and could be constrained by the haphazard manner in which they have developed (see Lines, 2017 for a detailed overview on the development of the international drug control regime). As a treaty organ under the Single Convention (1961) and the Convention on Psychotropic Substances (1971), the CND is bestowed with the significant authority to alter the listing of substances under international control according to their level of harm and perceived therapeutic value (Article 3 of Single Convention; Article 2 of the 1971 Convention). The CND is also bestowed with the same powers in relation to preparations and pre-cursor chemicals in the 1971 and 1988 Conventions (Article 3 of the 1971 Convention; Article 12 of the 1988 Convention). The first two conventions require the CND to make changes in the listing of substances on the basis of recommendations by the WHO, whereas the latter 1988 Convention requires the CND to take into account recommendations of the INCB.

Gimenez Corte (2010) offers an interesting overview as to how historical and political influences have largely shaped this scheduling process. The INCB, in particular, has been known to extend its remit, raising concerns and opinions regarding the science involved in drug policy, influencing the CND over and above the WHO. This happened in 2003 where the CND ignored the WHO's recommendations to reschedule dronabinol (a synthetic form of THC, the main active principle of cannabis), due to ostensible concern expressed by the INCB regarding insufficient evidence of safety (Ballotta, Bergeron and Hughes, 2008). Yet, times are changing. In January 2019, for the first time in history, the WHO's Expert Committee on Drug Dependence (ECDD) recommended changing the scheduling of cannabis, clarifying that the cannabis compound – CBD – is not under international control, and addressing longstanding inconsistencies in scheduling; in recognition of this plant's medicinal value (WHO, 2019a). This will have far reaching implications for national regulatory landscapes if accepted by the CND.

However, for as long as the international legal architecture remains in place, it is important to observe that the latter two conventions have also largely been shaped by economic, political and historical precedents, which has led several commentators to observe that the conventions are outdated instruments and products of their own time (Bewley-Taylor and Jelsma, 2011, 2012; Tupper and Labate, 2012). The actual existence of the latter two conventions could support this contention, since the Single Convention, as its title suggests, was designed to constitute a 'single' sole convention for all present and future international drug-related issues (Bewley-Taylor and Jelsma, 2011). But, rather than incorporate new substances within the Single Convention's amendment procedure, countries instead chose to adopt a new convention to respond to the emerging array of new 'psychotropic' substances.

The Convention on Psychotropic Substances

The Convention on Psychotropic Substances (1971) (1971 Convention) schedules largely synthetic psychoactives such as amphetamine-like stimulants, barbiturates and other sedative-inducing substances, and hallucinogens into four schedules according to their perceived harm and therapeutic value. This convention, ratified by 184 parties as of June 2019, therefore appears to operate in much the same way as the Single Convention (see the United Nations Treaty Collection, 2019g). Yet, a Senate of Canada (2002) report notes that tougher controls were placed upon the regulation of the three plants under the Single Convention than the newer mainly synthetic substances, as developed countries wished to retain more freedom over their own vested pharmaceutical interests. Once more then, interests of an economic nature pervaded the regulatory framework of the international drug control system, most notably at a time when many states were drafting their own domestic legislation to respond to these international obligations (see the UK's Misuse of Drugs Act, 1971; New Zealand's Misuse of Drugs Act, 1975; the US's Psychotropic Substances Act, 1978).

The titles of the conventions reveal a further discrepancy within the two instruments since the Single Convention on *Narcotic* Drugs (1961), includes psychoactives which would not ordinarily be defined as 'narcotics' – substances which produce a sedative effect (Saunders, 2007). For Arnao (1990), the term was deliberately purged of its scientific meaning and was employed as a legal bureaucratic term in order to legitimise the legal distinction between different types of psychoactives. He acknowledges that the semantics of the conventions, which notably conflate drug use with drug abuse, reveals the presence of a moral hegemony and a desire for nations to conform to one particular drug control paradigm (ibid).

These observations support the idea that drugs are a social construction, created for specific governmental purposes (Seddon, 2010, 2016). Derrida (1995: 229) further reiterates this line of reasoning through asserting that: 'the concept of drugs is a non-scientific concept that is instituted on the basis of moral and political evaluations'. The use of such terms could also demonstrate the dated nature of the conventions. For instance, the bureaucratic creation 'psychotropic' is not defined in any of the conventions, yet it is now imposed upon a group of substances whose only genuine connection is that they were all consumed within the same era. Hence, one could question the effectiveness of this regime, particularly in relation to the regulation of the new psychoactive substances (NPS) phenomenon.

Convention against Illicit Traffic in Narcotic Drugs and Psychotropic substances

The final Convention Against Illicit Traffic in Narcotic Drugs and Psychotropic substances (1988) (1988 Convention) goes some way to recognising the increase in the variety of psychoactives available, as it regulates precursor chemicals to substances controlled by the earlier two treaties (see Article 12 and Tables I and II of the 1988 Convention). However, the predominant focus is on countering increasingly powerful and sophisticated transnational drug trafficking. As of June 2019, the 1988 Convention is ratified by 190 parties (see the United Nations Treaty Collection, 2019h), and while its aims are largely focused on the issue of organised crime, this latter instrument is arguably the most punitive of the three for the individual user. For the first time, Article 3(2) requires the possession of substances for personal use to be a criminal offence, prior to this, it was debatable as to whether possession alone had to be criminalised.

Legal room for manoeuvre

According to Boister (2001), while Article 36(1) of the Single Convention requires parties to 'punish' the cultivation, manufacture, preparation, *possession*, etc. of controlled psychoactives, this provision can be viewed in light of its drafting history – which was originally entitled 'Measures against illicit Traffickers' (see Commentary on the Single Convention on Narcotic Drugs, 1973: 112). When regarded this way, states could reasonably deviate from penalising possession alone, given the overall nature of the provision. Moreover, both articles consider their provisions to be subject to a parties 'constitutional limitations/ principles' (see Article 36(1)(a) of the Single Convention and Article 3(2) of the 1988 Convention) and the 'basic concepts of its legal system' (ibid).

Lines (2017) also draws on a teleological approach to treaty interpretation, in order to interpret drug control treaty obligations in light of their object and purpose. Lines (ibid) carefully and systematically puts forth a convincing case for interpreting the UN drug control conventions in a way that should be dynamic and human rights-based. This is because the overarching goal, or *telos* of the drug conventions is to 'promote the health and welfare of humankind', through implementing their *utilitarian* object and purpose: 'to limit controlled substances to medical and scientific purposes' (ibid: 122, 126; preamble, the Single Convention).

Thus, nations have had considerable latitude when drafting their own legislation, and it is for this reason, domestic drug policies deviate to a considerable extent across the globe (see Eastwood, Fox and Rosmarin, 2016 for decriminalisation policies worldwide). The legislative inconsistency both within and between the three conventions has also facilitated civil liberties claims when arguing for a right to consume certain psychoactives (for more detail, see Chapters 4 and 5).

Such legislative inconsistencies include the discrepancy between Article 49 of the Single Convention which calls for the abolition of all quasi-medical/ traditional drug use within 15 or 25 years, and Article 14(2) of the 1988 Convention which requires parties to 'respect fundamental human rights' and to 'take due account of traditional licit uses, where there is historic evidence of such use'. Moreover, Articles 14(1) and 25 of the 1988 Convention state that its provisions should not derogate from any obligations under the previous drug control treaties, including the 1961 obligation to abolish traditional drug usage. Article 32(4) of the 1971 Convention also allows parties to make a reservation for plants traditionally used in 'magical or religious rites'.

There are however limits to the latitude afforded to states. Although the *telos* of the treaties may allow considerable room for manoeuvre, in relation to decriminalising psychoactives for personal use, and for the employment of an array of harm reduction measures, there is arguably no wiggle room to implement national regulatory policies for non-medical use outside of a 'traditional' 'magical' or 'religious' setting, given their *utilitarian* object and purpose. The INCB has made this position extremely clear in relation to the countries and the states in the US that are beginning to regulate cannabis for non-medical purposes (INCB, 2017a, 2018, 2019; see also Jelsma et al., 2018).

Despite the INCB's clear stance on limiting the use of drugs contained in the three Conventions to medical and scientific purposes, there are a range of options for states wishing to regulate controlled psychoactives and conform to their obligations under international law. Rather than simply withdraw from a drug treaty, states could denounce and then re-accede to a treaty with a reservation. This procedure was successfully employed in Bolivia in 2013, as this country was the first to denounce the Single Convention and re-accede with reservation allowing its citizens to chew the coca leaf (Doward, 2013).

However, the unique circumstances requiring Bolivians to protect coca as cultural patrimony, may not be transplantable to emerging cannabis policy environments, most notably in Canada, Uruguay, certain US states and Jamaica. Instead, Jelsma et al. (2018: 1) have suggested the more 'elegant' approach of *inter se* modification, this would require a special agreement among a group of like-minded states to modify certain treaty provisions (see also Boister and Jelsma, 2018 for more detail). The benefits of this approach are that it allows for international trade between regulating jurisdictions, it provides an element of protection against the *status-quo* orientated members of the international prohibition regime, and it has due regard for international law, as it allows for a temporary period of what could be called 'respectful non-compliance' (Jelsma et al., 2018: 11).

Ultimately, state parties to the three UN drug conventions are provided with some room to deviate away from the prohibitive norm, in light of certain treaty provisions (see, for example, Article 36(1)(a) Single Convention; Article 32(4) 1971 Convention; Article 3(2) and 14(2) of the 1988 Convention), especially when combined with a *teleological* or *utilitarian* approach to treaty interpretation. Besides, the drug conventions are not self-executing in contrast to most human rights treaties. Consequently, the UK has always been able to retain a measure of flexibility when drafting its own domestic drug control legislation.

The domestic drug control framework

The Misuse of Drugs Act

The Misuse of Drugs Act (1971) (MDA or the 'Act') is the dominant legislative instrument in the UK designed to control and restrict where necessary 'dangerous or otherwise harmful drugs' (see the Long Title, MDA 1971). The Act corresponds to the UK's treaty commitments under the three UN drug conventions and coincided with societal changes in relation to the increasing non-medical use of psychoactives (Shiner, 2009).

Other UK drug legislation prior to the Act also created an array of criminal offences, which largely conformed to previous international obligations (see the Dangerous Drugs Act 1920; the Dangerous Drugs Act 1925; the Dangerous Drugs Act 1932; the Dangerous Drugs Act 1951; the Dangerous Drugs Act 1964 and the Dangerous Drugs Act 1965). However, the majority of these were repealed when their provisions were consolidated by the MDA. The overarching purpose of the MDA is similar to that contained in the Single Convention's preamble, as it seeks to control substances which are 'capable of having harmful effects sufficient to constitute a social problem' (s1(2) MDA). This phrase is purposely broad to include not just direct, physical or mental harm to the user but to encompass societal harm as well.

In moving the Misuse of Drugs Bill to be read for the second time, Lord Windlesham classified drug use as a 'force' capable of threatening 'societies existence as a politically, socially or economically viable order' (HL Deb 14 January 1971: 224). Over time various UK drug strategies have emphasised the presence of substance-related harms to the individual, to potential victims, to families and to communities as a whole (Home Office, 1995; HM Government, 2008, 2010, 2017) (see Chapter 2 for a more detailed discussion on states' emphasising the harms individuals can cause communities and societies at large via illicit psychoactive use).

Although a couple of members of the House of Lords did consider that a criminal conviction under the MDA could also produce its own harmful effects, when reading the Misuse of Drugs Bill, very little recognition has been afforded to this notion in the official discourse since then (HL Deb 14 January 1971). Instead, to adequately assess the level of harm a substance is capable of producing, the MDA incorporates its own ABC classification system. When introducing the legislation in 1970, the then Home Secretary James Callaghan observed:

> The object here is to make ... a more sensible differentiation between drugs. It will divide them according to their accepted dangers and harmfulness in the light of current knowledge and it will provide for changes to be made in the classification in the light of new scientific knowledge. (HC Deb 25 March 1970: 1453)

While the classification of substances was largely modelled upon the schedules contained within the international conventions at the time (see House of Commons Science and Technology Committee, 2006), Callaghan's observation demonstrates that the MDA was envisaged as a flexible, organic statute where psychoactives could move up and down its classification scale, according to scientific evidence as it emerged.

Interestingly, the conventions do not even require the implementation of a domestic classification system which relates the classification of substances to the maximum criminal penalties which could be imposed. The UK makes it a criminal offence to import (s3 MDA), export (ibid), produce (s4 MDA; see also s6 MDA which refers to restrictions on the cultivation of cannabis), supply (s4 MDA), or possess (s5 MDA) any of the controlled substances listed in the Act's schedules. In the UK, the subsequent penalties which are imposed are designed to correspond with the level of harm perceived under the legislation's ABC system. Conversely, many other countries leave it to the courts to determine the relative harm of the substances in the sentences which are passed, to avoid arbitrarily applying their domestic legislation (Police Foundation, 2000).

Yet, in principle at least, the role of the Advisory Council on the Misuse of Drugs (ACMD) serves to mitigate against an arbitrary application of the Act. The ACMD is a non-departmental government body comprising of 23 members with various expertise in law, criminology, pharmacology, toxicology, etc. (ACMD, n.d.). Members are required to advise Ministers on the classification of substances alongside reviewing any situation of drug misuse, where again that misuse could have harmful effects sufficient to constitute a social problem (s1(2) MDA). Given their expertise and scheduling role, it could be argued that the ACMD is the domestic equivalent to the WHO, as they also provide their political counterpart the CND with scheduling advice and recommendations (Article 3(3) of the Single Convention). Additionally, s2(5) of the MDA specifies that the Secretary of State cannot amend the scheduling of a substance without consulting the ACMD first, which was presumably intended to help guard against any potential dogmatism on behalf of the state.

The Secretary of State for the Home Department (Home Secretary) has considerable powers under the Act to alter the regulatory measures attached to any of the substances currently controlled. In fact, although the Act is often presented as little more than a list of prohibited substances with various criminal penalties attached, the Home Secretary actually has the power to:

- make the possession, supply, import, export and production of any of the substances currently controlled (including the cultivation of cannabis), lawful if done in accordance with the terms of a license or other authority (s7 MDA);
- exclude the application of any provision of this act which creates an offence via regulations (s22 MDA); and
- make different provisions in relation to different controlled drugs, different classes of persons, different cases or circumstances, etc. (s31 MDA).

Needless to say then, the Act in theory corresponds well with its flexible, evolutive design, and as Walsh (2010) observes: the MDA in its current form actually allows for the implementation of every regulatory model found within Transform's *Blueprint for Regulation*, a document which proposes five separate models for legalising and regulating currently controlled psychoactives in the UK (Rolles, 2009a). What is more, the Misuse of Drugs Regulations (2001) (MDR) operates alongside the MDA and documents a variety of regulatory mechanisms which could be implemented. To put it simply, 'what the Misuse of Drugs Act prohibits the Misuse of Drugs Regulations 2001 permits' (Fortson, 2011: 29). Rudi Fortson QC, a practising barrister specialising in drugs law, asserts that the combined effect of these two instruments theoretically allows for the existence of a regulatory mechanism which is as flexible as the will of parliament and its Ministers (ibid).

We are beginning to see that flexibility, since the Home Secretary exercised the powers conferred by s7, s22 and s31 of the MDA to reschedule cannabis-based products for medicinal use into Schedule 2 of the MDR (see The Misuse of Drugs (Amendments) (Cannabis and Licence Fees) (England, Wales and Scotland) Regulations 2018). This means that there is now a legal route for cannabis to be prescribed by senior clinicians without the requirement for a Home Office licence, as this is required under Schedule 1 MDR (for more detail, see Chapter 4). This legal change is largely due to the well-publicised stories of Alfie Dingley and Billy Caldwell in 2018, two boys with life-threatening epileptic seizures, who responded well to cannabis treatment. The Home Secretary, Sajid Javid's willingness to review the situation and to issue emergency licenses to the two boys under s7 of the MDA (Home Office, 2018a), before rescheduling cannabis-based medicines under the 2018 Regulations, demonstrates the power of storytelling to engage policy makers on an emotive, human level by speaking directly to their values (Bone et al., 2018; Bone and de Hoedt, 2018; for more detail, see Chapter 2).

However, for the most part, the MDA has been criticised, as applying arbitrarily in practice (Police Foundation, 2000; House of Commons Science and Technology Committee, 2006; Nutt, 2009; Walsh, 2010; Fortson, 2011). While the Act is deemed to conform to its obligations under the HRA (see s19 HRA), Walsh (2010) questions whether the MDA is discriminatorily commandeered as it fails to regulate alcohol and tobacco on the basis of 'historical and cultural precedents' (Government Reply to the Fifth Report from the House of Commons Science and Technology, 2006: 24).

The UK government have failed to provide any further explanation as to whether this reasoning constitutes a lawful justification for the distinction. This is particularly problematic in light of the government's additional recognition that these two substances account for more deaths and health issues than any currently controlled psychoactives (ibid), and yet the overarching concern of the MDA is to reduce such harms. The MDA could thus be seen as regulating historically contingent taste, in much the same way as the international drug control framework, as the scheduling, inclusion and exclusion of certain psychoactives has been recognised to be morally, historically and culturally determined (Braithwaite and Drahos, 2000; Gimenez Corte, 2010).

Professor Nutt (2009), a former chairman of the ACMD, further highlights the lack of any rational, evidence-based approach to the current classification system. Along with his colleagues, he has produced a more systematic, transparent assessment for measuring the physical dependence and social harms from drugs, which has yielded a markedly different classification scale (Nutt et al., 2007). In this scale, alcohol and tobacco are ranked amongst the most harmful psychoactives. Other currently regulated class A substances are ranked amongst the least, and it is largely supported by drug policy reformers focusing on integrating a more evidence-based approach. It could be argued that Nutt et al.'s (ibid: 1047) 'rational scale' of harm is perhaps more in line with the application of the Act, as originally envisaged by parliament.

The Psychoactive Substances Act

One thing that could be said for the MDA though, is that it is at least premised on the idea of reducing harm – albeit ostensibly. In 2016, the UK government enacted the Psychoactive Substances Act (PSA), in response to the NPS, 'phenomenon'. NPS are defined by the UNODC (2013: 1) as:

> [S]ubstances of abuse, either in a pure form or a preparation, that are not controlled by the 1961 Convention on Narcotic Drugs or the 1971 Convention on Psychotropic Substances, but which may pose a public health threat.

The stated aim of the PSA is: 'to make provision about psychoactive substances'. A crucial difference between the PSA and the MDA is that the MDA controls specified substances, whereas the PSA applies to any non-exempted 'psychoactive substance' (Fortson, 2016). By imposing a 'blanket' prohibition on acts of producing (s12(1)(a)), supplying and offering to supply (s12(1)(b),(c)), importing or exporting (s12(1)(d),(e)), a non-exempted 'psychoactive substance', the PSA 'breaks a fundamental legal principle that "what is not forbidden is allowed"' (Stevens, 2017: 837). Stevens (ibid) considers that the enactment of the PSA reverses this principle and he argues; forbidding everything not expressly allowed goes too far in extending the reach of the state into the lives of its citizens. As discussed at length in Chapter 2, from a Millian liberal perspective, criminalisation (i.e. state interference), can only be justified if the conduct in question causes harm to others. In a similar vein, a legal paternalist would only justify criminalisation if it causes harm to oneself or to other people.

Removing all pretence of drug policy as being about reducing harm renders the PSA 'fundamentally illiberal' according to Walsh (2017a: 43). The enactment of the PSA can only be justified then from a legal moralist standpoint, since this deontological position is prepared to criminalise conduct believed to be immoral, even if there is no evidence to suggest the conduct causes harm (Feinberg, 1984). As noted in Chapter 2, it is thought that this position is heavily weighted towards the interests of the state in achieving cohesion, social stability and control. While legal moralists generally accept the notion that whoever holds political power can impose their morality on others (Stewart, 2010), a leading proponent of this philosophy, Lord Devlin (1959), accepts prohibitive laws if they are based on a *society's collective* judgment on whether conduct is immoral.

It is difficult to deduce the general public's judgment on how best to control NPS, since an effectual structured procedure of public and expert consultation about this issue failed to materialise; the debate was silenced before it had the chance to begin. The UK government dismissed the opinions of leading drug policy organisations Release and Transform on the Psychoactive Substances Bill, and they drafted provisions of the PSA before consulting their own experts, the ACMD (see Release and Transform, 2015; see also Burgess, 2016). Through analysing the parliamentary debates on the Psychoactive Substances Bill, Walsh (2017a) concludes that UK law-makers enacted the PSA due to concern with vulnerable young people most likely to take them, any associated antisocial behaviour and sudden deaths. While these are clearly important concerns, it is thought that the radical prohibitive stance taken in the PSA was informed in part by NPS media reporting, which is viewed by Alexandrescu (2017) as exaggerated and alarmist. A formal public consultation and a consideration of regulatory alternatives could have led to a very different approach (see All-Party Parliamentary Group on Drug Policy Reform, 2013; Fortson, 2016; Reuter and Pardo, 2017).

In 2013 Transform commissioned the renowned pollsters Ipsos MORI to measure the public's support for drug policy reform. Interestingly, the poll revealed that two-thirds of the public (67 per cent): 'support a comprehensive independent review of all the possible policy options (from legal market regulation to tougher enforcement) for controlling drugs' (Transform, 2013: n.d.). By failing to effectively consider *society's collective* judgment on the NPS issue, it could be argued that the PSA lacks democratic accountability, which incidentally is the main criticism levelled at the expansion of human rights law in a UK context (see O'Cinneide, 2017). Perhaps then, the PSA could even struggle to legitimise itself from a legal moralist perspective, if we are to accept Devlin's views on this philosophical position.

The purpose of the act can also be questioned since Stevens (2017) acknowledges that since the 1960s, there has been a trickle of new substances assimilating into the range of drugs consumed recreationally, though the late 2000s saw an increase in this development. For Potter and Chatwin (2018), separating out NPS as a different category of substances is unhelpful, dangerous and could have far-reaching consequences – in terms of policy making and user experiences. A consequence of conflating hundreds of NPS into a category which fails to objectively unite or delineate them from existing categories of drugs has led to an inflation of the size of the problem in the public discourse, and a return to more stringent forms of drug control, away from evidence-based, harm reductionist initiatives (ibid). The PSA fails to appreciate that NPS use should be viewed as part of a broader landscape of drug scene developments connected to globalisation, socio-technological and socio-economic shifts (ibid). For Potter and Chatwin (ibid), NPS should be viewed through this wider lens, rather than as a distinct phenomenon (see also Chapter 1 on 'The origin and value of human drug use').

While the premise of the PSA is problematic, its operation is arguably more so. In the PSA, a substance is defined as psychoactive 'by stimulating or depressing the person's central nervous system, it *affects* the person's *mental functioning* or *emotional* state' (s2(2)). Accordingly, all psychoactive substances fall under the PSA's remit, unless they are listed in Schedule 1 of the PSA as an 'exempted substance' (s2(1)(b)). The list of exempted substances currently includes 'controlled drugs (within the meaning of the MDA' (Sch. 1(1)), 'medicinal products' (Sch. 1(2)), 'alcohol' (Sch. 1(3)), 'nicotine and tobacco products' (Sch. 1(4)(5)), 'caffeine' (Sch. 1(6)) and 'food' (Sch. 1(7)). The PSA creates 'a legal fiction' according to Fortson (2016: 309) since the majority of the exempted substances are 'pharmacologically psychoactive', and it is difficult to distinguish between these arbitrary categorisations.

By way of example, two legal cases successfully argued in the first instance that nitrous oxide (commonly known as 'laughing gas') was covered by the medicinal products exemption (Sumnall, 2017). This led the Court of Appeal to clarify in the case of *R* v. *Chapman and Others* (2017) that canisters of nitrous oxide are not medicinal products if intended for recreational purposes. The PSA breaches the principle of legal certainly here, given that 'drug' categories are not mutually exclusive. The breach of this principle, which requires that the law is certain and precise (McGarry, 2011), is exacerbated further by the difficulty in proving 'psychoactivity', as required by s2(1)(a) of the PSA. The ACMD (2015: 2) acknowledge that 'the only way of determining psychoactivity is via human experience which is not usually documented'. The principle of legal certainty is also protected by Article 7 of the ECHR, which suggests that the PSA is not human rights compliant.

This potential breach of Article 7 and the failure of the PSA to be tied to the key concept of harm, implies that this Act is not fit for purpose. While the Home Office has conducted a review to measure outcomes before and after the implementation of the PSA, there is at present no legal room to deviate from the existing status quo (Home Office, 2018b; for more detail on the operation of the PSA, see Fortson, 2016; also see Chapter 5 for the religious rights implications of a blanket ban). Contrastingly, as previously highlighted, the legal mechanisms stipulated in the MDA could create alternative regulatory regimes for all of the psychoactives it currently controls. Of course, this legal architecture is threatened by the politicisation of our drug laws. The politicisation evident in UK government proposals to roll back our domestic system of human rights, also means that human rights could be less effective in challenging prohibitionist drug control laws (see Chapters 4 and 5 – 'Applying a human rights perspective').

Conclusion

It is clear that the nature, function and purpose of both the international human rights and drug control regimes have impacted upon their operation domestically. The international human rights framework has developed in a rather logical, coherent and consistent manner, whereby the terms of each new treaty informs and adds to the interpretation of others. While the HRA is a relatively recent construction, its successful operation is largely dependent upon a system of human rights established by the ECHR, which in turn was heavily influenced by the creation of the UDHR. Accordingly, human rights law is arguably intertwined and reciprocally influential at every level (Steiner, Alston and Goodman, 2008).

While international human rights instruments have a higher legal standing than international drug control instruments (by virtue of Article 103 of the UN Charter), and a higher institutional standing (since the creation of the HRCb in 2006), this international framework is not immune from political pressures. The high political standing afforded to the international system of human rights is waning. It is no longer enough to commend the procedural mechanisms in place to promote transparency and accountability by encouraging states, NGOs and other interested parties to enter into a 'constructive dialogue' with human rights bodies, if there exists a growing resistance to transnational forms of governance.

As detailed within this chapter and within Chapter 2, the rise of ideological nationalism poses a challenge to international and regional human rights bodies, as there is a perception that these bodies lack a clear democratic mandate. Moreover, the waning of a national political authority due to the forces of globalisation has facilitated a retreat to particularist positions which ground a sense of identity for people. It is this growing nationalistic sense of an identity which has been utilised by the UK Conservative party to promote the idea of a distinctly British Bill of Rights, the repeal of the HRA and/or the withdrawal from the ECHR; an instrument deprecated as a 'foreign' construction.

Chapter 3 exposes the legitimacy crises facing the UK system of human rights, despite revealing the substantial amount of freedom within the legal architecture (via s2 HRA, the principle of subsidiarity and the margin of appreciation doctrine), for British judges to develop 'home grown' case law unique to the changing standards of British society. While the international, regional and domestic systems of human rights are threatened by their politicisation, and a perception of counter-democratic overreach, this chapter nonetheless demonstrates the architectural mechanisms in place to advance social, moral and legal change, and predicts how the human rights framework could work in the future. What is more, this complexly intertwined and influential system of human rights is beginning to notably influence the international drug control framework, despite the weakening position of the human rights system when regarded in isolation.

Historically, the institutional bodies within the international drug control framework were criticised as operating without transparency or accountability, in direct contrast with the institutional mechanisms in place for the international human rights bodies. As demonstrated, this contributed to the continuance of a regime where moral, historical, political and economic hegemonies dominated. While this remains the case, to a large extent, given the haphazard way in which the three international drug control conventions have developed, the INCB and the CND are beginning to acknowledge their human rights obligations and allow for a very limited divergence from the global prohibitive paradigm.

This is partly due to bottom-up calls for reform from the producer countries most impacted by prohibition and from civil society engagement. Such pressures helped advance the UNGASS process, which further exposed the fragmented approach to drug control between states. Despite the UNGASS Outcome Document (UNODC, 2016) reaffirming the prohibitionist status quo, the UNGASS process facilitated a dialogue between states, civil society, NGOs, UN human rights institutions and other relevant stakeholders culminating in the increasing involvement of human rights bodies, i.e. the OHCHR, in typically CND-led policy discussions. Not only does this result gives credence to the idea that citizens value democratic self-government (see O'Cinneide, 2017), and the importance of facilitating empowered citizens and relevant stakeholders to have a legitimate input, it reveals how a human rights focus can help to shift the balance of power away from the dominant hegemonies.

Of course, for as long as the three UN drug conventions remain in place, their fundamental object and purpose is to limit controlled drugs to medical and scientific purposes. Accordingly, any legislative changes made domestically can only go so far, in order for a state to be legally compliant with its international drug control obligations. While some states are openly flouting the conventions, this chapter encourages the adoption of *inter se* modification instead, to maintain a healthy respect for the principles of international law. As demonstrated in the context of the legitimacy crises facing human rights, it is the belief in the *idea* of the international political order which is important.

While the UK's domestic system of drug control, in relation to the MDA, mirrors the biases and fallacious scheduling processes found within the three UN conventions, it is nonetheless a surprisingly flexible instrument, capable of allowing a diverse array of regulatory models, for all of the substances it controls. In direct contrast, the PSA allows no legal room for manoeuvre and it is criticised as not being human rights compliant. Ultimately, this chapter concludes that the legal architecture behind the human rights and drug control frameworks is changing both internationally and domestically. Barring the enactment of the PSA, the domestic human rights and drug control regimes are regulated by flexible, organic instruments – capable of evolving and adapting to most changing circumstances. However, this chapter also reveals how the international and domestic legal architecture for both systems can be politicised. Chapters 4 and 5 should be read in light of these turbulent times.

Part II

Applying a human rights perspective

Chapter 4

Health rights, autonomy rights and the drug control framework

This chapter will centre on the human right to 'health'. It will initially identify the difficulties associated with defining and understanding this human right, it will highlight the relationship between the individual and the state in relation to a state's positive and negative health obligations, and that conceptions of 'health' under a human rights lens are broad, and can complement health ideals highlighted within the international and UK drug control framework. This will emphasise the way that UK and comparable jurisdictions address some of the legal conflicts between the two regimes, when applying health rights and related autonomy rights to issues concerning drugs. A state's negative health obligations, in particular, are often given short thrift by the courts under the current drug control system, despite its capacity to accommodate them. Although, this is beginning to change, as some jurisdictions are demonstrating an increased willingness to promote a state's negative and positive health obligations and autonomy rights related to the human right to health as well.

Chapter 4 will draw on the conceptual arguments developed throughout the first half of this book that a human rights perspective, developed philosophically, politically and legally can:

1 Better reflect and understand human psychoactive use (Chapter 1);
2 Highlight and reconfigure conflicts between the state and the individual (Chapter 2); and
3 Demonstrate (to an extent) that the human rights and drug control frameworks are legally compatible (Chapter 3).

This perspective will be analysed in light of cannabis case law, which shows how the two frameworks work in practice. A focus on cannabis case law could allow for helpful comparisons to be drawn, given the variety of cannabis policies in comparable jurisdictions outside of the UK. Additionally, both health and autonomy rights have been employed when challenging the legality of cannabis prohibition, therefore, any overlaps or distinctions can be more easily highlighted. Ultimately, Chapter 4 acknowledges the potential and the limitations of applying a human (health and autonomy) rights-based perspective to drug control issues within national and comparable courts.

Sources of law to define 'health'

The notion of 'health' and how one defines what constitutes 'good health' is an idea which has been grappled with for centuries. From the Hippocratic Oath (Edelstein, 1943) to the WHO definition (1948), commentators have employed both medicalised (Boorse, 1975) and social constructionist (Freidson, 1970) definitions to varying degrees, in an attempt to clarify how our 'health' should best be considered. Medicalised definitions are often deterministic and hold that diseases are invariant to time or place and are universal (Conrad and Barker, 2010). Those who favour a medical model of health are perceived as naturalists, as they consider that health and disease are ubiquitous features of the natural world, and draw on descriptive definitions of health which are based upon biological function (Hamilton, 2010).

Social constructionist definitions, on the other hand, distinguish disease (the biological condition), from illness (the social condition), believing that the meaning and experience of the latter is shaped by social and cultural systems (Eisenberg, 1977). For Coggon (2012), such varied contextualisation of the notion of health can lead to a crucial tension in substantiating what is 'good' for us. For instance, there exist both internal perspectives of health – as perceived by the person in question, and external perspectives – that others may take of a person's state of health (Sen, 2004). An external perspective could invite the medical establishment and/or policy makers to commit to a more medicalised view on what they believe to be good for us, leaving the individual (i.e. the internal perspective) to grapple with a more social constructionist view on what they believe to be good for themselves. Epistemologically speaking, Sen (ibid) further highlights the dichotomy between observation-orientated methodologies and perception-orientated views when assessing individual states of health. The former places a greater reliance on *externally* observed medical statistics, whereas perception-orientated methodologies have been a mainstay of the social sciences, which give effect to *internal*, self-perceptions of health (for more detail on dichotomous health concepts, see Table 4.1).

While the idea that an external perspective commits to a more medicalised conception of health is a generalisation, since internal (i.e. individual) views can of course be medicalised (Rose, 2003) and vice versa, some health scholars are wary of the determinism perceived in external policy appeals to science and medicine (Coggon, 2012). There is arguably a good reason for this if such determinism facilitates a 'monistic creep' or 'moral imperialism through medicalisation' (Coggon, 2012: 30, 229). To link this observation explicitly to drug policy making, Stevens and Zampini (2018) consider the set of actors at the centre of English drug policy making to consist of the medical establishment and law enforcement bodies (non-exhaustively comprising public health professionals, doctors, the Home Office, the police and civil servants) (Stevens, 2017). Stevens and Zampini (ibid) consider that the aims and practices of public health and social control bodies overlap, as powerful actors are able to institutionalise their own normative preferences on what they believe to be good for us. Therefore, values relating to social control could be said to dominate the drug policy making process.

The tension between external and internal health perspectives is also visible when individuals assert their human right to health, since these rights can manifest as the *positive* legal duties a state has to provide us with basic health care (duties which tend to conform to a medicalised model centring on the provision of medicine). Placing the onus on the state corresponds more to an external state-derived conception of health. In contrast, the human right to health can afford individuals the *negative* right to live and construct their own lives as they see fit, free from external constraint. This corresponds more to an internal, individual conception of health (see Table 4.1). It is for this reason that Coggon (2012) commits to a political model when analysing health issues, as he recognises that allocating health responsibilities is always going to be contestable, since key tensions exist between the positive and negative duties a state has in relation to the health of its citizenry. Positive and negative duties arise from positive and negative rights; the former obliges the state to act, whereas the latter obliges inaction from the state.

The relationship between the state's positive duty to provide health care for its citizens and to some extent even determine the 'health' of its citizenry, is positioned against the individual's right to decide for themselves. While this state/individual binary mimics the one identified in the drug policy sphere (see Chapter 2), the 'human right to health' field perhaps affords a more obvious recognition to this tension. However, as will be demonstrated, the drug control framework complements health rights and related human rights legislation, and in principle at least, both regimes are able to accommodate each other.

The remainder of this section evidences complementary health norms within the two frameworks, by examining positive and negative health obligations in relation to the drug control framework. Additionally, negative health obligations relate to autonomy rights, so the contours of health rights relating to autonomy and autonomy rights relating to health will be discussed. The section concludes with a broad definition of health; capable of accommodating an external, internal, social constructionist and a medicalised viewpoint.

International positive 'health' obligations

In international legal instruments, the formulation of the right to health reads as the right to 'the highest attainable standard of health'. This standard initially appeared in the preamble to the WHO constitution in 1946 and Article 25 of the UDHR in 1948, prior to being enshrined in Article 12 ICESCR (1966), Article 24 of the Convention on the Rights of the Child (CRC) (1989), and Article 25 of the Convention on the Rights of Persons with Disabilities (CRPD) (2006). While the human right to health has been recognised in numerous international instruments,[1] the most authoritative interpretation of the right to health is outlined in Article 12 of the ICESCR, which documents the positive legal duties a state has to provide health care to its citizenry, and it recognises that '[e]veryone has the right to the enjoyment of the highest attainable standard of physical and mental health'. However, it should be reiterated that the ICESCR is not legally binding in the UK, as the UK has not ratified this convention (for more detail, see Chapter 3).

In May 2000, the Committee on Economic, Social and Cultural Rights (CESCR), which monitors the ICESCR, adopted a General Comment on the right to health (General Comment 14, 2000). General Comments more thoroughly clarify the nature and content of an individual's rights and a state's obligations. This General Comment acknowledges that the right to health does not entail the right to be healthy, rather the right contains both freedoms and entitlements (General Comment 14, 2000: para 8). An entitlement to a system of health protection requires states to provide *available* health care, goods, services, facilities and programmes (ibid: para 12a). A complementary requirement is that the health care provided is *accessible* for all within the shortest possible time (ibid, para 12b). Such procedural requirements are relevant when considering whether there is a right to controlled psychoactives, i.e. medical cannabis (see 'Providing medical cannabis in the UK' section).

Though, the General Comment observes that such obligations can only be fulfilled when states have the adequate resources to do so. As highlighted in the 'Providing medical cannabis in the UK' section, resource allocation issues are prevalent when considering a state's positive health obligations, as it is assumed that domestic authorities are best placed to assess its use of resources, its priorities and its social needs (see *Shelley* v. *UK*, 2008). Thus, the positive responsibility placed on states is grounded in instrumental as well as normative considerations, emphasising the difficulty in defining the human right to health.

Notwithstanding any instrumental considerations, the normative content of Article 12 ICESCR includes the provision of 'essential drugs, as defined by the WHO Action Programme on Essential Drugs', among the 'core obligations' of states (General Comment 14, 2000: para 12a; 43d). As detailed in Chapter 3, the WHO is firmly intertwined with the drug control framework, since a number of the WHO's (2017) model list of essential medicines reside in the UN drug conventions. For example, methadone and morphine feature on this list, while simultaneously residing in Schedule I of the Single Convention, which

1 The European Convention on Social and Medical Assistance, The European Social Charter, The United Nations Declaration on the Rights of Disabled Persons, The United Nations Declaration on the Use of Scientific and Technological Progress in the Interests of Peace and for the Benefit of Mankind, Principles for the Protection of Persons with Mental Illness and the Improvement of Mental Health Care, The European Convention on Human Rights and Biomedicine. For a more comprehensive list of international and regional legal instruments relevant to health and human rights, see The World Health Organisation (2002).

provides some the most stringent regulatory controls (except for those required for substances which additionally reside in Schedule IV; such as cannabis[2] and diamorphine) (see Article 2, the Single Convention; see also Chapter 3 for more detail on scheduling).

Though the controls are stringent, it is important to remember the dual purpose of the Single Convention and those which succeed it, as they facilitate *commodity control* as well as *penal control* (Boister, 2001; see also Chapter 3). Accordingly, the majority of the Single Convention and the 1971 Convention concern themselves with ensuring that psychoactive substances are available for medical and scientific purposes, by putting specific regulatory controls in place (see Preamble; Articles 2, 12, 19 and 20, the Single Convention; Preamble, Articles 8, 9 and 10, the 1971 Convention). Both conventions recognise a positive legal duty to protect and encourage the health of a state party's citizenry, in a similar vein to Article 12, ICESCR, requiring the provision of available and accessible health care (General Comment 14: para 12).

Alongside the provision of health care, the international drug control and human rights frameworks can embrace more social constructionist aspects of health as well. For instance, the right to health incorporates a wide range of socio-economic factors, reflecting the reality that social factors (i.e. nutrition, housing, etc.) do influence the health of individuals (ibid: para 4). The General Comment also targets certain groups such as those with mental disabilities, the terminally ill and indigenous peoples; comprehending the more nuanced, individual obligations a state has in this sphere (ibid: paras 18–29). This point will be returned to, particularly regarding the special appreciation a state should have regarding the cultural and traditional practices and medicines for indigenous peoples (ibid: para 27; see Chapter 5 for more detail).

Moreover, the drug conventions do not prevent broader harm reduction approaches which seek to minimise health harms related to substance use. In recent years, UN human rights monitors have been increasingly critical of a number of states who fail to embrace a harm reduction approach, with Lines (2017) and Bewley-Taylor (2012: 101) observing a tension between UN human rights and drug control bodies; reflecting diverging 'perspectives on the [drug control] regime's … norms concerning punitive prohibition' (see also Chapter 3). The UN Special rapporteur on the human right to health, Dainius Pūras, has also been prominent in explicitly linking a state's positive obligations to provide harm reduction services with the human right to health (Human Rights Council, 2016: A/HRC/32/32). Thus, harm reduction approaches (capable of recognising wider social determinants of health)

2 This situation is now changing for cannabis, given the recommendation from the WHO's (2019a) Expert Committee on Drug Dependence for cannabis to be deleted from the most restrictive schedule (IV) (in effect acknowledging its medical potential and – if the recommendation is passed by the Commission on Narcotic Drugs – ending the default prohibition of medical uses under the international drug control framework).

are becoming more prevalent within UN commentaries on the human right to health, despite the forgoing reticence from the UN drug control bodies (see Chapter 3 for more detail).

Nevertheless, the positive duties to provide available and accessible health care at an international level are arguably more likely to facilitate an external, medical model of health. This is because both the drug control and human rights frameworks rely on organisations such as the WHO, and bureaucracies such as the INCB, to determine which substances are 'essential medicines' or to advocate the controls and the restrictions relating to their administration (Articles 12, 19 and 20, the Single Convention; WHO, 2017). The purpose of the drug conventions further supports a more medicalised conception of health, since they are mandated to ensure the provision of essential medicines.

At the European level, the European Convention on Human Rights (ECHR) has become an important source of human rights law (this is especially true for the UK, see 'Providing medical cannabis' below). Human rights related to health such as privacy-related rights (Article 8, ECHR), the right to life (Article 2, ECHR), the right to dignity (Article 3, ECHR) and the principle of reproductive autonomy (Article 8, 12, ECHR) can be located within the ECHR. These rights can additionally relate to the positive obligations a state has to ensure the provision of health care (for more detail, see Wicks, 2007).

Furthermore, the European Social Charter of 1961 is the counterpart of the ECHR in the sphere of economic and social rights, and it includes the right to social and medical assistance. The Council of Europe, the organisation responsible for the ECHR and the European Social Charter has also drafted a more specific convention relating to health rights – The European Convention on Human Rights and Biomedicine (ECHRB) (1997). Finally, the EU Charter of Fundamental Rights derives from another important European organisation, the European Union. The EU Charter also recognises the right of access to preventive health care and the right to benefit from medical treatment (Article 35). The EU Charter applies to European Union institutions and its member states when implementing EU law.

Positive 'health' obligations in the UK

In contrast with the positive legal duty to provide health care at an international level, the UK has not specifically legislated for a human right to health care within its domestic legislation. The UK case law examples in this chapter which relate to the positive obligations a state has to ensure the provision of health care are drawn from privacy-related rights contained within the ECHR. Article 8(1) of the ECHR states that: 'Everyone has the right to respect for private and family life, home and correspondence'. This article imposes positive obligations upon contracting states to facilitate the conditions which can ensure the respect for private life, this can include the provision of health care (see 'Providing medical cannabis' below).

Notwithstanding privacy-related rights, other rights related to health (i.e. the right to life, the right to dignity) can also be drawn upon here (see Wicks,

2007). Furthermore, while the UK is not a signatory to the ECHRB, this Convention's principles and provisions are of persuasive authority. The ECtHR may give advisory opinions in relation to the interpretation of the ECHRB, and the UK is required to 'take into account' any judgment from the ECtHR that is of relevance to a case in question, by virtue of section 2 of the Human Rights Act (HRA) (1998) (see Chapter 3 for more detail on the human rights legal architecture).

Despite the lack of any specific domestic health rights legislation, the UK was one of the first countries in the world to develop a national provision of health care services through the creation of the National Health Service (hereafter the NHS) in 1948. More recent health statutes in the UK, the Health Act (2009) and the Health and Social Care Act (2012) focus predominately on the quality and delivery of NHS service providers, as opposed to the provision of health care per se. The latter instrument is particularly controversial as it has been criticised for providing a legal framework for the increased privatisation and marketisation of the NHS (Patients4NHS, 2018). Although resource allocation issues will be considered in this chapter, it is beyond the scope of this book to evaluate the impact of recent NHS reforms (see Exworthy, Mannion and Powell, 2016 for a more comprehensive evaluation on the impact of these reforms).

By narrowing the focus to the discourse contained in national health legislation and official NHS documents, this section illustrates the scope for capturing a broad conceptualisation of health, when considering the UK's positive obligations to provide health care and to promote conditions which are conducive to a healthy life. The Health Act (2009) makes provision about the NHS Constitution, a document which 'establishes the principles and values of the NHS in England' and your rights as an NHS patient (Department of Health, 2015: 2). A regularly updated Handbook to the NHS Constitution provides a more in-depth explanation for each of the core principles, the first and possibly foremost being that it provides 'a comprehensive service, available to all' (Department of Health and Social Care, 2019: 14).

The NHS was designed to meet the needs of everyone since it incorporates a 'wider social duty to promote equality through the services it provides' (ibid: 17). Such an integral focus on equality through working across organisational boundaries, and in conjunction with local communities and the wider population (ibid: Principle 5), suggests that any domestic obligations to provide health care could be well suited to the universal discourse of human rights and could encompass a more welfarist agenda. To further reiterate this point, another core principle enshrines the NHS as a patient-centred service (ibid: Principle 4). It is perhaps fair to suggest that the positive duties placed on the NHS accommodate an internal and social constructionist conception of health as well as a medicalised and/or external one, as the NHS constitution considers wider social diameters and advocates for a person-centred approach. This encapsulates health into the wider category of welfare; which Coggon (2012) advocates given the political relevance of the concept of 'health'.

It could be argued that the Misuse of Drugs Act (1971) (MDA), as the primary UK statute restricting and controlling 'dangerous or otherwise harmful drugs' (Preamble, MDA), also incorporates this wider definition of health. Section 1(2) of the MDA makes provision for the Advisory Council on the Misuse of Drugs (ACMD), and their primary objective is to review drugs 'capable of having harmful effects sufficient to constitute a social problem'. Again, this social aspect is a key concern and requires the ACMD to opine on matters relating to the provision of: substance treatment, rehabilitation, education, research and community service co-operation (ibid); indicating that the act has the potential to encompass a broader definition of health in a similar vein to the NHS.

In direct contrast, the Psychoactive Substances Act (2016) (PSA) does not refer to the concept of harm, when making provision for psychoactive substances in response to the novel psychoactive substances phenomenon (NPS) (see Chapter 3 for more detail). By limiting its focus to imposing a blanket prohibition on psychoactive substances which are not on an exempted list, the PSA fails to account for the potential harms caused by drugs or drug policy; hence any corresponding positive health obligations on behalf of the state cannot exist. For the purposes of completeness, the Medicines Act (1968) (MA) is the other principal psychoactive statute which relates to the positive legal duties the UK has to ensure the health of its citizenry. The MA retains a more medicalised function since it relates to the provision and control of medicines for health care purposes. As such, its aims are perhaps more broadly related to the international positive duties placed upon states relating to access to essential medicines, as discussed above.

For the most part, the overall discussion on the positive duties the UK has internationally and domestically to provide health care indicates that in theory there exists scope to move beyond its mere provision, to ensure that broader 'health' needs are met. A comprehensive focus on the positive duties placed upon the UK suggests a potential allowance for an internal, social constructionist view of health, as well as a more medicalised one. Though in practice, a medicalised, external view is preferred (see 'Providing medicinal cannabis: an overview' subsection). In any event, both the health rights framework and drug control frameworks (with the exception of the PSA), are complementary in principle, and purely on a definitional level, both systems have the capacity to be legally compatible.

International negative 'health' obligations and related autonomy rights

The right to health contains freedoms as well as entitlements, and the General Comment (2000: para 8) recognises that such 'freedoms include the right to control one's health and body ... and the right to be free from interference'. The General Comment (ibid: para 3) further stipulates that the right to health is closely related to and dependent upon other human rights such as the right to life, non-discrimination, equality, privacy and the enjoyment of the benefits of scientific progress and its applications. Although such rights are well documented within the UDHR, the ICCPR and the ECHR (for the right to life see Article 3 UDHR; Article 2 ECHR; Article 6.1 ICCPR; for the right to privacy see Article 12 UDHR; Article 8, ECHR; Article 17, ICCPR), additional human rights such as the free development of personality will also be shown to link to a human right to health in the case law.

Hence, a negative health obligation – which obliges inaction on behalf of the state – and affords the autonomous liberty for humans to live and construct their own lives as they see fit (see Chapters 1 and 2 according to Mill, 1859/2001; Berlin, 1969) is closely linked to existing civil and political rights which are grounded in the concept of personal autonomy. Consequently, a human right to health can be difficult to quantify. Tobin (2012: 132) notes that the right to health should not be inflated to such an extent that the rights relevant to these matters are automatically subsumed within the right to health:

> The principle of the interdependence of human rights and the requirement for system coherence demands that the potentially colonizing effects of the right to health must be avoided.

To avoid this, Chapter 4 will delineate 'positive health obligations', 'negative health obligations' and 'autonomy rights' in the case law subsections, to account for their *lex specialis* status, whilst simultaneously acknowledging the interdependent, indivisible nature of human rights. As will be demonstrated, the contours of negative health obligations can overlap with autonomy rights (see 'Critiquing Quayle'), and autonomy rights can also be closely related to the human right to health (see 'Moving beyond the human right to health'). Autonomy is a complex concept to define. The word 'autonomy' is derived from autos (self) and nomes (law) and it relates to 'a broader freedom to determine how to live one's own life' (Wicks, 2007: 61). For the purposes of this book, a distinction – regarding protection of the choice to take drugs – is made between human rights rooted in autonomy arguments, where there is no need for any justification based on health grounds and health-based human rights which require such a justification.

Negative health obligations and autonomy rights are more expansive in their character since individuals can make their own decisions in relation to their own health, subject to the restrictions explored in the liberal doctrine (see Chapter 2 according to Mill and Berlin), which can manifest in the limitations contained within human rights legislation. Wicks (2007) highlights several ECHR cases which rely on a number of human rights (most notably those contained in Article 3, 8 and 9, ECHR), to claim non-interference from the state in relation to an individual's health. Thus, a larger element of subjectivity can potentially be afforded to the individual when defining 'health', beyond a narrower external (i.e. state-derived) or medicalised understanding of the concept.

The international drug control regime has a similar capacity to recognise the breadth of the negative duties a state has to its citizenry in relation to their health and autonomy rights. As highlighted in Chapter 3, the international drug conventions are renowned for their legislative inconsistency in relation to human rights claims. The so-called safeguard clauses, specifying that drug convention obligations are subject to domestic or constitutional law, means that there are several grounds where negative rights to health, or related autonomy human rights, could be afforded to the individual within this sphere (see the Commentary on the 1988 Convention (1988: 41) for a detailed list of these grounds). Two of the most well-known safeguard clauses, the Single Convention (Article 36(1)(a)) and the 1988 Convention (Article 3(2)), refer to the fact that their provisions are subject a state party's constitutional limitations/principles. More specifically, the 1988 Convention (Article 14(2)) requires parties to 'take due account of traditional licit uses where there is historic evidence of such use', thus implying an allowance for negative health obligations and a potential respect for 'traditional' medicinal use.

Since many western constitutions were formulated during the enlightenment period and are based upon the liberal values of freedom and personal autonomy (values which are relied upon when enforcing negative rights), it is possible to accommodate a state's negative health obligations and human rights grounded in personal autonomy. Furthermore, the UN special rapporteur on the right to health (Human Rights Council, 2016: A/HRC/32/32, 114b) has welcomed states to:

> [s]eek alternatives to punitive or repressive drug control policies, including decriminalization and legal regulation and control, and nurture the international debate on these issues, within which the right to health must remain central.

Thus, alternative regulatory policies to prohibition such as decriminalisation and legal regulation, which can facilitate 'the right to control one's health and body' (General Comment 14, 2000: para 8), can be justified normatively using the right to health and related human rights.

Negative 'health' obligations and related autonomy rights in the UK

Negative health obligations in the UK and related autonomy rights are covered via the ECHR as incorporated into domestic law by the HRA 1998. Along with imposing positive obligations on states to foster conditions conducive to ensuring respect for private life (which can include the provision of health care), Article 8(1) ECHR protects a broad range of privacy interests, and it promotes negative health obligations, since the core of Article 8's protection is the prevention of arbitrary interference by the state.

The sphere of 'private life' is extremely broad. An array of privacy interests are protected here, including ones which relate more specifically to health including (but not limited to): reproductive rights (see *A B and C* v. *Ireland*, 2010); preventing forced medical treatment and compulsory medical procedures and end of life issues (European Court of Human Rights, 2019). Since the sphere of private life has roots in the concept of autonomy which requires self-determination for how to live one's own life free from state interference, it follows that Article 8(1) extends to the right to personal development and autonomy-based rights more generally as well (ibid). For the purposes of completeness, there is no common law protection of the right to privacy. Nevertheless, English common law does recognise a state's negative health obligations in relation to self-determination, by recognising an individual's right to refuse medical treatment (*Re T*, 1992).

With specific regard to the UK's negative health obligations, the philosophy of the NHS aspires to put the patient 'at the heart of everything the service does', and 'rather than being passive recipients of health care, patients also play a key role in managing their own health' (Department of Health and Social Care, 2019: Principle 4). This is further reflected by the duties placed upon commissioners in the Health and Social Care Act (2012), which stress the importance of involving individuals in their own care and treatment. Yet, although these principles could be interpreted as respecting patient autonomy and the rights of patients to control their own treatment etc. (see 'Critiquing Quayle'), there nonetheless remains a tension, for the state to protect personal autonomy while simultaneously promoting the welfare of all of its citizenry. While these two values are not mutually exclusive, in relation to substance use at least, the line becomes increasingly blurred.

The NHS goes to lengths to promote the health of people through campaigns aimed at healthy eating, stopping smoking and reducing the citizenry's alcohol intake (Public Health England, n.d.). Such campaigns, combined with deterrents such as higher taxes, etc., highlight the tension which exists between positive and negative health obligations in this sphere. These obligations refer to the duty to protect an individual's health, and the duty to refrain from acting in a way that unjustifiably interferes with an individual's health or personal autonomy in consuming these substances.

The application of the domestic drug control framework fails to accommodate this tension as it presently stands. For instance, the psychoactives restricted under the MDA and the PSA can be legally distinguished from those which are subject to little or no control under the criminal justice framework: alcohol, sugar and tobacco. While the MDA's legislative provisions are flexible, and when read in conjunction with the Misuse of Drugs Regulations (MDR) (2001), can facilitate an array of regulatory possibilities without attaching the current criminal sanctions (see Chapter 3); in practice, the MDA controls substances via prohibitionist ideology, and without due regard to the international safeguard clauses. The PSA goes even further and actively contradicts the idea of freedom from state interference, by imposing a blanket ban on everything which is not on a specified list of exempted substances (see Chapter 3 for more detail).

Moving towards a broader definition of health

With the exception of the PSA, both the international and domestic (UK) human rights and drug control frameworks are compatible here at a definitional level. For the most part, both of these legislative regimes have the capacity to work systemically in the UK, and there exists flexibility in all of the key conventions and statutes, barring the PSA. Social constructionist and medicalised definitions on what constitutes ones 'health' are present within both frameworks. While it is arguably straightforward for negative health obligations and related autonomy rights to embrace both views of health, since they facilitate a more internal, individual conception, it is interesting that the positive duties placed upon the UK to promote its citizenry's health, also encompass both medicalised and social constructionist views. The capacity of the drug control and human rights frameworks to account for both interpretations of 'health' is a key theme throughout this chapter. In theory, at least, it demonstrates the potential of the two frameworks to cater for the complexities of human drug use, and our multiple drug-using purposes (for more detail, see Chapter 1).

There exists a common normative environment between the human rights and drug control frameworks, when the contours and content of 'health' are fully explored therein. Both frameworks are also intertwined with the WHO, an organisation which employed a broad definition of health long before the creation of the three UN drug conventions, or the most authoritative instrument on the right to health, the ICESCR. The WHO's (1948/1998) definition of health states: '[h]ealth is a state of complete physical, mental, spiritual and social well-being and not merely the absence of disease or infirmity'. Although this definition has been criticised as unrealistic, unclear and impractical (Huber et al., 2011; Tobin, 2012), its sheer breadth and ambition are the reasons it has barely altered since 1948 (Bone and Seddon, 2015).

The WHO definition accommodates both positive and negative definitions of health, and it is aspirational and utopian in its aims, thereby complementing human rights ideals (see Chapter 1 according to Brems, 2009). The definition's refusal to be constrained by arbitrary considerations of what constitutes 'health' further facilitates external, internal, medicalised and social constructionist interpretations. This is important since there exists a strong presumption in international law against normative conflict (Koskenniemi, 2006). Favouring a broad definition of health can therefore help to dynamically interpret drug control and human rights treaties, in a way that strives for consistency with other treaty obligations (see Article 31 of the Vienna Convention on the Law of Treaties, 1969). This can then feed down into domestic understandings of the meaning of health, as applied to drug control issues.

Toebes (1999) goes even further in suggesting that the meaning of health in international law should solely evolve via the application of the human right to health before international and national courts. Lines (2017) also favours an adjudicative approach, in order for dynamic interpretations of drug control law to take place. As discussed in Chapter 3, Lines (ibid) draws on a teleological approach to treaty interpretation, in order to interpret international human rights and drug control treaties in light of their overarching object and purpose. Since the overarching *telos* of the drug control conventions is to 'promote the health and welfare of humankind', this affords judiciaries considerable latitude to interpret drug control and human rights legislation in a legally compatible way.

Yet, there are limits as to what the courts are willing or are able to do to mitigate the legal conflicts between the drug control and human rights regimes, by recognising a more expansive definition of health. For instance, judiciaries could be constrained by the utilitarian object and purpose of the drug conventions, which limit the production and use of controlled drugs 'exclusively to medical and scientific purposes' (Article 4(c) the Single Convention). Moreover, Lines (2017: 154) recognises that courts can engage in 'active nullification' here, deciding that the objectives of drug prohibition are so important that human rights obligations need not be considered (either at all, or in a robust manner), or that drug control law supersedes human rights protections. As will be demonstrated in the 'Critiquing *Quayle*' section, the UK and US judiciaries can conform to an external view of health, rooted in prohibitionist ideology. Thus, a broader human rights perspective (developed philosophically and politically, as well as legally in Part I) is also necessary, to illuminate how the drug control and human rights frameworks actually operate in practice, and the potential for a more concurrent approach.

This section reveals that both frameworks can understand and respond to drug use as a complex human phenomenon, given their capacity to accommodate various conceptions of health and related autonomy rights (see Chapter 1 for more detail on the philosophical perspective). Moreover, a rights-based focus on the positive and negative obligations the UK has to both protect its citizenry's health (*positive*), and to not interfere with an individual's health choices (*negative*), and any related autonomy rights has been highlighted within the human rights and drug control legislation (see Chapter 2 for more detail on the political perspective). State obligations are clearly outlined from these sources of international and domestic law. This should serve to reinforce the UK policy makers' and courts' unwillingness or inability to engage with both frameworks in practice, particularly when compared to case law from other jurisdictions.

It should be acknowledged that Table 4.1 is a generalisation since medicalised views can be internal* and social constructionist views can be external*. Indeed, this section reveals that positive state obligations to provide health care can also accommodate social constructionist views. Regardless, presenting such health dichotomies is important, as it shows the potential of both the human rights and drug control frameworks to accommodate a broad conception of the human right to health and related autonomy rights in *theory* – even if this is not often the case in *practice* (see case law sub-sections below).

Table 4.1 Defining health

Health perspective	*View of health*	*Set of actors*	*State obligations*
External	• Medicalised *(*also social constructionist)* • Positivist epistemology • Observation-orientated methodologies	• State institutions • The medical establishment	• Positive obligations to provide health care
Internal	• Social constructionist **(also medicalised)* • Subjective epistemology • Perception-orientated methodologies	• The individual person who uses drugs	• Negative health obligations to refrain from acting in a way that unjustifiably interferes with the right to health • To respect autonomy-based human rights (i.e. privacy, private life, personal development, the free development of personality)

Positive health obligations: providing medical cannabis in the UK

Since the international drug control system has created no judicial body where dynamic interpretations of drug control law can take place, the most influential actors interpreting the conflicts and tensions between the drug control and human rights frameworks are the domestic and regional (i.e. the ECtHR) courts. This section covers a state's positive health obligations and considers whether a change in the law on the provision of medical cannabis in the UK could invite legal challenges in the future. The procedural rights of patients in respect of access to medical cannabis will be considered by drawing upon relevant ECtHR and domestic case law. Canadian case law will also be drawn upon for comparison purposes. This section reveals an historic judicial reluctance to become involved in whether or not there is a right to treatment in the UK and a preference for an external, medicalised conception of health from the medical profession. This view persists despite the potential for the drug control and human rights frameworks to accommodate internal, social constructionist perceptions of health in relation to cannabis use.

Providing medicinal cannabis: an overview

In June 2018, the UK Home Secretary announced a review to look into the scheduling of cannabis under the MDR (2001). The first part of the review was conducted by Professor Dame Sally Davies, the Chief Medical Officer (CMO) for England. The review recommended that the whole class of cannabis-based products for medicinal use (CBPMUs) be moved out of Schedule 1 of the MDR (2001), since Schedule 1 drugs have little or no therapeutic value by definition (see Chapter 3), and that CBPMUs should reside in Schedule 2 of the MDR (Davies, 2018). In the second part of the review, the Advisory Council on the Misuse of Drugs (ACMD) (2018) agreed that 'cannabis-derived medicinal products' should be rescheduled, subject to certain conditions.

Consequently, on the 1st November 2018, the Misuse of Drugs (Amendments) (Cannabis and Licence Fees) (England, Wales and Scotland) Regulations (2018) (the 2018 Regulations) amended previous regulations, to reschedule CBPMUs in humans to Schedule 2 of the MDR (2001). Effectively, this means that there is now a legal route for cannabis-based products for medicinal use to be prescribed by doctors without the requirement for a Home Office license. A CBPMU (a cannabis-based product for medicinal use) has been defined by the government as a medicinal product or as a substance used in the preparation of a medicinal product, which contains; cannabis, cannabis resin, cannabinol or a cannabinol derivative, and it is produced for medicinal use in humans (see s3 of the 2018 Regulations).

The changes to the UK law do not explicitly state which medical conditions could benefit from cannabis medicines. In *theory*, any patient with a medical condition where there is a clear published evidence of benefit, and where all other licensed treatment options have been exhausted, is potentially eligible for medicinal cannabis (see the 2018 Regulations; Department of Health and Social Care, 2018). In *practice*, the early professional guidance is focused on cannabis use for a very small number of medical conditions including chemotherapy-induced nausea and vomiting, pain (both neuropathic and in a palliative care context), spasticity in multiple sclerosis, and paediatric epilepsy conditions (see the British Paediatric Neurology Association (BPNA), 2018; The Royal College of Physicians (RCP), 2018). Initially, it is likely that these conditions will be seen as more suitable for unlicensed CBPMUs; effectively excluding other medical conditions until further evidence or guidance becomes available.

Only specialist medical practitioners (basically, hospital consultants) on a specialist register can prescribe cannabis medicines in the UK (the 2018 Regulations). The guidelines for specialist clinicians (to be supplemented by an ongoing National Institute for Clinical Excellence (NICE) review (expected publication date, October 2019)), have been criticised as unduly restrictive (ibid), it could be argued that they prioritise an external, medicalised view of health. The British Paediatric Neurology Association (2018) guidance considers the evidence base for the efficacy and safety of most CBPMUs to be extremely limited, and along with the Royal College of Physicians (2018: 3) guidance, there is a clear preference for reliance on randomised control trial (RCT) data since '[a]necdotal positive reporting is not a mechanism to protect public safety'. Although RCTs are perceived as constituting the 'gold star' standard for evidence, practical reasoning dictates that a more open-minded epistemology would lead to a deeper understanding of all of the evidence pertaining to medicinal cannabis. For Sen (2004), *externally* observed medical statistics and *internal* perception-orientated studies ought to inform each other to gain a more complete picture.

When considering the provision of medical cannabis around the world, a rather unique evidential picture is presented. It has often been the case that bottom-up anecdotal evidence and activist campaigns (as opposed to top-down quantitative RCTs), initially altered the medical community to the plant's potential therapeutic use, given the restrictive scheduling constraints placed upon research (see Bone, Klein and Potter, 2018 introducing a Special issue in *Drugs and Alcohol Today*, which includes human stories from cannabis activists and patients). Internal, social constructionist conceptions of health recognise that individuals and groups produce their own view of reality, and that knowledge itself is the product of social dynamics (Conrad and Baker, 2010). Acknowledgement of perception orientation studies, which give effect to internal, self-perceptions of health, alongside externally observed RCT data, could help to build a body of research in this area and improve a clinician's education. The Medical Cannabis Clinicians Society (MCCS) and the All-Party Parliamentary Group (APPG) on Medical Cannabis under Prescription (2019a) report that part of a general reluctance to prescribe is due to a lack of education about medical cannabis, as well as the *perceived* external view in the early guidance pertaining to the lack of research.

As of March 2019, the MCCS and the APPG on Medical Cannabis under Prescription (2019a) were aware of only six private prescriptions that had been written and not a single NHS prescription. Medical cannabis consumers in the UK should be aware that there is little judicial protection for a right to treatment domestically, given the reality of allocating scarce resources, particularly within the NHS (Wicks, 2007). In addition, the ECtHR accords a wider margin of appreciation to contracting states in matters of health care policy. For example, in *Shelley* v. *UK* (2008), the ECtHR found the claimant's court application – to compel prison authorities to provide UK prisons with needle exchange programmes – to be inadmissible. The reasoning process here regarded the jurisdiction in question to be presumably more knowledgeable than the ECtHR on matters pertaining to their own state priorities, resources and social policies which relate to the health of their populace (ibid).

Although there is generally no right to treatment in the UK, upon presenting an overview of the provision of medical cannabis, it appears that medical cannabis (for the most part) is neither available nor accessible; contra to the General Comment on the right to health (2000: para 12) (also see *A B and C* v. *Ireland*, 2010 below). What is more, the ECtHR and domestic case law have more recently indicated that individuals are entitled to expect some minimal procedural requirements when their health care access is decided by the medical profession and/or the government.

Procedural aspects of a right to treatment

In *A B and C* v. *Ireland* (2010), the ECtHR rejected the argument put forward by three applicants that Article 8 (ECHR) conferred a right to abortion. The substantive complaints of the first two applicants concerned the negative health obligations placed on the Irish state. The core argument being that the prohibition of abortion sought for health or well-being reasons disproportionately restricted their right to respect for their private lives (see 'Negative health obligations' section). Contrastingly, the third applicant's complaint concerned the positive obligations placed on states under Article 8 to ensure procedural proprietary when determining access to health care. The court found that Ireland had violated the ECHR by failing to provide an *accessible* and *effective* procedure by which a woman could have established whether or not she qualified for a legal abortion under Irish law at the time.[3]

Although this case concerned the provision of a health care service, this principle could potentially extend to the provision of medicine, i.e. a CBPMU. In the *A B and C* case, the ECtHR considered the impact on the third applicant of 'a discordance between the social reality and the law' (para 248) and that the framework relating to the legal provision of an abortion should be:

> [s]haped in a coherent manner which allows the different legitimate interests involved to be taken into account adequately and in accordance with the obligations deriving from the Convention. (para 249 citing *S.H. and Others* v. *Austria*, no. 57813/00, § 74, 1 April 2010)

Since the UK is a party to the ECHR at the time of writing, they are required to 'take into account' the ECtHR's decision here in line with s2 of the HRA (see Chapter 3). In light of this, it is questionable whether the legal framework on the provision of medical cannabis has been 'shaped in a coherent manner' allowing for the 'different legitimate interests involved to be taken into account adequately'. The MCCS and the APPG on Medical Cannabis under Prescription (2019a) report that clinicians are erroneously interpreting the existing guidance on prescribing as mandatory. This potentially excludes potential patients for whom cannabis could have a therapeutic effect, and the 'different legitimate interests involved', as the law has a broader applicability than the very small

3 There was an Irish referendum in 2018 informed by a citizen's assembly, which helped contribute to a change in the law, legalising abortion in Ireland (see 'The Conclusion' chapter for a more detailed discussion on the efficacy of citizen assemblies in the policy making process).

number of medical conditions focused on in the guidance. Excluding general practitioners from prescribing could also affect the 'different legitimate interests involved' since cannabis is a symptom treatment, as opposed to a cure for many conditions (ibid). General practitioners are therefore well placed to adopt a more holistic approach to medical cannabis prescribing (ibid).

Additionally, in the *A B and C* case, the ECtHR noted that the Irish medical guidelines on abortion provided no framework where a difference of opinion could be examined, contributing to the overall decision that the Irish government had not provided an effective or accessible procedure to determine whether a woman could qualify for an abortion. The clinical guidance available at the time of writing also fails to provide a framework which allows for a difference of opinion. NICE ought to take account of this decision when publishing their own supplementary guidance. Indeed, the MCCS and the APPG (2019b: 10) have produced their own guidelines, where it is recommended that specialists do not 'refuse prescription based on their own lack of understanding, but seek to work with an expert cannabis physician'.

Resource allocation issues

In considering whether the government has established an accessible and effective procedure to determine whether a patient can qualify for medical cannabis, it is also important to illuminate how the decisions are made and to highlight the need for consistency between patients (see Newdick 2005). Yet, there are clear resource allocation issues given the limited funds available in the NHS. In the UK, all cannabis medicines, apart from Nabiximols (marketed as Sativex) and Nabilone, are currently unlicensed.[4] In *theory*, a specialist clinician is able to prescribe an unlicensed medicine, Nabilone, or Sativex – a product which has a market authorisation and resides in Schedule 4 of the MDR. However, in *practice*, NICE (2014) guidelines do not recommend that Sativex is prescribed on the NHS due to its high cost. Nabilone's use is also infrequent, it is a synthetic cannabinoid and it is only recommended when other treatments have failed under the close supervision of a specialist doctor (NHS, 2018). In addition, NHS Trusts and/or Clinical Commissioning Groups have reportedly told clinicians in some instances that CBPMUs are too expensive to prescribe, since each prescription is on a 'named patient' basis and has to be individually imported, until bulk supply can be made available in the UK (MCCS and APPG, 2019a).

Resultantly, the predominant route through which to provide medical cannabis in the UK, at the time of writing, is via a private prescription, which could cost the patient between £600 and 700 a month and an additional £200 for an appointment (Jacobson, 2019). It could be argued that this is not 'in accordance

4 A third medicine, Epidiolex, owned by GW Pharmaceuticals, is currently under regulatory review for childhood epilepsy and is expected to become licensed in 2019.

with the obligations deriving from the Convention' (*A B and C*, 2010: para 249), most notably Article 14, which when read in conjunction with Article 8 ECHR, protects patients from discrimination. It could be reasoned that the cost of a private prescription in the UK places an excessive, discriminatory burden upon less wealthy patients. However, in *A B and C*, the ECtHR found that although the first applicant was adversely affected by Ireland's prohibition of abortion, by virtue of her financial status, this was insufficient to ground a complaint under Article 14 of the ECHR.

Even if CBPMUs are to become more widely available in the UK in the future (thereby lessening the chasm between an accessible and effective procedure to obtain medical cannabis in theory and in practice), the cost of CBPMUs could still provide a legal justification to prevent the NHS from prescribing them. Despite the fact that the NHS constitution imbues equality and a patient-centred approach; striving to ensure that 'patient interest comes before institutional interest' (Department of Health and Social Care, 2019: Principle 5), resource allocation issues could nonetheless affect its implementation in practice. For example, while the Court of Appeal criticised the way in which the health authority refused three transsexuals gender reassignment surgery in *R* v. *North West Lancashire Health Authority, ex p. A, D, and G* (1999), the court considered that the decision itself was still acceptable, if it was made on the basis of prioritising finite resources.

The Court of Appeal doubted whether the Authority really regarded transsexualism as an illness, since there was a near 'blanket policy' in place prohibiting gender reassignment surgery (para 993). As such, the court required the health authority to reformulate its policy to make effective provisions for exceptions in individual cases; to avoid blanket policies by considering each case on its individual merits. With regard to providing medical cannabis in the UK, this decision could help to mitigate against moralistic decision-making, and potentially prevent health authorities from subscribing to prohibitionist ideology by enacting a blanket ban. This case confirms that while there may not be a general right to treatment under English law, the medical establishment and the government are required to make decisions in a procedurally fair manner. While this procedural lens can highlight whether the legal framework to provide medical cannabis in the UK is fair and transparent, a broader distributive perspective could still consider the refusal of cannabis treatment – on the basis of limited resources alone – to be morally questionable since the UK is reported as being the biggest producer and exporter of medical cannabis in the world (INCB, 2017b).

Medical cannabis markets are rapidly changing around the world. In view of this section, countries should be aware of the requirement for procedural proprietary when providing a legal framework for the provision of medical cannabis. Indeed, any country party to the ECHR should take into account the *A B and C* case and the principles extrapolated here. When read in conjunction with the *ex p. A, D and G* case, it appears that individuals in the UK are entitled to expect some minimal procedural requirements when their health care access is decided by the medical profession and/or the government. While this section focuses on providing medical cannabis, similar arguments could apply in the future to the provision of psychedelic therapy, as the law begins to respond to the research outlining the therapeutic efficacy of certain psychedelics (Sessa, 2017, 2018; Denver Psilocybin Initiative, 2019).

The Parker *and* Hitzig *comparison*

In the absence of a general right to treatment, UK citizens are mostly limited to challenging the procedures in place when their health care access is decided by the medical profession and/or the government. Contrastingly, the Canadian cases of *R* v. *Parker* (2000) and *Hitzig* v. *Canada* (2003) actually challenge the constitutionality of their drug laws in relation to cannabis, resulting in a transformative shift in domestic cannabis policy; from its prohibition to its legal regulation for medicinal use.

In *R* v. *Parker* (2000), the Ontario Court of Appeal held that an absolute prohibition on cannabis without any medical exemption violated the defendant's right to life, liberty and security of the person under s7 of the Canadian Charter, and it declared the blanket prohibition of cannabis to be unconstitutional. In July 2001, Health Canada implemented the Marihuana Medical Access Regulations (MMAR) in response to *Parker*. In *theory*, the MMAR allowed for the access to and use of cannabis for medical patients, yet medical consumers had no legitimate access in practice, since the regulations provided no legal source of supply. Parallels could be drawn with the UK here, because as a result of *Parker*, medicinal cannabis was legal in *theory* but inaccessible in *practice*. Accordingly, in *Hitzig*, the Ontario Superior Court declared that the regulations were unconstitutional.

As a consequence of *Hitzig*, Health Canada was authorised to dispense cannabis to medicinal consumers via centralised state-run programs. These cases show how the judicial process can be particularly influential in altering regulatory policies pertaining to medicinal cannabis. Canadian case law facilitated policies which created legal exemptions for the medicinal use of cannabis and the Canadian judiciary further directed the state to actively create regulations to dispense cannabis to medicinal consumers. The Canadian judicial process is therefore capable of actively constituting drug policies which are shaped from a human rights perspective, as opposed to predominately challenging any procedural impropriety (however, as discussed in Chapter 3, the Canadian government have also demonstrated their willingness to openly flout the international drug control conventions in relation to establishing a legal regulatory framework for cannabis in 2018).

Of course, it should also be noted that the constitutional differences for the Canadian and ECtHR judges here are highly significant. Since s7 of the Canadian Charter of Rights and Freedoms was violated, the Canadian court could exercise its increased judicial power to place positive obligations upon the

Canadian government and enforce a judicial remedy (under s24 of the Canadian Charter in *Parker*). In contrast, contracting states to the ECHR (i.e. the UK), enjoy a wide margin of appreciation, particularly in relation to providing health care, as it is assumed that the state is best placed to assess its use of resources, its priorities and its social needs (see *Shelley* v. *UK*).

The Ontario Court of Appeal in *Parker* also employed one of the 'safeguard clauses' contained within the UN drug conventions to argue that their obligations under the international drug control framework are subject to Canada's 'constitutional principles and the basic concepts of its legal system' (see Article 3(2) the 1988 Convention). In other words, if s7 of the Charter makes growing and possessing cannabis for medical reasons unconstitutional, then the government can enact a regulatory framework for the provision of medicinal cannabis without violating the UN drug conventions; demonstrating the legal flexibility and compatibility of the human rights and drug control frameworks. Though, of course, it should be explicitly acknowledged that this flexibility is confined to *medical* cannabis given the utilitarian objective of the drug conventions, limiting activities relating to controlled substances solely to 'medical and scientific purposes' (Article 4(c), the Single Convention).

Politically speaking, UK courts are more constrained, due to a deference to health professionals in relation to resource allocation within the NHS. Therefore, regarding the UK state's positive obligations to provide health care, there is a limited focus on the procedural aspects of a right to treatment in the UK courts. Constitutionally speaking, the UK courts are also required to interpret drug control legislation in a compliant way (s3 HRA), or else make a declaration of incompatibility (s4 HRA) (see Chapter 3). It is then left to parliament to remedy any legislative defects. In contrast with the Canadian judiciary, the UK courts cannot declare the legislation unconstitutional or otherwise create legal exemptions for medicinal cannabis use.

What is more, the ECtHR generally defers to the government's policies and procedures when considering a state's positive health obligations, given the margin of appreciation doctrine. UK citizens who consume controlled psychoactives, such as cannabis, could therefore look to a state's negative health obligations. Such obligations require inaction on behalf of the state, given the right to control one's own health and body and to be free from state interference.

Negative health obligations: critiquing *Quayle*

It has been alleged that the lack of access to medicinal cannabis in the UK has driven people to buy 'street cannabis' (Health and Social Care Committee, 2019: Q194), or to otherwise grow their own (Klein and Potter, 2018). With that in mind, it is important to consider the negative health obligations placed on the UK government, and the potential and the limitations of applying a state's negative health obligations to the drug control framework. While this section predominately focuses upon a medical cannabis case in the UK, the analysis could be applied to other controlled psychoactives as well. This section will also draw on comparable case law examples from the US, to demonstrate the legal and political limitations placed on the UK courts.

When drug policy and human rights legislation conflict in the UK, this section additionally reveals how the case law example fails to allow for a broad definition of health which incorporates both a medicalised and a social constructionist definition, in a similar vein to the WHO's definition. The section questions both the willingness of the judiciary and (from a human rights perspective), the appropriateness of incorporating a definition of health, in relation to a state's negative health obligations, which moves beyond a deterministic outlook rooted in prohibitionist ideology. It is thought that a broad view of health, incorporating external, internal, medicalised and social constructionist views could more accurately reflect and respond to human drug use. A distinction will also be made between human rights rooted in autonomy arguments, where there is no need to justify the choice to take drugs, and health-based human rights, which require such a justification.

Critiquing Quayle: a medical cannabis case

In the leading medical cannabis case in England and Wales, *R* v. *Quayle*; *R* v. *Wales*; *R* v. *Taylor and another*; *R* v. *Kenny*; *Attorney General's Reference (No. 2 of 2004)* (2005) (*Quayle*), the appellants suffered from a range of medical conditions. These included (but were not limited to): phantom-limb pain, multiple sclerosis, AIDS and pancreatitis, and they sought to alleviate the conditions by consuming cannabis. The majority of the individuals in this joint appeal were convicted at their first trial under the MDA for either possession, possession with intent to supply, for the cultivation, importation and/or the production of cannabis. Four of the five appellants sought to challenge the legitimacy of their verdicts by claiming that the common law defence of necessity should be applied where cannabis was used for medical purposes.

Conversely, the Attorney-General was also appealing a case whereby one defendant, Mr. Ditchfield, was acquitted at his trial, as the jury accepted his defence of medical necessity for supplying cannabis to multiple sclerosis and cancer sufferers. The judges dismissed the appeals and answered the Attorney-General's question that the common law defence of necessity was not available to defendants who intended to supply cannabis to others, for the purposes of alleviating pain.

Closing down Article 8 ECHR

Perhaps somewhat erroneously, the appellants in *Quayle* and Ditchfield also tried to argue that their Article 8 rights under the ECHR would be infringed if the common law defence of necessity were not extended. It is difficult to disagree with the Court of Appeal's reasoning process here. The drug control legislative framework provides clear instruction that cannabis possession, supply, etc. should be criminal, and in the event that it is used medicinally, there exist clear instructions as to how to provide for its medical use, i.e. through rescheduling. The implications of which, for a medical cannabis consumer's human rights, are discussed in detail in the 'Providing medical cannabis' section above.

Accordingly, the Court of Appeal reasoned that to contradict the clear effect and purpose of the drug control legislation, by extending the common law defence of necessity is not possible, since the common law is only effective until: 'Parliament can legislate to draw a line or map out a new path' (para 56 quoting from *McLoughlin* v. *O'Brian*, 1983).

Perhaps then, the appellants ought to have relied on Article 8 ECHR on its own merits, in order for the Court of Appeal to assess the compatibility of human rights and drug control legislation, as applied to medical cannabis consumers? Article 8(1) ECHR (incorporated into UK law via the HRA) provides that '[e]veryone has the right to respect for his private and family life'. As already established (see the 'Sources of law' section), the right to private life is closely related to the human right to health. It could therefore ground a negative health obligation on behalf of the state to not interfere with an individual's health choices.

Under Article 8(2), ECHR this right can only be interfered with if it is:

> <u>[I]n accordance with the law</u> and is <u>necessary in a democratic society</u> in the interests of national security, public safety or the economic well-being of the country, for the prevention of disorder or crime, for the protection of health or morals, or for the protection of the rights and freedoms of others.

Drug control legislation in relation to the prohibition of cannabis is 'in accordance with the law'. To assess the compatibility of this legislation with Article 8 Convention rights, the prohibition of cannabis must have been taken in pursuit of one of the legitimate interests outlined above. It must further be shown that the prohibition of cannabis 'is necessary in a democratic society'. As such, the interference should correspond to 'a pressing social need' and 'be proportionate to the legitimate aim pursued' (see *The Observer and the Guardian* v. *UK*, 1991: paras 71–72). As noted in the judgment, the question of assessing whether the restriction of these individuals' Article 8 rights was proportionate to the legitimate aim pursued by the policy of cannabis prohibition was not directly raised (paras 65–67). Consequently, the judges did not feel in a position to consider either interpreting the drug control legislation in a compliant way (s3 HRA) or making a declaration of incompatibility (s4 HRA).

Hence, the Court of Appeal fell short of being able to invoke judicial balancing and proportionality tests to suitably assess these individuals' rights-based claims (para 66). This is unfortunate, especially since subsequent case law considers that the *Quayle* case forecloses the option of an Article 8 challenge to drug prohibition on the basis of medical use (see *R* v. *Altham*, 2006). Incidentally, the option of an Article 3 challenge was also closed down in *Altham*, as the judges considered that the state had done nothing to subject Altham to inhuman or degrading treatment by prohibiting cannabis, and following *Quayle*, that the defence of necessity is in conflict with the purpose and effect of the drug control legislation.

The narrow application of Article 8 in *Quayle*, to extend the common law defence of medical necessity, is also problematic, since the defence proves superfluous to adequately weighing up the legal conflicts involved. The judicial reasoning process could only ever be conducted superficially here, since this defence implies that there exists some wrongdoing on the defendant's part, which is then justified through the necessity of the action. Therefore, the defence of medical necessity fails to adequately challenge the status quo, and whether in fact, it is the prohibition of cannabis (as opposed to its use), which is 'wrong' through infringing these individuals' human rights to health. The following section presents a hypothetical scenario of how the case could have been reasoned if the human rights perspective – developed theoretically throughout this book – were to be applied, and the likely outcome of a compatibility assessment in practice, given the doubtful tone which pervaded throughout the judgment, in relation to its potential success.

A hypothetical scenario

If the Court of Appeal were to assess the human rights compatibility of drug control laws, as applied to medical cannabis consumers, then for Alder (2006), a typical adjudication process would involve judges engaging in consequentialist rather than deontological reasoning. When weighing up state interests in prohibiting cannabis use, Alder (ibid) perceives the balancing exercise to lend itself more easily to a cost/benefit analysis, at the expense of really considering the intrinsic value attached to an individual's rights. Alder (2006), Beck (2008) and Tsakyrakis (2009) acknowledge the artificiality which is inherent when balancing incommensurable values in human rights disputes, though this of course failed to emerge in *Quayle*. If the judges were able to engage with the moral value the defendants attached to their cannabis usage on a consequentialist basis, then there was ample room for a more detailed external perspective on the medical benefits and risks here.

There were several instances where the Court of Appeal judgment referred to the expert evidence which was adduced from earlier judgments, concerning the medicinal benefits the defendants' gained from their cannabis use (paras 2(i), 2(ii), 2(iii), 2(iv), 3(iii), 4(v), 5(iv), 16, 23). Most notably, was the evidence adduced from Dr Reynolds, a fellow at the Royal College of Anaesthetists and a member of the Pain Society, since he firmly concluded the defendant Mr. Quayle's evaluation by stating 'there is no question in my mind that this patient has taken cannabis with benefit to his chronic symptoms' (ibid: para 2(i)).

Though the judges were unable to discuss any of this evidence in relation to the appellants' Article 8 arguments, they were clear in their deference to parliament, demonstrating a level of 'active nullification' (Lines, 2017: 154). The Court of Appeal believed parliament and the elected government of the day were better placed to determine 'social, medical and legislative policy' (*Quayle*: para 68), because for the court to do so it 'would involve an evaluation of the medical and scientific evidence' (ibid), and 'a greater understanding of the nature and progress of the tests of cannabis which have taken and are taking place' (ibid).

If a broader approach to Article 8 as assessed against the MDA were taken, then as Buchanan (2008) observes, the correct application of human rights norms would involve drawing upon reliable, factual, and relevant information, to guard against parochialism, and an arbitrarily restricted set of moral values. Though the judges were not put in a position procedurally to determine the compatibility of the UK's drug control legislation with the ECHR (see Mance LJ, para 66), the tone of the judgment nevertheless reflected a clear parochial desire to maintain the prohibitive status quo; as the judgment consistently referred to the prevailing 'legislative scheme' (paras 54, 67). Hence, Alder's (2006) typical adjudication process was not as forthcoming as it could have been when contemplating the appellants' Article 8 human rights from a medical and consequentialist perspective.

Though, as noted throughout this chapter, to fully engage with a state's negative health obligations, a broader conception of health is needed. As demonstrated, both the drug control and human rights frameworks are capable of accommodating a social constructionist, internal conception of health, as well as a medical, external one. Along with Hayry (2004), Tsakyrakis (2009) and Walsh (2010), I consider the defendants' individual values and beliefs to be an intrinsic part of the judicial reasoning process. To interfere with an individual's health choices without any sound deontological or consequentialist reasoning invites a deterministic response which fails to adequately address the state/individual binary.

If the Court of Appeal were able and/or willing to allow for any internal deliberations, then judicial balancing and proportionality tests could have been invoked to guide judges when weighing the relevant moral considerations (for a detailed focus on the application of such judicial tests, see 'Moving beyond the human right to health' section and Chapter 5). The legitimate aim pursued by cannabis prohibition could have been weighed against individuals' health and well-being interests, to determine whether the blanket ban was proportionate. The potential benefits of empowering individuals to make their own health choices (see Csordas and Kleinman, 1996; Coomber, Oliver and Morris, 2003; Waldstein, 2010; Department of Health, 2015; Department of Health and Social Care, 2019) could also have been discussed along with contemplating the notion that if an individual convinces themselves that cannabis is beneficial therapeutically, this goes a long way towards it actually being such (Csordas and Kleinman, ibid). The NHS constitution supports this wider conception of health, as discussed in the 'Sources of law' section, it advocates a patient-centred approach, and considers that patients 'play a key role in managing their own health' (Department of Health and Social Care, 2019: Principle 4).

Contrastingly, the Court of Appeal in *Quayle* appeared to be more deferential to the hegemonic medical profession. For instance, the court considered that even if the defence of medical necessity were applicable, it would be limited to immediate sufferers and would not be extended to those involved in supply. As Szasz (2003: 66) observes:

> [T]oday in therapeutic societies, only the physician is allowed to dispense 'dangerous drugs'. If anyone else does so he is called a 'pusher', and is again condemned and punished regardless of the consequences of his efforts.

One could question the deference to the medical profession here, since Csordas and Kleinman (1996) note social control to be an implicit component within the therapeutic process. The authors observe how the paramount issue within therapy is one of control, be it pharmaceutical, political, financial or even social control of the values which are implicit within illness behaviour (ibid; see also Stevens and Zampini, 2018 who regard social control as implicit within the drug policy making process).

Yet, where does this position leave individuals who are engaging in self-care and who wish to take greater control over their own health and well-being? Coomber, Oliver and Morris (2003), Jones (2006) and Waldstein (2010) have all observed the expansion of self-care practices in relation to cannabis use, taking control away from dominant health care practices, which can result in better health outcomes; since it increases the level of autonomy and self-sufficiency for the individual. Arguably, the Health and Social Care Act (2012) and the recent NHS constitution value these goals as well, since they both advocate patient autonomy and stress the importance of patients having control over their own care and treatment (Department of Health, 2015; Department of Health and Social Care, 2019).

By viewing the *Quayle* judgment through this lens, one could argue that closing down any debate on the rights of two of the appellants to supply cannabis to HIV patients and cancer sufferers through their holistic clinic was perhaps deterministic, and that the issue warranted further exploration. While important legal distinctions have been made between possession for personal consumption and supply (see 'Moving beyond the human right to health' for more detail), the appellants' situation could fall within the ambit of personal consumption, since the cannabis was shared amongst a closed group of patients and was not distributed to third parties. Incidentally, the legal status of the cannabis social club model rests upon this important distinction in the law, but a thorough discussion on the legality of cannabis social clubs is beyond the scope of this book (see Marks, 2019).

Arguably, Coggon's (2012: 254) 'monistic creep' prevailed here as this judicial restriction in relation to cannabis suppliers mirrors a strong external conception of health, one which is rooted in prohibitionist ideology. This conception is further reinforced through the implied concern that the appellants may derive pleasure from their cannabis use, as opposed to it solely relieving them of pain (para 77). Rather than accepting pleasure as a valued, legitimate health outcome in line with the WHO's broad definition of health (encompassing 'complete well-being'), the notion of pleasure is negated or frowned upon. Of course, if the reliance on Article 8 rights were grounded in autonomy-based arguments here, as opposed to justifying an Article 8 challenge on health grounds, then any concern that the appellants may derive pleasure from their use, would in fact be sidestepped.

In any event, through employing an arbitrary external conception of what is good for our health, judges and policy makers risk being ill-informed of individual interpretations of health and the significance they hold for the person. Even if the judges, in this case, were able to conduct a compatibility assessment between human rights and drug control legislation, it is highly likely that they would have ruled that the drug control legislation does not conflict with the appellants' human rights. Mance LJ explicitly indicated this to be the case within the judgment (para 69), and the judgment arguably adopted a deferential tone to parliament and the presiding government throughout. Moreover, if a similar case were to go before the ECtHR, it is likely that this court would hold that the prohibition of cannabis sought for health or well-being reasons does not disproportionately restrict a citizen's Article 8 rights. The *A B and C* ruling, in respect of the first two applicants, recognised the breadth of the margin of appreciation to be enjoyed by the state in cases which raise sensitive moral or ethical issues (para 232).

The US comparisons

At the time of writing, 33 US states have legalised and regulated medicinal cannabis, and 10 have created a regulatory framework for recreational cannabis,[5] however, the possession of cannabis remains illegal under US federal law for any purpose via the Controlled Substances Act (1970). While the Rohrabacher-Farr amendment (2014) prohibits the federal government from spending funds to interfere with the implementation of state medical cannabis laws, the Cole Memorandum (2013), which also provided a level of protection in this regard, has since been rescinded during the Trump presidency. The case law pertaining to the US's negative health obligations not to interfere with a citizen's health choices has been legally inconsistent.

Prior to the amendment and the memorandum, in *Gonzales* v. *Raich* (2005), the Supreme Court concluded that the homegrown consumption of cannabis by Raich for the purpose of treating her serious medical conditions, and alleviating her constant pain, would substantially affect interstate commerce 'in

5 See procon.org for regular updates: https://medicalmarijuana.procon.org/view.resource.php?resourceID=000881 [Accessed 23rd June 2019].

both the lawful and unlawful drug markets' (para 19). This decision reinforces the centrality of economic interests in the drug policy sphere (as discussed in Chapter 3). It reveals how the operation of opposing policies in state and federal law can lead to inconsistent judicial decisions, given that Raich's use complied with California's Compassionate Use Act (1996). Conversely, in *City of Garden Grove* v. *Superior Court* (2007) the California Court of Appeal ordered the police department in California to give back a defendant's cannabis stating: 'because the act is strictly a federal offense, the state has no power to punish … it … as such' (para 380). Any further interference by the Trump administration to broaden the discrepancy between state and federal law could create even more legal inconsistencies in this area.

While these cases are not strictly speaking applicable to a UK context given the UK's unitary[6] (as opposed to federal) system of democratic governance, a focus on the inconsistency between state and federal law nevertheless highlights the complexity of the binary between the state and the individual. As demonstrated, the 'state' itself can be a multi-layered concept, and in federal democracies at least, it can incorporate a multitude of conflicting policies driven by different values; values which are weighted either towards the perceived harms or the perceived benefits derived from medicinal cannabis (see Chapter 2 for more detail on this dichotomy of interests).

Although the *Quayle* decision could not assess the compatibility of the appellants' Article 8 rights with the drug control legislation, the tone of the judgment nevertheless suggests that this issue had been politicised. A judicial reasoning process which mirrored the tone in *Quayle* can be seen in *US* v. *Oakland Cannabis Buyers' Cooperative* (2001). This case involved the potential applicability of the medical necessity defence for manufacturing and distributing cannabis. The US court held that the medical necessity defence could not be read into the Uniformed Controlled Substances Act 1970, since the defence: 'cannot succeed when the legislature … has made a determination of values' (para 491).

Given the procedural limitations placed on the UK court system, and the value-driven politicisation of the UK's drug control laws (also see Chapter 3), the judiciary may not consider that the state has contravened its negative health obligations by prohibiting cannabis in the near future. Although the rescheduling of CBPMU's could demonstrate a thawing of the current political climate in relation to medicinal cannabis, cannabis activists and other medicinal cannabis consumers are 'acting as if' the drug laws have already been changed through implementing the cannabis social club model or otherwise cultivating and growing their own (see Bone and de Hoedt, 2018; Klein and Potter, 2018; Decorte et al., forthcoming). In any case, it is arguably autonomy-based human rights arguments which can challenge prohibitionist drug laws to the greatest degree,

6 A unitary system of government is governed as a single entity, although some powers in the UK have been devolved to Scotland, Wales and Northern Ireland.

since the onus is placed on the state to justify their own prohibitionist drug laws to the court. This requires a clear exposition of a state's values, and such autonomy-based arguments have been successful in the landmark Mexican and South African judgments in 2018.

Moving beyond the human right to health: autonomy rights and the drug control framework

It is clear that in the UK, courts are constrained more constitutionally and procedurally than the US or Canadian judiciary, as they are limited to issuing a declaration of incompatibility, if drug control laws are found to be incompatible with human rights obligations. Contrastingly, the landmark judgments in Mexico and South Africa in 2018 demonstrate the potential of human rights case law to not only transform domestic drug policies in their respective jurisdictions, but they go even further and broaden out the type of human right argument which can be successful before a national court. While the human right to health forms an integral part of the complainants' legal arguments which are correlative to the consumption of cannabis, these cases reflect the capacity of the human rights framework to move beyond a limited conception of health; by considering broader autonomy-based human rights related to health, as opposed to health rights which relate to the concept of personal autonomy. Indeed, human rights rooted in autonomy arguments – where there is no need for any justification based on health grounds – could better reflect a variety of drug-using purposes (see Chapter 1 for more detail).

Constitutional and procedural mechanisms

Firstly, in relation to constitutional and procedural mechanisms, The Mexican judicial system is peculiar in that Supreme Court rulings only generate rights upon the plaintiffs involved. Supreme Court decisions will only become law when the court rules five consecutive cases in the same way. *Amparo in Review 237/2014* (also known as *the SMART case*), first challenged cannabis prohibition laws as the complainant's set up a cannabis social club named the *Mexican Society for Responsible and Tolerant Consumption* (*SMART*, for its acronym in Spanish). *SMART* was refused permission from the Mexican Health Authority to cultivate and consume cannabis for personal use, and the complainant's consequently sued the Mexican government arguing that their rights to health, privacy, self-ownership and free development of personality were violated.

The Supreme Court agreed with the plaintiffs and four more cases followed. These cases culminated in the 5th *Amparo in Review 548/2018*, which effectively created jurisprudence to force judges throughout the country to issue their judgments in accordance with the criteria established by the Supreme Court. The criteria allow individuals to plant, cultivate, harvest, prepare, possess and transport cannabis (excepting any acts of commerce). The Mexican

Congress of the Union had a period of 90 days to repeal the drug control provisions declared 'unconstitutional' and to regulate the activities related to the use of cannabis.

In a similar vein, the Constitutional Court of South Africa in *Minister of Justice and Constitutional Development and Others* v. *Prince (Clarke and Others Intervening); National Director of Public Prosecutions and Others* v. *Rubin; National Director of Public Prosecutions and Others* v. *Acton (CCT108/17)* (2018) (hereafter *Prince and Others*, 2018), also declared legislation criminalising the use, possession and cultivation of cannabis unconstitutional. The court suspended its order of invalidity for a period of 24 months, to give parliament an opportunity to remedy the constitutional defects. As a way of providing interim relief, Zondo ACJ read-in the drug control legislation that it would not be a criminal offence for an adult to use, possess or cultivate cannabis in private. Interestingly, if parliament fail to remedy the constitutional defects within the allocated time period, Zondo's reading-in will become law; highlighting perhaps to the greatest degree, the potential of human rights case law in comparable jurisdictions to transform drug policy.

Defining autonomy rights relating to the use of cannabis

The five Mexican judgments including *the SMART case* and *Amparo 548/2018*, and the South African *Prince and Others* (2018) judgment, adopt a broad approach towards conceptualising the human rights violated by a blanket prohibition on cannabis-related activities. In *the SMART case*, it was considered that a blanket ban restricted the complainant's human rights to:

> [P]ersonal identity, self-image, free development of personality, self-determination and individual freedom, all in relation to the principle of human dignity and the human right to health. (para 2)

The Supreme Court agreed with the complainant's contention that the state has adopted a paternalistic stance in enacting its cannabis policy, and that the state should not interfere with the inherent negative freedom to control one's own body and health (see also General Comment 14, 2000: para 8).

The Supreme Court, in *the SMART case*, drew specifically on the human right to the free development of personality, closely related to the right to privacy, by recognising that an individual has their own 'personal sphere' (para 33), that each human being (as opposed to the state) can best judge their own interests, and that the state should recognise the natural ability of the human person to determine the meaning of their existence according to: 'her own values, ideas, expectations, tastes etc.' (para 32). The court acknowledged the importance of empowering individuals to make their own life choices in relation to consuming cannabis, in contrast to the tone of the judgment in *Quayle* or the *A B and C* case when exploring a state's negative health obligations.

The Constitutional Court in *Prince and Others* (2018) similarly considered whether the legislative framework on cannabis limited the human right to privacy. The court drew on numerous international and national case law recognising 'a very high level of protection given to the individual's personal sphere of life ... beyond interference from any public authority' (para 48 citing *Bernstein* v. *Bester*, 1996). All of the rights conceptualised above involved a discussion of the tension between the state and the individual (see Chapter 2 for more detail); with the courts acknowledging state paternalism to pose a threat to individual freedom in this sphere (*SMART*: para 33). This broader view of autonomy-based human rights, relating to cannabis use, challenges the prohibitionist paradigm. This is because these judgments *actively engage* with the state/individual conflict to determine whether a person's rights have been limited (cf. *Quayle* and the *Oakland Cannabis Buyers' Cooperative* cases which defer to the legislature and the executive).

The judicial tests

While the courts in both jurisdictions acknowledge that human rights to free development of personality, privacy, health, etc. have been violated by prohibitionist cannabis policies, judicial tests considering whether the limitation is reasonable and justifiable, or proportionate to the legitimate aim pursued by prohibition, helped to guide the judges through their legal analysis. This facilitated both a consequentialist and a deontological reasoning process. The Mexican Supreme Court in *SMART* and *Amparo 548/2018* conducted a proportionality analysis in four stages.

First, the Supreme Court held that the constitutionality of the aims pursued by a blanket ban on cannabis was not valid, by adopting a Millian liberalist and a deontological analysis that every individual ought to be free adopt their own life plan, while not affecting others (*SMART*: para 48). Second, the court assessed the suitability of the blanket ban, engaging thoroughly with consequentialist reasoning in relation to evidence concerning the harmfulness of cannabis. The court noted that while cannabis use does not pose a significant risk to health (except when consumed chronically or excessively, and that the plant is less dangerous or similar to the dangers posed by alcohol and tobacco), the ban is a suitable measure, in light of its aims to protect public health and order.

Third, when contemplating the necessity of the measure, the Mexican Supreme Court made comparisons with other countries that have regulated or decriminalised cannabis, acknowledging that these alternatives can be accompanied by health and educational policies to more effectively address the aims pursued by the ban. Fourth, when considering the strict proportionality of the measure, the court highlighted the imbalance between the 'intense' degrees to which the complainant's rights to the free development of personality were infringed against the minimum degree to which the legislative aims of cannabis prohibition were met. The court held that a complete ban was not considered to be effective in promoting public health or order, and on the contrary led to more individual and societal harm (*SMART*: para 74; *Amparo 548/2018*: para 11).

Likewise, in concluding that a complete cannabis ban was not constitutionally valid, the South African court adopted a deontological and consequentialist reasoning process through conducting a justification analysis. Drawing on an earlier High Court judgment, the Constitutional Court pointed out that the state bore the burden of looking at whether the human rights limitation was reasonable and justifiable. The blanket ban was also considered to be unreasonable since it casts the net so wide, that even uses that were thought to pose no risk of harm were covered (*Prince and Others*, 2018: para 76 citing *Prince*, 2002: para 81).

The court engaged with consequentialist reasoning, by weighing up the evidence and noting the absence of medical evidence in relation to the amount of cannabis that needed to be consumed to cause harm. The court also noted that the state did not effectively respond to the expert evidence adduced in the case (see 'the Shaw report', paras 29–30 citing *Prince v Minister of Justice and Constitutional Development and Others; Rubin v National Director of Public Prosecutions and Others; Acton and Others v National Director of Public Prosecutions and Others (4153/2012)*, 2017 – hereafter '*Prince and Others*, 2017'), which cast doubt on the state's position in relation to the harmfulness posed by cannabis. The court similarly looked at other jurisdictions which have legalised or decriminalised activities relating to cannabis to determine that the ban was unreasonable, and therefore unjustifiable.

It is clear then that both the Mexican Supreme Court and the South African Constitutional Court avoided engaging in the process of 'active nullification' (Lines, 2017: 154). These judgments considered the relevant human rights questions in a robust manner, with the latter court placing the burden on the state to justify the blanket ban, as opposed to deferring to prohibitionist ideology and state legislatures', to hold that drug control law supersedes human rights protections (cf. *Quayle* and the *Oakland Cannabis Buyers' Cooperative* cases). Additionally, on a deontological level, the South African court in *Prince and Others* (2018), concluded that the ban was 'quite invasive' (para 66), and also acknowledged the state's moralistic construction of prohibitive cannabis laws; considering them to be 'replete with racism' and 'characterised by the racist footprints of a disgraceful past' (para 65 citing *S* v. *Nkosi* at para 753; at para 34 citing *R* v. *Malmo Levine* at para 108).

Questioning the ideology of prohibition

The Constitutional Court explicitly recognised the racist origins of prohibition, and the ideological commitment to a deeply divisive, segregated system which punishes some groups of people over other, more privileged groups, depending on the substance used (see also Taylor, Buchanan and Ayres, 2016). The *Amparo 548/2018* judgment similarly recognised the underlying fallacies of the prohibitionist paradigm, based on 'prejudice' 'moral valuations and not on scientific studies' (*548/2018*: para 5). These courts refused to engage in 'active nullification'; somnambulistically deciding that the prohibitionist objectives of drug control can trump human rights obligations (Lines, 2017: 154; see also Sachs, dissenting judgment in *Prince v. President, Cape Law Society and Others*, 2002: para 154).

The Mexican and South African courts engaged with relevant human rights questions, through following the relevant judicial tests. These judgments engaged in deontological reasoning as well as consequentialist reasoning, thereby challenging Alder's (2006) contention that judiciaries prefer the latter process (see 'A hypothetical scenario' subsection). This is because these courts questioned the very ideology of prohibition when considering the intrinsic value the complainants attached to their cannabis use, as opposed to indiscriminately deferring to state legislatures that have clearly made 'a determination of values' (*Oakland*, 2001: para 491; cf. *Quayle*).

The legal compatibility of the human rights and drug control frameworks

Finally, *Amparo 548/2018* specifically cites Article 3(2) of the 1988 Convention, acknowledging that the UN drug control provisions are subject to a state's 'constitutional principles and the basic concepts of its legal system' in relation to personal consumption. This safeguard clause was cited in relation to the fundamental right to the free development of personality, as a prerogative derived from the Mexican constitution, to legally justify the ruling declaring the prohibition of cannabis to be unconstitutional. As highlighted in the 'Sources of law' section, this thereby substantiates the legal compatibility of the drug control and human rights laws.

The Constitutional Court of South Africa similarly invoked this legal provision from the 1988 Convention to justify their ruling in relation to possession for personal consumption. The court adopted a teleological approach to treaty interpretation, by recognising that Article 3(2) made a fundamental distinction between possession, purchase[7] and cultivation for personal use, and trafficking and dealing which was considered to be 'serious' (*Prince and Others*, 2018: para 112 citing *Prince and Others*, 2017: para 109; see also the Commentary on the 1988 Convention, 1988: 48–49). While a declaration of invalidity was made in relation to the use, possession and cultivation of cannabis for personal use, the court had arguably taken the teleological approach to interpretation to its zenith here. As discussed in Chapter 3, the drug conventions provide no wriggle room for implementing specific regulatory policies for *non-medical* drug use.

7 The Constitutional Court distinguished its ruling from the earlier High Court judgment by refusing to confirm the declaration of invalidity in relation to the purchase of cannabis, since it would, in effect, be sanctioning dealing in cannabis.

Therefore, judiciaries around the world are still constrained by the international framework as it currently stands. *Prince and Others* (2018: para 35 citing *Prince and Others*, 2017: para 112) therefore held that:

> It was not for the court to prescribe alternatives to decriminalisation of the use of cannabis for personal use and consumption. It is for the legislature and the executive to decide on a suitable option or alternatives which can be made after these have been the subject of a deliberative process which is inherent in the idea of Parliament.

It is in this vein then that the 'Conclusion' chapter identifies potential approaches to policy making that can flow from the human rights analysis conducted throughout this book.

Conclusion

This chapter sought to understand the potential and the limitations of applying health rights and autonomy rights to drug control issues within the UK courts, the ECtHR, and courts in other comparable jurisdictions. Though the chapter focused on cannabis over other psychoactives, this should not restrict the significance of the chapter's findings, which are applicable to the drug policy field more broadly. This chapter reveals that both the international and the UK drug control and human rights frameworks share a common normative environment when the contours of 'health' are fully explored; one capable of facilitating a broad conception of this human right encompassing: medicalised, external, social constructionist and internal definitions. However, in practice, the Court of Appeal in *Quayle* and the ECtHR predominately defer to an external, state-derived view of health when drug control and human rights laws conflict.

The continued politicisation of drug control issues demonstrates the limitations of applying health rights to issues of drug control, especially in relation to cannabis. Nevertheless, case law from comparable judiciaries outside of the UK demonstrates the potential of human rights to transform drug policy; even while operating within a prohibitionist paradigm. The Canadian case law adopts a broader approach to interpreting a state's drug control and human rights obligations, facilitating a legal regulatory framework for medicinal cannabis.

Moreover, the recent landmark Mexican and South African judgments demonstrate the potential to move beyond justifying cannabis use on health grounds alone. The arguments employed here rest upon an individual's autonomy interests and related rights to privacy, to better reflect and respond to the meanings one attaches to their own drug use. Thus, the contours of health rights relating to autonomy and autonomy rights relating to health are fully distinguished here.

A state's positive and negative health obligations are also highlighted throughout this chapter, drawing attention to the power dynamic between the state and the individual. This dynamic necessitates fundamental normative questions concerning: how much/little responsibility the state has to both provide treatment, or at the very least to ensure procedural proprietary and adhere to the principle of equality when making health care decisions, while simultaneously respecting an individual's own health choices and/or their rights to be left alone. The UK and the ECtHR case law examples allude to the politicisation of drug control issues here, since the courts predominately defer to parliament and the elected government of the day, to avoid engaging with the relevant human rights questions; a process Lines (2017: 154) terms 'active nullification'.

The *Quayle* case and the *Oakland Buyers Cannabis Cooperative* case further demonstrate that the state can retain a monopoly on the morality of prohibition, given the judicial reluctance to assess the compatibility of drug control and human rights laws where the legislature 'has made a determination of values' (*US* v. *Oakland*, 2001: 491). The idea that prohibition is rooted in 'power politics and trade' (Seddon, 2013: 5; also see 'Introduction' chapter) deserves further exploration too, in light of a case which elevates the government's economic interests (see *Gonzales* v. *Raich*, 2005).

While the UK courts are more constrained procedurally and constitutionally (see s3, s4 HRA), which limits their capacity to directly transform drug policy, all judiciaries in jurisdictions which are party to the international drug conventions are constrained to an extent; since the constitutional safeguard clauses only apply to activities relating to personal consumption. Moreover, although the utilitarian object and purpose of the international conventions also limit the possibility of implementing regulatory policies for non-medical use, the broader teleological approach adopted in the South African and Mexican cases, highlight just how broadly construed human rights challenges can be, when grounded in the concept of personal autonomy.

Chapter 5

Religious rights, related rights and the drug control framework

Much like Chapter 4 which highlights the potential and the limitations of applying health rights and autonomy rights to the drug control framework, this chapter employs human rights to religion and related rights to the same effect. These rights will be analysed conceptually, demonstrating how a human rights lens can alter our perception of drug control issues. Unlike the medical use of psychoactives, which is recognised as a legitimate practice throughout the international drug control regime, religious drug use can be placed at a considerable disadvantage. The drug control regime developed out of a specific homogenising and colonial worldview. There exists a particular cultural hegemony throughout international and domestic drug control legislation, which cannot be as easily accommodated from a human rights perspective. Therefore, any conflicts between the state and the individual highlighted in this chapter serve to exacerbate the drug control regime's prescription to a distinct worldview.

This chapter explores the inherent difficulties in reconciling religious ideals under a human rights lens with those highlighted within the current drug control framework. Chapter 5 defines human rights to religion and related human rights, and explores legal conflicts regarding religious and related drug use in UK case law, and in case law from other jurisdictions, most notably the US. The chapter reiterates the complex and nuanced nature of human drug use, revealing the limitations and the potential of human rights, as applied to drug control issues, and it considers how a human rights perspective could better recognise the often enmeshed contexts of use.

Sources of law to define 'religion' and 'religious manifestations'

'Religion' is notoriously difficult to define, within any context, let alone a legal one. There is no definitive definition of religion in either international or UK legislation, despite the numerous instruments which protect religious rights (Gunn, 2003). Non-legal scholars have considered definitions of religion which are: parochial and have a theological or a confessional basis, to quasi-theological definitions which have a sacred or spiritual basis, to those shaped by western conceptual ideas such as colonialism or philosophical dualism (Martin, 2005). The varieties of religious experience can be so conceptually broad that the eminent philosopher William James considered 'religion' to embrace:

> [O]ne's understanding of the world, of one's part in it; as such everyone has their own 'religion' and the individual in question can be the only true arbiter of what 'counts'. (Walsh, 2014: 212 paraphrasing James, 1961)

According to Martin (ibid), some scholars even admit defeat in their definitional endeavour for 'religion', and argue for its integration into the umbrella category of 'culture' instead; posing the then more formidable job of defining 'culture'. The idea of 'culture' is so conceptually broad, that dialogues concerning cultural policy can fail at the extreme. Participants at a UNESCO discussion concluded that 'culture permeated the whole social fabric and its role was so pre-eminent ... that it might indeed be confused with life itself' (Tomlinson, 1991: 5). Hulsether (2005: 491) offers a similarly embracing definition which was surmised by his children as 'the ways of a people'. Such broad conceptualisations pose a definitional challenge since 'religion' may then simultaneously refer to almost anything and nothing in particular (ibid).

One way to address this challenge is to adopt a grounded approach, which is a fundamental part of the religious studies method (ibid). This approach involves analysing the case studies of practices which are conventionally understood as religious, and focusing on the self-understandings of the people involved (ibid). In a similar, more legalistic vein then, this section grounds its definitions by analysing the human rights instruments which protect religious drug use, and it assesses their compatibility with the drug control framework, in order to gauge a working definition.

As shown in Chapter 1, psychoactive use can be a fundamental part of the human condition, occurring across all times and geographical space (Weil and Rosen, 1983; Siegel, 2005; Smail, 2008), and can therefore constitute 'the ways of a people' in the broadest sense of the term. However, it is noted throughout this chapter that the legislation, case law, policies, scholars and the practitioners which shape the interplay between religious rights and drug policy, tend to focus on specific drug cultures, or rather 'indigenous' or 'traditional' use; thereby detracting from the general human experience of intoxication (for more detail, see Chapter 1). For the sake of coherency, legal definitions of religion are grounded according to this narrow focus, to better illuminate the dominant cultural hegemony within the drug control regime.

Yet, this chapter acknowledges broader conceptualisations of 'religion' where relevant, to further the symbiotic aim of demonstrating how a human rights perspective can better address drug control issues, and how the complex reality of human drug use can shape the flexible, evolutive design of human rights. As Hulsether (2005: 493) observes, there exists a habit of thinking about cultural difference in ways that emphasize 'the noble but doomed ways of exotic "others"'. The protections afforded to religious drug use embrace a particular narrative order, with a focus on 'othering'. Nevertheless, our increasingly globalised and pluralistic world necessitates a broader view of what constitutes a religion. This particular narrative order is illuminated throughout Chapter 5, and related human rights to the freedom of belief, spirituality and thought are also explored.

The initial subsections explore sources of law to define 'religion' within UK and international law. After demonstrating the sheer definitional breadth from a human rights perspective, these 'definitions' subsections consider how the international drug conventions and domestic (UK) drug policies have narrowed the way in which 'religions' are conceived; before analysing whether (if at all), psychoactive use can constitute a *bona fide* 'manifestation' of a religion or a belief within a UK and a US context for comparison purposes. This comprehensive exploration of what constitutes a 'religion', a religious 'manifestation' or the 'manifestation' of a 'belief' legally, should emphasise the expansive potential of these rights, and how they are often constrained by an external, political conception in relation to psychoactive use. As an important aside, the human right to 'freedom of thought' will be shown as capable of expanding such conceptualisations. Though, this human right will be analysed in full in the final case law section (see 'Beyond religious freedom'), which takes this idea to its zenith.

Defining 'religion' and related rights under the human rights framework

Many international and regional human rights instruments guarantee human rights to religion without explicitly offering a definition of the concept.[1] There has only been one major international effort to explain the rights protected under the notion of religion or belief (see the Declaration on the Elimination of all Forms of Intolerance and Discrimination Based on Religion or Belief, 1981). Many of these international rights additionally guarantee human rights to freedom of thought and belief, thereby expanding the concept in line with James' (1961) broad idea of religion (see Article 18, UDHR; Article 18, 27 ICCPR; Article 9, ECHR).

While various international instruments recognise that everyone has the right to freedom of religion or belief and to manifest this, the General Comment to Article 18 ICCPR, demonstrates the sheer breadth of this right at an international level. The General Comment 22 (1993: para 2) stipulates that: 'Article 18 protects theistic, non-theistic and atheistic beliefs, as well as the right not to profess any religion or belief'. This broad construction of the terms 'religion' and

1 See Article 18, UDHR; Article 18, 27 ICCPR; Article 14, Convention on the Rights of the Child, Article 12, International Convention on the Protection of the Rights of All Migrant Workers and Members of Their Families; Article 8, African Charter of Peoples Rights; Article 9, ECHR.

'belief' fits with the conceptual breadth James identified earlier on (Walsh, 2014 citing James, 1961). The General Comment further provides that there are no 'limitations whatsoever on the freedom ... to have or adopt a religion or belief of one's choice. These freedoms are protected unconditionally...' (1993: para 3). International legislation clearly facilitates an expansive view of what constitutes a religion or a belief, and since the incorporation of the ECHR via the HRA, this is mirrored domestically.

Article 9(1) ECHR (as incorporated by the HRA, 1998) provides:

> Everyone has the right to freedom of thought, conscience and religion; this right includes freedom to change his religion or belief and freedom, either alone or in community with others and in public or private, to manifest his religion or belief, in worship, teaching, practice and observance.

In theory, the notion as to what legally constitutes a 'religion' is wide-ranging, particularly since Article 9 does not just protect 'religion', but 'conscience' more broadly. All 'beliefs' are protected under the auspices of Article 9, not only religious beliefs (see the 'Beyond religious freedom' section for a more detailed discussion on this point). In interpreting Article 9 ECHR, the ECtHR recognise that the provision constitutes 'a precious asset for atheists, agnostics, sceptics and the unconcerned' (*Kokkinakis* v. *Greece*, 1993: para 31). However, prior to the HRA (1998), the UK adopted a narrower, theistic approach to defining religion, perceiving a religion to concern one's relationship with God, rather than accepting a belief in the platonic concept of the ideal (*Barralet* v. *Attorney General*, 1980).

Post-HRA, the UK case of *R (Williamson)* v. *Secretary of State for Education and Employment* (2005) (*Williamson*, 2005), adopts a more expansive approach in providing that a belief must:

> [B]e consistent with basic standards of human dignity or integrity ... possess an adequate degree of seriousness and importance ... be a belief on a fundamental problem ... be coherent ... and capable of being understood. (para 23)

The test is undoubtedly broad since Lord Nicholls adds:

> Overall, these threshold requirements should not be set at a level which would deprive minority beliefs of the protection they are intended to have under the convention.... (ibid)

The ECtHR case *Eweida and Others* v. *the UK* (2013: para 81) (*Eweida*, 2013) confirms the court's approach of protecting those views that 'attain a certain level of cogency, seriousness, cohesion and importance'. Alongside *Williamson*, this rather broad view (encompassing theistic and non-theistic approaches), should serve to answer criticisms, at a *definitional* level at least, that certain religious groups are afforded preferential treatment (see Bedi, 2007; Wright, 2007; Dworkin, 2013).

However, in *practice*, religions or beliefs which are not formalised in structure – for example, those relating to shamanic drug use – are at a disadvantage. As highlighted by Wicks (2014: 10) and in the case law subsections, establishing that a non-theistic religion or belief is sufficiently serious, etc. is much harder to do – 'in the absence of a widely respected body of opinion which presents an agreed solution to transcendental issues'. Though, any exemptions some religious groups may be afforded from facially neutral laws (such as policies pertaining to drug prohibition), usually relate far more to the actual *manifestation* of their religious practice, and the extent to which this threatens the cultural, political and historical hegemony embedded within the UN drug conventions, as explored below.

Defining 'religion' and related rights under the drug control framework

Despite the fact that human rights policies are cultural policies, given their cultural identity within the western tradition (Boiteux, Peluzio and Souza Alves, 2014; see also Chapter 1), their status as living evolutive instruments and their universalist intent, facilitates their capacity to embrace a broader view of religion, belief, spirituality, culture and free thought. Unfortunately, the conceptual framework to acknowledge these human rights is considerably narrower within the international drug control regime, as the UN drug conventions are 'based in an underlying moralism and pharmacological reductionism' (Tupper and Labate, 2012: 26). Human rights to religion, belief, spirituality and free thought are all essentially social constructionist concepts. There is no materialistic basis for these concepts, in contrast with medicalised definitions for the human right to health (see Chapter 4). As such, human rights to religion, belief, spirituality and free thought are perhaps even more susceptible to political influence, and a subscription to a particular worldview.

Certainly, for Tupper and Labate (ibid), the conventions are systemic legacies of a patriarchal, colonialist belief that the consumption of 'exotic' psychoactive plants, and the medley of motivations behind this, can either be controlled, suppressed or eradicated. The Single Convention (1961: Article 49), in particular, called for the eradication of all 'traditional' or 'quasi-traditional' uses of opium within 15 years, and the cocoa leaf and cannabis within 25 years of it coming into force. As alluded to throughout Chapters 1–3, provisions such as these have their roots in myth and xenophobia, and are based upon moral, geopolitical and economic reasoning, as opposed to being based upon any empirical analyses of harm or consequentialist philosophies (see also Gimenez Corte, 2010).

From a deontological standpoint, it is clear that a legal moralist position prevailed when writing the Single Convention, as an arbitrary negative value was attached to any motivation behind consuming these raw material products. Any definitional basis for what constituted a human right to religion or related rights was therefore irrelevant. However, the creation and implementation of the latter two drug treaties incorporate a more cultural relativist position, as they explicitly acknowledge the existence of a human right to religion and culture for a small minority of people. The 1971 Convention (Article 32(4)) allows state parties to make a reservation for plants 'which are *traditionally* used by certain small, clearly determined groups in magical or religious rites....' In a similar vein, the 1988 Convention (Article 14(2)) requires parties to 'respect fundamental rights', and 'take due account of *traditional* illicit uses where there is historical evidence for such use....'

While these provisions recognise religious contexts for use, there is little attempt made to define these contexts. Instead, the word 'traditions' was criticised in negotiations regarding the content of Article 14 (see Commentary on the 1988 Convention, 1998). The Official Commentary on the 1988 Convention observes the criticisms put forward by the intergovernmental expert group, responsible for examining a draft of this provision in 1987, as they noted that 'traditions' are often subject to change (ibid: 295). Tupper and Labate (2012) are similarly critical of Article 14, observing that cultural practices are not isolated, static and they do not necessarily originate from a pure origin. Hence, the drafters' assumption of this reality is unnecessarily homogenising, as it fails to appreciate the evolution of such practices, and the human rights of those who partake in them, in an increasingly globalised, pluralistic and transnational world (ibid).

Additionally, the preoccupation with 'traditional' psychoactive use emphasises the tendency, as observed earlier by Hulsether (2005: 493), to focus on 'exotic others'. The UN drug conventions reflect this stance through protecting 'small, clearly determined groups' which embrace this particular narrative order (Article 32(4) the 1971 Convention). However, all drug use is cultural since psychoactive consumption stretches back into deep history and occurs across most cultures (Siegel, 2005; Smail, 2008; see Chapter 1). As Derrida (1995: 229) frankly points out: 'there are no drugs in nature'. Rather, the use and regulation of all psychoactives are embedded within a particular cultural, historical and political paradigm (ibid; Seddon, 2010; 2016). If we are to accept that the law has no ontological reality since, 'no rule, treaty or custom, no matter how special its subject matter ... applies in a vacuum' (Koskenniemi, 2006: para 120), then it is easy to conceive of the UN drug conventions as political creations.

The existence of the 'safeguard clauses' – provisions designed to prevent conflicts with a state party's constitutional principles or human rights obligations – (see Chapters 3 and 4), further emphasise the political nature of the conventions. This is because the existence of escape clauses are quite rare in international law, as they can act in contrast to Article 27 of the Vienna Convention on the Law ofTreaties, which encourages state compliance (Boiteux, Peluzio and Souza Alves, 2014). Arguably this rare room for deviation exists, in part, because the conventions' homogenising division between illicit/licit psychoactives, fails to appreciate the human rights of citizens in countries which subscribe to different religious contexts for drug use. Moreover, the general application of the safeguard clauses, where convention provisions are subject to a parties 'constitutional limitations/principles' (see Article 36(1)(a) of the Single Convention and Article 3(2) of the 1988 Convention), provides some room to protect a broader view of human rights to religion, belief and free thought under the existing regime.

In practice, the UK has failed to interpret the conventions liberally, since the Misuse of Drugs Act (1971) (MDA) likewise regulates historically and culturally contingent taste. By way of example, the UK government's failure to incorporate alcohol and tobacco into the prohibitive drug control framework is admittedly due to 'historical and cultural precedents' (House of Commons Science and Technology Committee, 2006: 24; see also Chapter 3). Additionally, the Psychoactive Substances Act (2016) (PSA) imposes a blanket ban on activities relating to any non-exempted psychoactive substance. The PSA's all-encompassing nature is particularly problematic for anyone wishing to consume psychoactives, not previously caught within the ambit of the MDA, for religious, spiritual or thought expanding purposes; since there is no consideration for the religious and related rights implications of a blanket ban within this Act.

Though the international and domestic human rights and drug control frameworks (excepting the PSA) are capable of embracing a broad definition of 'religion' and any related rights to 'belief' and/or 'free thought', the analysis above demonstrates that drug control legislation is far more restrictive in the way it conceptualises religious or 'traditional' drug use. Additionally, while the right to have a religion, or a belief, or the human right to freedom of thought constitute absolute rights, the right to manifest these rights can be limited. Except where it is explicitly legislated for, the question of whether psychoactive use constitutes a legitimate 'manifestation' of a religion or a belief is left to the judiciary. For comparison purposes, the following section analyses: what constitutes a legitimate manifestation of a religion or a belief, within both a UK and a US context.

Psychoactive usage as the 'manifestation' of a religion or a belief

Prior to the enactment of the HRA, the UK judiciary were reluctant to consider whether drug use had any religious legitimacy. Instead, the courts would historically protect religious freedom as a negative freedom. As such, individuals were free to manifest their beliefs and their religion as they wished, unless such a manifestation were restrained by common law or statute (Sandberg, 2011). It is perhaps unsurprising then, that early Rastafari cases (comprising the bulk of religious drug use cases in the UK), failed to accord any weight to the defendants' religion. As I have noted elsewhere, in *R* v. *Williams* (1979), R v. *Daudi* and *Daniels* (1982) and *R* v. *Dalloway* (1983), the judges were more preoccupied with possession versus supply issues (Bone, 2014a). In fact, prior to the HRA, these were the only three cases whereby the defendants were actually recognised as Rastafarians (Poulter, 1998). As an important aside, it is unclear at this stage whether human rights protections under the auspice of religious freedom will decline if the HRA is repealed and replaced with a British Bill of Rights (BBR). Even so, it is unlikely that the UK government will be able to withdraw from the ECHR without parliamentary legislation, following the *Miller* (2017) case (for more detail, see Chapter 3).

In all three of the aforementioned Rastafari cases, the defendants' religious status was deemed to be irrelevant, because the fact that cannabis possession or supply was expressly prohibited by law was regarded as definitive (ibid). Thus, there was no interference with these defendants' human rights to manifest their religion. For Sandberg (2011), this judicial reasoning process is unfortunate at the definitional stage, since the same outcome could be reached on a more expansive view of religion. Perhaps then the judicial focus should not be on whether the defendants' right to manifest their religion has been interfered with (ibid). Rather, for the most part, judges should accept drug use as a legitimate 'manifestation' of a religion, belief, etc. and focus their attention upon whether any interference with this right is justified. For example, in *Williamson* (2005: 57), Lord Walker doubted whether it was correct for the courts 'to impose an evaluative filter' at the definitional stage, since excluding a claim at the outset prevents the courts from truly engaging with the merits of a case.

Regardless, the UK courts are more accommodating at the definitional stage post-HRA (though it remains to be seen whether this will be the case if the HRA is repealed). In *Eweida*, the ECtHR also clarified the definitional breadth as to what counts as a manifestation, within the meaning of Article 9. Though, it cannot be said that every act constitutes a manifestation of a belief:

> [T]he act in question must be <u>intimately linked to the religion or belief</u>. An example would be an act of worship or devotion which forms part of the practice of a religion or belief in <u>a generally recognised form</u>. However, the manifestation of religion or belief is <u>not limited</u> to such acts; <u>the existence of a sufficiently close and direct nexus</u> between the act and the underlying belief must be determined on the facts of each case. In particular, there is <u>no requirement on the applicant to establish that he or she acted in fulfilment of a duty mandated by the religion in question</u>. (para 82)

This test is arguably broader in comparison than the sincerity and centrality tests adopted in the US. The sincerity requirement tests the knowledge of the defendant's beliefs and the extent to which the manifestation is religious in nature, whereas the centrality test requires the manifestation to be central to the defendant's religion (Bone, 2014a). As I have acknowledged elsewhere, these tests can discriminate against minority religions, and those who do not subscribe to an orthodox, westernised conception of religion (ibid). The US tests are particularly epistemologically challenging for the Rastafari, as their movement is racial, cultural and political in nature, and is not solely religious (ibid).

Not all of the Rastafari consume cannabis as a religious sacrament either. Hence, its member's claims could well fail at the definitional stage in the US (see *Robinson* v. *Foti*, 1981; *Reed* v. *Faulkner*, 1988). Accordingly, while the US may have the strongest juridification of religious freedom claims (see 'Comparable case law from jurisdictions outside of the UK' section), its manifestation tests are more stringent than the UK's post the HRA, and particularly in light of *Eweida*, an ECtHR case which clarifies Article 9 jurisprudence.

Despite the definitional breadth of *Eweida*, potentially accommodating drug use which constitutes a manifestation of a belief, as well as a religion – providing there is a 'sufficiently close and direct nexus' between the two – only the latter manifestation is really accommodated by the courts in relation to drug use at present (for more detail, see the 'Beyond religious freedom' section). While it is unnecessary in theory to warp drug use experiences into a form which approximates those of recognised religions, in practice judiciaries are reluctant to consider manifestations outside of an orthodox religious context. To my knowledge there have been no UK cases which consider the right to consume drugs as a genuine belief or a philosophy.

In the US, two notable cases involved defendants who argued their drug use constituted a legitimate religious manifestation, despite the case facts indicating that the manifestations were of a more or secular nature; involving a particular belief or philosophy (*Leary* v. *US*, 1967; *US* v. *Kuch*, 1968). It was thought that religious claims would be more successful here (Lander, 2014; see 'Beyond religious freedom' section for more detail). Historically, domestic courts and comparable jurisdictions outside of the UK have been unduly restrictive, holding not only for the drug use to be: 'religiously important to its user but also an essential part of a traditional rite of communal significance' (Bakalar and Grinspoon, 1984). Bakalar and Grinspoon (1984: 32) continue with an analogy:

> It is as though mountain climbing were regarded as generally so dangerous and useless that climbers would be fined and jailed unless they could prove they were making a pilgrimage to a holy site on the peak certified by an established church.

Such a restrictive approach fails to reflect the complexity, the nuances and the multiple purposes behind human drug use. For instance, Labate and Feeney (2012) note that shamanic drug use practices are rooted in ontological definitions of nature and culture, as opposed to being recognised as religious under western standards. Moreover, such practices are medically, artistically, culturally and spiritually enmeshed (ibid). Therefore, it is difficult to isolate a specific context for use. Since conceptualisations for religion, culture, etc. are so wide-ranging, this issue is problematic at the definitional stage.

Perhaps suggestions similar to Mhango's (2008) that – manifestation tests should protect the Rastafari irrespective of whether political, cultural or religious factors dominate their claims – should be utilised throughout this area.

Any legal definition for religion invites the courts to consider a plethora of issues, and even the entire answer to the scope and limits of religious liberty (Ahdar and Leigh, 2005). Thus, avoidance of this issue may well be justified. Since both human rights and drug control frameworks are (for the most part) capable of embracing broad conceptualisations of religion, belief, etc., the question of whether the drug use is justified should arguably be what constitutes the prime judicial focus, as explored below.

UK case law: critiquing *Taylor*

While both the human rights and drug control frameworks are capable of embracing broad definitions of religion and belief in relation to psychoactive usage, in practice, only certain drug use is legitimised on this basis. The diverse employment of various manifestation tests demonstrates that while human rights are legally and philosophically designed to have universal applicability (for more detail, see Chapter 1), they retain a perennial weakness through their westernised, culturally bound conceptions of religion. The UN drug conventions further exacerbate this weakness, because for drug use to be accepted on the above grounds, use should be 'traditional' (Article 32(4) the 1971 Convention; Article 14(2) the 1988 Convention). Thus, a bias is revealed in favour of those who conform to the exotic 'other' narrative order. Several case law examples from jurisdictions outside of the UK conform to this narrower perspective, as preferential treatment is afforded to particular cultural drug use, and to 'small clearly determined groups' (Article 32(4) the 1971 Convention; see the 'Comparable case law' section).

On the other hand, UK domestic case law refuses to accord preferential treatment to any particular group, deferring instead to the UN drug conventions and the legislature. This section analyses the reasoning process of the UK's judiciary when balancing an individual's human rights to freedom of religion and belief against the interests of the state. In a similar manner to Chapter 4, this section highlights the failure of the judiciary to adequately address the binary between the state and the individual, and it emphasises the legal compatibility of the human rights and domestic drug control frameworks, if a broader conception of religion were to be adopted. This section also highlights the legal distinction between a substance such as cannabis, which falls within the ambit of the MDA (1971), and those which fall under the remit of the PSA (2016). Since the latter statute is *not* concerned with reducing harm, a hypothetical scenario will be discussed to explain why this situation is wholly illiberal and could contravene the judicial reasoning process that a human rights approach is supposed to engender.

Moreover, there is no domestic case law which centres on the human right to use psychoactives to manifest a heartfelt 'belief'. While it will be noted that other jurisdictions have implicitly or explicitly analysed these issues (*People* v. *Woody*, 1964; *Leary* v. *US*, 1967; *Kush* v. *US*, 1968; *MAB, WAT, J-AYT* v. *Canada*, 1994), the UK has focussed upon the more orthodox 'religion' component of

Article 9 ECHR. The most prevalent UK case law in this area concerns the human rights of the Rastafari to consume cannabis as a religious sacrament (see Bone, 2014a for more detail). Similar to the *Quayle* case in Chapter 4, the courts have a leading case on religious drug use which has been deferred to in subsequent cases, despite the fact that that the judicial reasoning process is arguably lacking. *R* v. *Taylor* (2001) (*Taylor*) is the leading case in England and Wales on the legal conflict between religious rights and the drug control framework: it has had far-reaching consequences for succeeding cases, and for a case concerning connected rights to freedom of thought (*R* v. *Hardison*; see 'Beyond religious freedom' section). For this reason then, much like *Quayle*, *Taylor* will be analysed in full.

Critiquing Taylor*: an overview*

Taylor was one of the first cases post-HRA to consider the tensions between religious freedom and the global drug prohibitionist framework. The defendant was searched by the police when approaching a Rastafari temple and was found to be possessing roughly 90 g of cannabis. He argued that he was a practicing Rastafarian and admitted his intention to supply it to other Rastafari for religious purposes. Literature on the Rastafari movement indicates that their cannabis use is much more than a religious practice. Rather, it is bound up with their race, culture, politics and it is integral to the identity of Rastafarianism itself (Barrett, 1977; O'Brien and Carter, 2002–2003; Bone, 2014a).

However, Taylor's claim centred solely upon the religious component. Upon arrest Taylor stated 'I'm a Rasta, it's part of my religion' (para 5), and at trial, he argued that his actions should be interpreted as a manifestation of his religion under Article 9(1) ECHR. There were no definitional issues at trial as the prosecution conceded that Rastafarianism was a religion and perhaps more surprisingly, that the cannabis was a legitimate manifestation of Taylor's religion – 'destined for use in connection with Rastafarian religious purposes' (para 14). Such progression at the definitional stage in the UK is discussed briefly above and is outlined more thoroughly elsewhere (Bone, 2014a). Needless to say then, Article 9(1) was engaged, but the court held that that Taylor's rights were limited by the provisions of Article 9(2). As with *Quayle*, the legality of cannabis remained a central concern. Deference was made to the UN drug conventions, to the exclusion of all other considerations specific to Rastafarianism.[2]

The limitations contained in Article 9(2) are similar to those in Article 8(2) and the court considered whether either article could be relied upon here. Article 9(2) provides:

2 To avoid confusion I employ the term 'Rastafarianism' when referring to the religion as a whole. However, it should be recognised that the followers of the Rastafari religion would not approve of this terminology, since they reject any form of 'ism' (Glazier, 2001).

> Freedom to manifest one's religion or beliefs shall be subject only to such limitations as are prescribed by law and are necessary in a democratic society in the interests of public safety, for the protection of public order, health or morals, or for the protection of the rights and freedoms of others.

Rose LJ articulated the reasoning process of the trial judge through noting that the limitations on cannabis supply are 'prescribed by law' since they are imposed via the MDA, 1971. Of central importance then was whether the limitations were 'necessary in a democratic society' and 'proportionate' to the perusal of the legitimate aims contained within in the limitations.

The judicial reasoning process

The judge relied heavily on the UN drug conventions as evidence that the total prohibition of cannabis was necessary and proportionate, in order to 'combat public health and public safety dangers' (ibid: para 14). However, the very existence of the UN drug conventions was enough to substantiate this claim. As highlighted in Chapter 4, Lines' (2017: 154) process of 'active nullification' is evident here, since the Court of Appeal deferred to the UN drug conventions and prohibitionist ideology, to hold that drug control law supersedes human rights considerations. The prosecution drew the courts attention to *United States* v. *Whyte* (1984: 1021), where it was accepted that the court should not take into account 'evidence minimising the dangers from marijuana abuse', since to do would usurp the legislature who have seen fit to 'control a substance on a rational basis' (ibid: 26). Yet, by refusing to engage with the available evidence, the 'rational' aspect remains to be seen. Arguably, the Court of Appeal here made a similar 'determination of values' response, as highlighted in the previous chapter.

Like in *Quayle*, the judge was keen to defer any conflicts with a defendant's human rights to parliament, since the granting of any religious defence was perceived as the province of the legislature and not the courts (para 27). While predictable, this approach was unfortunate since the Crown Court, and later Rose LJ in the Court of Appeal, refused to explore any evidence relating to the significance cannabis held for the individual and for the Rastafari religion in general, as well as the impact of cannabis on health. Mr. Owen Davies QC, acting on behalf of Taylor, argued that the court's justification process was not 'necessary' or 'proportionate' as they refused to analyse this evidence (paras 19, 21). Davies relied upon case law from other jurisdictions which more adequately engaged with the binary between the state and the individual, as these judiciaries allowed expert evidence to be adduced pertaining to the religious and cultural significance psychoactives could have for the individual and their religion (see below for *People* v. *Woody*, 1964; *Prince*, 2002). By failing to consider the wealth of historical, religious, medical or sociological material on Rastafarianism, the key issue of proportionality was instead determined 'by reference to international legal documents of general application' (Edge, 2006: 85).

Even if the court thoroughly weighed up the appropriate evidence, as highlighted in Chapter 4, the balancing conceit favours a consequentialist approach. This approach lends itself far more easily to a cost/benefit analysis, at the expense of engaging with the intrinsic value attached to an individual's human rights (Alder, 2006). Though, for Tsakyrakis (2009), the principle of proportionality merely pretends to be rational, objective and extraneous to moral reasoning. He puts forward a compelling argument that the proportionality test rests upon the illusory assumption that conflicts of values can be reduced to issues of 'degree' or 'intensity', and that these concepts can be measured via a common metric (ibid: 474).

An earlier debate between Habermas (1996) and Alexy (2003) led both parties to conclude that the human rights adjudication process concerns itself with whether something is adequate, inadequate, appropriate, intensive or far-reaching, as opposed to determining whether something is right or wrong in itself. Thus, human rights are transformed into something which appears to be quantifiable, but in reality cloaks the evaluative questions that a human rights approach entails. If we are to accept that human rights are rooted in human nature (see Chapter 1), then this often comprises of competing and irreconcilable impulses, such as the desire for sociability (which feeds into the state's interests), against the need for autonomy (an individual's interest) (Alder, 2006). Articles 8–11 ECHR are especially concerned with the expressive values of an individual, and with their very sense of self-identity (ibid). Alder (ibid: 8) observes how the rational consequentialist approach can crush the subjective experience and identity of the individual, through citing Sedley LJ's assertion that:

> [I]f a balancing exercise between a human right and the public interest is taken seriously, in a majoritarian democracy the public interest would always win.

It is easier to discern then why the decision in *Taylor* was made solely by reference to public interest concerns, which were substantiated via the existence of the UN drug conventions. Yet, Beck (2008: 224) acknowledges that the very appeal to consequences during the judicial balancing exercise between a human right and a limitation is in itself contentious, since: 'rights by their nature are designed to trump consequentialist, utilitarian or majoritarian considerations'. This 'rights as trumps' observation feeds into Tsakyrakis's (2009) argument that a *bona fide* adjudication process involves a thorough understanding of what one values about the human right in question, and contextualising this alongside other moral and political values. Hence, the moral issues should be openly spelled out, weighed up and engaged with from a deontological, normative standpoint as well. Both deontological and consequentialist arguments should be employed in tandem, to better inform the judicial reasoning process, as demonstrated in the Mexican and South African cannabis judgments in Chapter 4. Otherwise, the proportionality principle can invite the courts 'to make value judgments behind the veil of legal objectivity' (Beck, 2008: 237).

Indeed, it is somewhat ironic that the legal provisions Rose LJ relied upon in *Taylor* (most notably Article 36(1)(a) of the Single Convention and Article 3(2) of the 1988 convention) could easily have been interpreted so as to find for the defendant (paras 11, 13). As detailed in Chapter 4, while these provisions criminalise our actions relating to the consumption of certain psychoactives, they are also considered to be 'safeguard clauses' and subject to a state parties 'constitutional limitations/principles' (ibid). It is this rare room for deviation that has in fact allowed other jurisdictions to find for the defendant, and for their human rights to religion and culture (see Boiteux, Peluzio and Souza Alves, 2014). However, a more typical 'active nullification' process arose in *Taylor* (Lines, 2017: 154). The judge drew clear inferences from the UK's subscription to the UN drug conventions, to concoct what Walsh (2010: 435) views as 'a worst-case scenario', through relying upon vague 'public health and safety' stipulations, in order to justify an expansive reading of the limitations contained in Article 9(2).

The Smith *logic*

Furthermore, the Court of Appeal accepted the prosecution's argument *per curiam* which drew its reasoning from the US case of *Employment Division* v. *Smith* (1990). This case held that a distinction could be drawn between:

> [L]egislation prohibiting conduct because it relates to or is motivated by religious belief and legislation which is of general application but prohibits, for other reasons, conduct which happens to be encouraged or required by religious belief. (para 22)

Though endorsed by some (see Wright, 2007), this reasoning has been repeatedly criticised. McConnell (as cited in O'Brien, 2001) is especially critical of this logic which perceives drug laws to be facially neutral, hence they should apply to everyone without exception. He notes that unlike with race, sex or gender issues, minority religions actually strive to be different and to not be accorded the same treatment as others (ibid). Leaving aside the much thornier issue of why some religions, cultures or belief structures ought to be accorded protection from facially neutral drug laws and others ought not to for the moment, criticisms of the *Smith* logic should still carry some weight. Whether drug laws can ever be neutral when they engender incommensurable values such as public health or safety concerns and rights to religious freedom or privacy, remains to be seen. If judiciaries accept the *Smith* logic, then it arguably obfuscates key justificatory issues. As Waldron (1996) and Beck (2008) observe, by failing to address any underlying incommensurables, judiciaries may trivialise the idea of human rights, which destroys their moral force.

Not only did Rose LJ defer any normative (consequentialist and deontological) questions to the legislature in *Taylor*, but he also refused to answer definitively on whether a different outcome could have been reached if the case concerned the possession of cannabis as opposed to its supply. He only stated that such an occurrence 'raises different considerations' (para 17). This vague approach, combined with the lacking normative – consequentialist or deontological – foundation in the judicial reasoning process is regrettable. Especially, since *Taylor* has become a key authority for UK cases which consider the conflict between religious freedom and prohibitionist drug policies, and any connected human rights to freedom of thought (see *R* v. *Andrews*, 2004; *R* v. *Hardison*, 2005; *R* v. *Aziz*, 2012; *R* v. *John Lewis*, 2013).

A small concession

Although, one way in which the judge perhaps alleviated the conflict presented between the state and the individual, and engaged with the moral normative dilemma at the heart of this case, was by ruling that the defendant's original 12-month long sentence was 'significantly too long' (para 34). As well as looking at the defendant's personal circumstances, Rose LJ highlighted that the supply was for religious purposes as opposed to commercial ones, to justify substituting *Taylor*'s custodial sentence to five months. While this possibly stands as a very small concession to the defendant's religious rights, this mitigation is nevertheless more accommodating to the defendant than domestic Rastafari cannabis cases prior to the enactment of the HRA.

In *R* v. *Williams* (1979), *R* v. *Daudi and Daniels* (1982) and *R* v. *Dalloway* (1983), the judges all downplayed the religious element, or else made it clear that they would not discriminate in favour of the defendant's religion. Contrastingly, post-HRA, the Court of Appeal in *R* v. *Andrews* (2004) and *R* v. *John-Lewis* (2013) both considered Rose LJ's reasoning during sentencing. While this consideration was accepted in the latter case and the defendant's sentence was reduced, in the former case, the defendant's religious motive was held not to apply, given his more serious offence of cannabis importation.

I have alluded elsewhere to the judicial pre-occupation with possession versus supply issues in these cases (Bone, 2014a). Such pre-occupation with possession, supply or importation arguably demonstrates a more rational basis for ruling in favour of the state, given concerns relating to public safety, health, etc., than merely deferring to the legality of a substance does. An exploration of these issues also indicates a more thorough engagement with the international drug conventions, since two of the safeguard clauses – facilitating legal room to deviate – are thought to be applicable to 'personal consumption' (Article 3(2) 1988 Convention) and not to 'more serious offences' (Article 36(1) Single Convention). The comparable case law examples are also dominated by such issues. More importantly, several of these cases undermine the Court of Appeal's reasoning process, through recognising the individual's human rights arguments, since the judges here engaged in a comprehensive balancing exercise. This balancing exercise, weighing up the individual's interests against the state's, directs us to all of the relevant, normative considerations, as opposed to deferring solely to the UN drug conventions and the ideology of prohibition.

The Psychoactive Substances Act: a hypothetical case

Of course, even if UK judges limit themselves in future cases to deferring to *Taylor* and the UN drug conventions, the very least that can be said for substances controlled by the MDA (1971) (such as cannabis), is that this statute is premised on reducing harm (at least ostensibly). As discussed in Chapter 3, the PSA (2016) creates a blanket ban on trade in *any substance capable of producing a psychoactive effect*, unless the substance resides in one of the arbitrary exemptions listed within the act. Crucially, the PSA contains no reference to harm, despite the fact that the judicial reasoning processes examined throughout Chapters 4 and 5, largely rests on the – albeit 'worst-case scenario' – assumption (Walsh, 2010: 435), that the prohibition of certain psychoactives is necessary to protect the public. Walsh (2017a) reiterates the point strongly that the qualifiers contained in Article 9(2) are rooted in a presupposition of harm: the PSA is not.

For the purposes of this chapter, the all-encompassing nature of the PSA means that psychoactive plants which were not thought to be caught up within the ambit of the MDA, such as ayahuasca, are now banned (see Walsh, 2015, 2017b for a thorough discussion on the legality of ayahuasca in the English courts). Consequently, the PSA is discriminatory on a religious basis by prohibiting these plants or 'plant medicines': 'typically taken ... with a view to therapeutic healing and/or spiritual enlightenment' (ibid: 41–42). While this chapter highlights that the domestic courts have progressively found it easier to overcome the first legal hurdle – that a person's human rights in relation to controlled substances have been limited, the second legal hurdle – pertaining to whether or not this limitation is justified – is now even harder to overcome in relation to the PSA.

This is because the PSA is not even premised on any consequentialist evaluations of harm. Though the Court of Appeal in *Taylor* (cf. the comparable case law below) predominately failed to engage in deontological or consequentialist reasoning – deferring instead to UN Conventions, the PSA *actively* promotes this process of 'active nullification' (Lines, 2017: 154). Imposing a blanket ban on all substances (excepting those which are government-approved), with no reference to the concept of harm, encourages judges to defer to the ideology of prohibition. Hence, if a case came before the UK courts in the future, involving plant medicines prohibited by the PSA, this controversial statute supports the judicial conclusion that drug control laws automatically supersede human rights considerations.

Comparable case law from jurisdictions outside of the UK

Although domestic case law in this area has gradually stumbled over the first legal hurdle – recognising when an individual's religious rights have been limited, the second legal hurdle – questioning whether or not this limitation is justified, has proven trickier to overcome. This section covers comparable case law which thoroughly engages with the first legal hurdle on a deontological basis (cf. the UK); as it acknowledges the significance a person accords their religious drug use. However, overcoming the second legal hurdle poses a challenge for courts in other jurisdictions (most notably, the US and South Africa) as well. While judiciaries may not automatically rule that UN drug control law supersedes relevant human rights considerations, the comparable case law drawn on in this section engages in consequentialist reasoning, to hold that the limitation on an individual's religious rights to consume psychoactives is justified. This section explores whether or not this reasoning is actually justified, or whether judges are merely hiding behind Beck's (2008: 237) 'veil of legal objectivity' (see the 'Possession versus 'more serious offences'' and Drug discrimination subsections). The section finally offers an example of how to carefully craft a religious legal exemption to answer any public interest concerns, and it looks at the disadvantages of relying upon the human right to freedom of religion. This ground is narrowly construed in practice, when applied to human drug use. It can therefore fail to reflect the reality of lived experience when consuming psychoactives.

Recognising the significance of religious drug use

When asking whether the state has 'shown a proportionate, necessary justification for prosecuting Rastafarians for supplying others of their religion?' the defence counsel in *Taylor*, Mr Owen Davies QC, cited two comparable case law examples (para 21). In his first example, *People* v. *Woody* (1964), the Supreme Court of California acknowledged the significance that peyote – a small spineless cactus containing psychoactive alkaloids – held for Native Americans in their Church ceremonies. The discourse used in the Supreme Court judgment adopted an unusual spiritual quality, which mirrors the reality of peyote use within the Native American Church (NAC). The court recognised that the plant was at the 'theological heart of the defendant's religious practices', facilitating 'familial and social bonds' through allowing NAC worshippers to 'experience the deity' (para 721). Consequently, the court upheld the right of Native Americans to use peyote in accordance with their religion.

The second case cited by Mr Owen Davies QC was the South African case of *Prince* v. *The President of the Law Society of the Cape of Good Hope* (2002) (*Prince*). This case similarly acknowledged the religious significance that cannabis held for Mr Prince, a practicing Rastafari and a law graduate. Four of the nine judges agreed with Mr Prince that denying him access to the bar (the legal profession), because of his religious cannabis use, amounted to a disproportionate infringement on his religious freedom. When exploring whether the Rastafari ought to be exempted from drug laws prohibiting cannabis, the judgments demonstrated a keen knowledge of the Rastafari way of life in a way that had not been seen previously. The Constitutional Court of South Africa explored the many ways in which the Rastafari consume cannabis, and appreciated medical evidence which suggested that cannabis use does not necessarily cause harm (para 24).

As alluded to within Chapter 4, it is unusual to examine judicial discourse which does not predominately accentuate the dangers an illicit psychoactive poses, though this is beginning to change. This more open approach was embraced by two Justices in particular; Justice Sachs and Justice Ngcobo, as their dissenting judgments were especially strong. These Justices focussed on the *value* of the human right in question. Hence, they favoured Tsakyrakis's (2009) normative approach; an approach which was so lacking in *Taylor*. For this reason, it is worth repeating Justice Ngcobo's observation pertaining to the effect cannabis prohibition has for the Rastafari religion. For him, this total restriction constitutes:

> ...a palpable invasion of their dignity. It strikes at the very core of their human dignity. It says that their religion is not worthy of protection. The impact of the limitation is very profound indeed. (para 51)

Justice Ngcobo clearly spelled out the deontological moral issues through recognising the significance cannabis holds for the Rastafari and their religious practices. Justice Sachs added that the real difference between the dissenting judgments and the majority rests on how much trouble the state ought to go to in order to accommodate the religious rights of the Rastafari. He determined that: 'the constitution obliges the state to walk the extra mile' (para 149). The conflict between the *perceived* public interest in maintaining a blanket ban on cannabis, and the individual's religious interest was clearly accentuated here, which directed the court to develop a moral argument about the correct 'balance' between these two values; as the Justices openly and comprehensively detailed the moral values at issue. *Prince* could therefore serve as an example to judiciaries across the globe of how to actively engage with the human rights issues at stake. Of course, it is important to note that the judges were applying a constitutional right in *Prince*. Other jurisdictions are more constrained procedurally and constitutionally. As highlighted in Chapters 3 and 4, the UK courts, can at most, interpret drug control legislation in a legally compatible way with convention rights (s3 HRA), or issue a declaration of incompatibility (s4 HRA), requiring parliament to remedy any legislative defects.

While there are difficulties in comparing two cases in different jurisdictions, applying different rules, the *Prince* judgement nonetheless placed very little emphasis on the existence of the UN drug conventions, in comparison with *Taylor*. Instead, the majority in *Prince* were predominately concerned with the hypothetical difficulties a religious legal exemption could pose. The judges demonstrated an understanding of Rastafari culture through recognizing the lack of any rigid doctrines or organisational structures within Rastafarianism, given the movement's rejection of colonialist, hierarchical attitudes (Bone, 2014a). However, it was this understanding which raised practical concerns with regard to enforcing a legal exemption. Consequently, this became the primary justification for limiting the law graduate's human rights, as explored in detail in the 'Crafting a religious exemption' subsection below.

Possession versus 'more serious offences'

Once the comparable case law overcomes the first legal hurdle, by comprehensively engaging with the relevant human rights questions, and determining that the defendant's freedom of religion has been limited, the second legal hurdle deals with the thorny issue of whether such a limitation is justified. Unlike *Taylor*, the *Prince* case explicitly considered the distinction between possessing cannabis, and producing and trafficking cannabis when contemplating this justification issue (although, Rose LJ in *Taylor* did implicitly acknowledge the distinction between supply for religious purposes and commercial supply, given the reduction in sentence). For Justice Ngcobo, the production and trafficking of drugs is inherently harmful, and yet the policy of a blanket prohibition casts the net so wide that uses that pose no risk of harm are caught up (para 81). Therefore, limiting a defendant's human rights for possession alone could not be justified in the minority judgments.

Besides, the first legal case to find in favour of a Rastafari defendant was also dominated by the distinction between possession and more serious offences involving supply and importation. In 2012, the Italian Supreme court (Judgment No. 14876) upheld an earlier ruling which quashed a Rastafari defendant's conviction for possessing approximately 97 g of cannabis with the intent to supply it to others. Despite focusing less on the broader tension between religious rights and drug prohibition, and more on possession versus supply issues, this focal point is preferable to deferring straight to the legislature. Unlike *Taylor*, this case did not rule that drug control law supersedes human rights obligations, without actively engaging with the normative values at stake. Empirically considering the distinction between possession, supply, production and importation demonstrates a willingness to rationally balance the level of harm an individual could pose to others on a consequentialist basis, since supply, production and importation offences are thought to be more serious than possession alone. Such deliberations stimulate the more evaluative questions a human rights approach engenders.

Of course, these distinctions would be largely redundant if there was no system of global prohibition, and the government legally regulated the psychoactives currently controlled by the drug control framework. In the absence of this, the courts have the unfortunate task of choosing between 'criminalisation' and 'non-regulation'. Judiciaries can either rule against the defendant – ensuring that their actions continue to be criminalised – or else they can rule in favour of the defendant – despite the fact that no legal regulatory framework for the defendant's drug of choice exists. It is perhaps of little wonder then that judges are reluctant to create limited legal exemptions in the religious liberties field, given the potential for diversion into the black market, since any religious exemption would exist within this wider prohibitive context.

Drug discrimination

Indeed, the dominant rationale for the majority in *Prince*, when ruling that the limitation of the defendant's religious rights was justified, centred upon the potential abuse of a crafted legal exemption which protects the religious rights of Rastafari cannabis users:

> [I]t is difficult to imagine how the island of legitimate acquisition and use by Rastafari for the purpose of practicing their religion could be distinguished from the surrounding ocean of illicit trafficking and use. (para 130)

In a similar vein, the practicalities of enforcing a religious exemption for the Rastafari weighed heavily on the minds of US judges, and yet it was not an overriding concern in relation to the NAC and their religious peyote use. Several Rastafari cases in the US, including *Olsen* v. *DEA* (1989), *State* v. *McBride* (1989) and the *Smith* case (1990) analyse why preferential treatment is afforded to the NAC here, since, at the time of writing, both cannabis and peyote reside in Schedule I of the Controlled Substances Act (CSA) (1970), and both groups attach religious and/or cultural significance to these substances. The dissenting judgments in these cases highlight the cultural favouritism behind these decisions (Bone, 2014a). Judge Blackburn's dissent in *Smith* (1990) is particularly noteworthy for its unfavourable comparisons. He stated that peyote use by the NAC in a closed ritual setting was 'far removed from the irresponsible and unrestricted use of unlawful drugs' (para 913). The implication that peyote use is not unlawful, irresponsible, or recreational suggests that Rastafarianism was viewed as no more than a yardstick through which to assess the reasonableness of other religious liberties claims.

Moreover, the somewhat surprising judicial acceptance of the broad nature of the NAC's religion is possibly why their regulatory exemption is so unrestricted; the judiciary and the US government noted very early on (prior to the enactment of their national drug control legislation, the CSA), that Native Americans regard 'peyote as a deity' (Drug Abuse Control Amendment Hearings, 1970: 118). This culminated in a legislative exemption which effectively allows the unlimited use of peyote, since the only restrictions relate to its manufacture (CSA (21 C.F.R. § 1307.31, 1990)). Yet, the fact that any minority group is awarded a regulatory exemption on a religious basis harks back to a fundamental dilemma to be exposed throughout this chapter, and within religious jurisprudence more generally:

> Why are some individuals afforded rights to consume psychoactives for religious or related purposes and not others, particularly if just as much significance is accorded to their use?

Arguably, the rare example of positive judicial discourse in *People* v. *Woody* (1964), contemplating the religious and cultural benefits peyote use holds for the NAC, further emphasises Hulsether's (2005: 493) observation that cultural difference is perceived and afforded to 'the noble but doomed ways of exotic others'. One of the ways the US judiciary justifies its cultural favouritism or bias is to emphasise the special duty the US has to protect the integrity of Native Americans, in light of the trauma and colonisation inflicted upon this group historically (*State* v. *McBride*, 1989). As previously highlighted, much like with the existence of the UN drug conventions, judicial decisions are clearly shaped by a particular cultural, historical and political paradigm.

The fact that the UN drug conventions restrict any religious reservations for certain plants to those used by 'certain, small, clearly determined groups' (Article 32(4), 1971 Convention), also suggests that economic considerations play a key role here, since this provision cannot apply to international trade (ibid). The lack of any codified cannabis exemption for the Rastafari, in direct contrast to the NAC, is possibly due to the fact that cannabis is a highly marketable commodity. Reflecting back on the comparable health case law examples in Chapter 4, one of the primary reasons *Raich*'s (2005) claim to use cannabis medicinally failed, was due to the economic ramifications at federal level, if US states allowed individuals to cultivate their own cannabis. The popularity of this plant emphasises that in practice it is not religious nor any related human rights-based concerns which ultimately influence regulatory exemptions. Rather, a particular historical, cultural and political paradigm is always in play, and as noted in Chapter 3, the global prohibitionist regime is shaped in large part by vested economic interests.

Yet, it is important to concede that a religious legal exemption for cannabis could be more open to 'abuse' and potential diversion into the black market, than one for less popular psychoactives. Therefore, perhaps the problem rests with trying to craft a religious legal exemption in the first place? The South African High Court in *Prince* v. *Others* (2017) (which eventually concluded in the landmark *Prince and Others*, 2018 ruling as outlined in Chapter 4) made a crucial comparison between the *Prince and Others* (2017) case and the earlier *Prince* (2002) ruling, since the latter case was focussed on a limited question:

> [N]amely whether the failure to provide an exemption in respect of the use of cannabis for religious purpose by Rastafari infringed their religious rights under the Constitution. (*Prince*, 2002: para 94)

Significantly, in the earlier *Prince* (2002) ruling, Mr Prince did not dispute that the blanket ban on cannabis served a legitimate government purpose, rather according to the majority ruling, 'he accepts that it does but contends … the legislation ought to have made an exception … permitting such use for religious purposes' (ibid: para 113). However, the latter two cases could be described as 'a broader constitutional challenge to that which confronted the Constitutional Court in *Prince*' (*Prince*, 2017: para 20). By challenging the constitutionality of the prohibition of cannabis on broader autonomy grounds, Mr Prince and his fellow applicants challenged the very ideology of prohibition itself. Crucially, this ground avoids calling on the judges to carefully craft an exemption within a prohibitive framework – a difficult task given the popularity of cannabis. Thus, by relying on broader autonomy arguments, Mr Prince and his fellow applicants avoided a situation where judges can seemingly provide a pragmatic rationale for restricting an individual's religious rights, whether this is done objectively or behind a discriminatory veil. Relying on the broader human right to privacy dismantles the prohibitionist paradigm, as the issues raised on autonomy grounds apply to everyone, regardless of religion. For this reason, it is worth repeating *Prince*'s (2017: para 20) founding affidavit in full:

> The substantive questions in this matter are to what extent and in what way government may dictate, regulate or proscribe conduct considered to be harmful as well as what is the threshold the harm must cross in order for government to intervene. Can government legitimately dictate what people eat, drink or smoke in the confines of their own homes or in properly designated places? Privacy concerns dictate and our constitution recognises that there should be an area of autonomy that precludes outsider intervention.

Crafting a religious exemption

Since courts in the UK have provided no religious exemptions for psychoactive use, it is unlikely that a legal case will succeed, at present, on broader autonomy grounds; particularly since drug users perceive a protective power attached to religious or therapeutic use, as the UN's drug control framework explicitly recognises health and religious rights (preamble, the Single Convention; Article 14(2) the 1988 Convention; Article 32(4) the 1971 Convention; Walsh, 2014). As explained in this book's introductory chapter, most of the successful case law, in jurisdictions outside of the UK, concerns the infringement of an individual's religious or health rights when the drug control and human rights regimes conflict. It is also worth reiterating that a court can only find for an individual on broader autonomy grounds in relation to personal consumption (see *Amparo 548/2018* and *Prince and Others*, 2018), and there is no wiggle room for the courts to implement specific regulatory policies for non-medical use outside of a 'traditional' or 'religious' setting, given the *utilitarian* object and purpose of the UN drug conventions.

More to the point, claiming the label of religious usage when trying to exempt oneself from the prohibitive framework could also be a genuine description of a person's motivations (Walsh, 2014). Thus, it is still important to explore how judiciaries can effectively craft a religious exemption, in the event a defendant can overcome both legal hurdles: first, that their human right to manifest their religion has been limited, and second, that this limitation cannot be justified.

The *Gonzales* v. *O Centro Espírita Beneficente União do Vegetal* (2006) (*Gonzales*) judgment provides a useful example as to how the consequentialist logic relied upon to restrict an individual's religious rights (as explored above), could potentially be overcome with a carefully crafted legal exemption; capable of addressing the practicalities of enforcement. In 2006, the US Supreme Court in *Gonzales* allowed members of a religious organisation, the União do Vegetal (UDV), to hold an exemption permitting them to consume ayahuasca tea – a psychoactive brew containing the controlled compound DMT.

The UDV and the Drug Enforcement Administration (DEA) eventually reached an agreement on the handling of an exemption, which defined how ayahuasca for UDV ceremonies in the US must be handled as a result of this decision (see *O Centro Espirita Beneficiente Uniao do Vegetal* v. *Holder*, 2010). In very general terms, the injunction stipulates that the UDV must import its tea properly, its use must be limited to church members, susceptible members must be warned about the effects of the drug, and if the government believe that the substance could negatively affect church members – or that the DMT levels are too high – they can apply for an 'expedited determination' as to whether the churches' license should be suspended or removed (ibid). Arguably, these restrictions answer health and safety, public health, and public order concerns; those which, in a UK context, would be articulated under Article 9(2) ECHR. Regulations such as these also emphasise the correlativity of the rights and duties doctrine – a doctrine often forgotten in practice given the rise of individualism – but it is nevertheless capable of reconfiguring the binary, as discussed in Chapter 2.

Of course, it may have posed less of a problem for the judges in *Gonzales* to rule in the UDV's favour, since, in 2006, the UDV were a largely unknown non-theistic religion, and ayahuasca and it's religious/cultural elements were relatively unfamiliar in the western world. Therefore, the foreignness of the UDV's practice may have provided a degree of deference to the principle of religious liberty (Labate and Feeney, 2012). Yet again then, this case could be said to operate within a particular cultural paradigm, since a higher degree of protection is thought to be afforded to the exotic 'other' (Hulsether, 2005). On a consequentialist basis, there would also have been less concern of diversion into the illicit market than with cannabis here (ibid), given the relative unfamiliarity of this psychoactive in comparison. Regardless though, the restrictions contained within the *Gonzales* exemption serve to counter such diversion arguments and the implications this has for public health and safety, etc. Accordingly, the tension between the state and the UDV is balanced more fairly, since both parties' interests have been affected.

In comparison, the Court of Appeal in England and Wales unsurprisingly gave short thrift to its own ayahuasca challenge presented by the defendant Peter Aziz, an ayahuasca shaman. When considering whether Article 9 had been engaged or breached, Judge Roach held that any breach was proportionate and necessary under the qualifying provision – Article 9(2) (see *R* v. *Aziz* (2012).Yet, the European situation highlights a much sketchier regulatory picture. Feeney and Labate (2013: 127) observe there to be a 'patchwork of regulatory schemes' throughout Europe. Courts in European jurisdictions including in Spain, the Netherlands, France, Italy, Germany and the UK disagree as to whether the religious use of ayahuasca poses a sufficient risk to public health and safety, and whether or not both legal hurdles can be overcome (ibid).

Not only that, the religious recognition for this practice has been hotly contested across Europe in particular (Feeney and Labate, 2013), since its shamanic nature has led several jurisdictions (most notably France; see the About-Picard Law, 2001) to question its religious status. This thereby limits the possibility for individuals to overcome the very first legal hurdle – that their freedom to exercise their religion has been limited, if the nature of their religion is disputed from the outset. This harks back to the definitional issues outlined in the 'Sources of law' subsections; despite the definitional breadth of what can constitute a religion or a belief under Article 9 ECHR (see *Eweida*).

According to Feeney and Labate (2013), European jurisdictions would benefit from undertaking a broader approach to conceptualising this 'religious' practice, because the unique social setting in which ayahuasca is consumed, calls for soliciting input from affected groups, as well as emphasising anthropological considerations when weighing up 'harm'. To return to this psychoactive's original Latin American home, this reasoning informed a Brazilian Resolution regarding the religious use of ayahuasca in 2010 (*Conselho Nacional de Politicas sobre Drogas's* Resolução n. 01, 2010) (CONAD Resolution No. 1/2010). The rules norms and ethical principles here are mainly moral, emphasising a less invasive form of social control (ibid). Although, there are prohibitions on commercial distribution, tourism, advertisement and the therapeutic use of ayahuasca to mitigate against harms (ibid). Since the CONAD Resolution evolved through a participatory process with groups who consume ayahuasca, the regulations are thought to better reflect the modality of ayahuasca use in Brazil (Labate and Feeney, 2012).

The acknowledgement that ayahuasca use extends beyond a religious setting, as it is entangled within an encompassing medicinal, spiritual and cultural context as well, has been a topical subject within the drug policy sphere in recent years (ibid; Blainey, 2015; Labate, Cavnar and Gearin, 2017), as have discussions pertaining to the increasing globalisation of ayahuasca (see Tupper, 2008; Labate and Jungaberle, 2011; International Center for Ethnobotanical Research, Education and Service, 2019). This gives credence to the argument that human psychoactive usage is occurring in an ever-increasing globalised context (Courtwright, 2002; see also Chapter 1).

And yet, the UK still struggles to properly engage with the first two legal hurdles – is there a limitation on the defendant's right to exercise their religion and is this limitation justified? Even the case law examples which more comprehensively explore these two hurdles, fail, for the most part, to overcome the second legal hurdle. Of course, the justification hurdle is easier to overcome if: the religious drug use is limited to small groups, cultural sensitivities play a part and/or the religious group conforms to a particular 'exotic other' narrative. A distinct lack of economic consequentialist considerations helps too. In the unlikely event that a religious legal exemption is granted, the case law examples (with the possible exception of the NAC) often neglect to account for enmeshed contexts of use.

Beyond religious freedom: case law which enmeshes human rights to freedom of belief, freedom of thought and the notion of cognitive liberty

Although this chapter has focussed extensively on religious rights to use cannabis, ayahuasca, and peyote, a reminder should be made at this point that these substances serve to demonstrate the central aim of highlighting the potential and the limitations of applying a human rights lens to the drug control framework. The case law analysis has thus far focussed on drug use which could be protected under the auspices of religious freedom, since it is easier to satisfy the definitional tests here, as non-religious beliefs (particularly those that are non-formalised in structure), are placed at a disadvantage (Wicks, 2014). This perennial weakness within the human rights framework is the reason why some cases brought legal action, or else compiled their defence on religious grounds, when the case facts suggest that their psychoactive usage was mandated by a much broader conception of 'religion' than is currently applied in practice. In fact, human rights to manifest a belief or a philosophy, or rights to freedom of thought could all be applicable to the following cases, as well as employing a broader conception of what should constitute religious freedom in relation to psychoactive use.

The UK *Williamson* (2005) case acknowledges that primary regard should be had for the subjective experience the individual attaches to their religion, as opposed to opting for any external conception of how religions should be conceived. Dworkin (2013), in particular, takes umbrage with the judicial preference for theistic religions, as he considers that it is difficult, nigh on impossible, to find a principled basis for confining a human right to a theistic religion. He argues for a more general right to 'ethical independence' whereby people are free to express and act upon profound convictions, which can be limited by the government to prevent harm (ibid: 130–131). Indeed, this is exactly what Article 9 ECHR purports to do (see *Eweida*). Though freedom of religion jurisprudence is aware of the dilemma posed between being either too exclusionary, or else expanding the concept beyond any workable scope (Horwitz, 2014), Dworkin's expansion of religion, and the definitional breadth of Article 9, should nevertheless be welcomed within the drug policy sphere. Especially, if we are to accept that religious rights to consume psychoactives are enmeshed with rights to health, cultural rights, and rights to manifest beliefs or human rights to free thought.

The globalisation of shamanic practices, in particular, is a game changer, as it poses problems for contemporary human rights and drug policy laws. So far, this book has shown that human rights predominantly afford protection to a more arbitrary conception of religion, a more external state-derived conception of health, and the rights of small, often historically vulnerable, established groups within the drug policy sphere. Yet, the complex reality of human drug use calls for the human rights framework to adapt the protection it can afford to the individual here. For instance, Blainey (2015: 287) observes that the Santo Daime – another ayahuasca using religious group – consider this psychoactive as a form of 'entheogenic therapy'. The definition of an entheogen is 'becoming divine within' (*Oxford Dictionaries*, 2019: n.p.). Accordingly, this form of therapy is thought to interweave health, spirituality, religion and culture, as shamanic traditions in particular regard life as a whole, and consume psychoactives in a way which engenders a dialogue between spiritual and medical-scientific health and knowledge. Ayahuasca is just one of the many psychoactives that is consumed within these indigenous and newer syncretic settings (see Labate and MacRae, 2010; Labate and Jungaberle, 2011; Blainey, 2013).

Others (non-exhaustively) include cannabis, psilocybin, peyote and the iboga root (see McKenna, 1992). Rastafari cannabis use further provides a useful example here, as this movement is not solely religious, and Rastafari cannabis consumption serves a similar entheogenic purpose to that of older ancient Hindu and Buddhist traditions (Barrett, 1977). In fact, a more recent English Rastafari case, *R* v. *John-Lewis* (2013), centred upon the defendant's medicinal use of cannabis as well as his religious use. However, any entheogenic approaches which cater for enmeshed and multiple contexts of use, clearly conflict with mainstream Euro-American laws which, in practice, generally afford protection to isolated, arbitrary contexts of use. Narrow conceptions of religion have been elevated here, since the application of human rights in practice, fails to uphold their interdependent, interrelated and indivisible goals (World Conference on Human Rights, 1993; see also Chapter 3).

Therefore, this section outlines case law which rests on the human right to manifest a belief in relation to psychoactive use, before exploring the utility and the success of broader autonomy-based arguments, including human rights to the freedom of thought and the notion of cognitive liberty. The employment of domestic (UK) and comparable case law further demonstrates how the human rights framework is capable of responding to the complex phenomena of human psychoactive use, and reflecting the reality of lived experience, since drug use can occur in multiple enmeshed contexts. Though, in practice the human rights framework is rarely harnessed in this way.

Freedom of belief

The UN's Human Rights Committee (HRCa) in *MAB, WAT, J-AYT* v. *Canada* (1994) demonstrates the potential shortcomings of relying on the human right to manifest a 'belief' ground within the drug policy field. This case involved leaders of the 'Assembly of the Church of the Universe'. The members' beliefs involved worshipping and consuming cannabis as the 'sacrament' of the church. The UN's HRCa refused to accept the worshipping of cannabis as a philosophical belief at a basic definitional level, noting that: 'a belief consisting primarily or exclusively in the worship and distribution of a narcotic drug cannot conceivably be brought within the scope of Article 18 ICCPR' (para 4.2). This decision is troubling since it appears that the HRCa concluded that the belief in question was incapable of protection, as opposed to questioning the genuineness of the defendant's beliefs. Scepticism over the belief could be inferred through the use of inverted commas, coupled with the argument that the 'belief' was no more than a device for legitimising criminal behaviour (ibid).

As Sandberg (2011) notes when reiterating the analysis in *Williamson* (2005): it is not for the courts to judge the validity of a faith, rather they should concern themselves with whether the belief was made in good faith, or better yet conduct a straightforward analysis as to whether the restriction of a belief (religious or not), is justified. Given the increasing infiltration of certain psychoactives into the mainstream westernised conscience (see above for the globalisation of ayahuasca example), it is arguably more prudent that such cases satisfy the definitional stages outright. Judicial efforts can then focus on analysing the fundamental moral issues such cases produce.

The much earlier case of *US* v. *Kuch* (1968) also elicits such issues given the provocative facts of the case. The defendant was indicted for obtaining and transferring cannabis and for the unlawful sale, delivery and possession of LSD. She argued that she was an ordained minister of the Neo-American Church, an incorporated religion in the New York State, which advocated the use of psychedelics as a spiritual endeavour. The consumption of psychedelics was regarded as sacramental foods and as manifestations of 'the grace of God', and as such it was contended that they should belong to everyone (para 443). Given the centrality of the Churches practice, one prong of the US's manifestation test is clearly satisfied.

However, the churches motto was 'victory over horseshit'; its official hymns were 'puff the magic dragon' and 'row row row your boat'; it was headed by Chief Boo Hoo and its symbol was a three-eyed toad (paras 444–445)! Accordingly, the judge felt the Church was mocking established institutions, and he declined to accept it as a religion within the context of the first amendment of the US constitution which protects the free exercise of religion (ibid). Judge Gesell contextualised his reasoning at the time through commenting that: 'A nihilistic, agnostic and anti-establishment attitude exists' (paras 445–446). The late 1960s was historically a time of great social and political change given the rise of the counterculture, the proliferation of civil rights movements, and the growing demands for individual freedom.

Cases like *Kuch* therefore exemplify the partisan approach between the state and the individual to the greatest degree. While the *Kuch* case produces key moral and philosophical questions such as what can constitute a *bona fide* belief system, such issues run deeper since the human right to freedom of expression (Article 19 UDHR; Article 10 ECHR) could arguably have been utilised here, to secure rights of defendant's like *Kuch* to actually throw down the gauntlet and legitimately mock these established institutions. Arguably, it is through testing or 'mocking' the status quo that broader conflicts between the state and the individual can be more clearly illuminated.

It is perhaps unfortunate then that the prominent psychedelic advocate, Dr Timothy Leary, failed to draw upon either his membership in the Neo-American Church or on his own religion, the 'League of Spiritual Discovery', when conducting his defence for the possession and trafficking of cannabis in 1967. These actions were deemed to be a federal offence at the time under the Marihuana Tax Act (1937). Leary sought to base his defence on a more established conception of religion, and the then-recent *People* v. *Woody* (1964) ruling, through arguing that as a practicing Hindu the cannabis was used as a spiritual tenet of his religion. This attempt to warp the consumption of psychedelics into an act endorsed by a well-known religion, reiterates the failure of the human rights system to fully appreciate psychoactive usage as part of a broader non-theistic belief system, or as the manifestation of a philosophy; in line with James's (1961) or Dworkin's (2013) broader conception. While there has been progression at the definitional stage for secular belief systems (see *Williamson*, 2005; *Eweida*, 2013), any resulting judicial balancing act can potentially be even more politically charged and transparent, as demonstrated below.

Freedom of thought and the notion of cognitive liberty

As well as the religious challenges, Leary's legal team additionally put forth a more secular argument that as an expert on various psychoactives, Leary was entitled to experiment as he saw fit (Lander, 2014). The discourse embraced here facilitated a broader notion of religion: 'as a matter of political morality and philosophical depth' (Dworkin, 2013: 109). When commenting on the case, Leary declared his motives to be 'clearly spiritual, interior and not ulterior' (Conners, 2010: 216–217). He passionately observed that: 'Liberty was at stake here, freedom to access your own body and brain, a right I believe was protected by the Constitution…' (Leary, 1990: 239). For Boire (2000), a major proponent of cognitive liberty, any prohibition on the formation of certain mind states, which are engendered by the use of psychoactives, effectively strangles the free mind itself. Thus, 'free expression is made meaningless' (ibid: 11). For Boire (1999/2000, 2000, 2003a, 2003b), freedom of thought is intrinsic to all other rights. Boire (1999/2000: 12) describes the concept of cognitive liberty, which is underpinned by the freedom of thought, as follows:

> The right to control one's own consciousness is the quintessence of freedom. If freedom is to mean anything, it must mean that each person has an inviolable right to think for him or herself. It must mean, at a minimum that each person is free to direct one's own consciousness; one's own underlying mental processes, and one's beliefs, opinions and worldview. This is self-evident and axiomatic.

When commenting on the operation of the US legal system, Boire (2003b) notes that the first amendment, which protects rights to free speech, the free exercise of religion, free association, free press, etc. are all moot if the necessary mentation or thought processes which underlie these actions is constrained by the government. Through prohibiting the 'freedom to think as you will and speak as you think' (Boire, 2003b: n.p. citing Justice Brandeis in *Whitney* v. *California*, 1927), all other forms of freedom are lost since '...freedom of thought ... is the matrix, the indispensable condition, of nearly every other form of freedom' (Boire, 2003b: n.p. citing Justice Cardozo in *Palko* v. *Connecticut*, 1937).

By failing to rely upon his own conception of religion, and the (in)famous 'turn on tune in drop out' mantra, the case of *Leary* v. *US* (1967) exemplifies a preference for certain, more conventional, constructions of rights and freedoms over others. Leary (1983: 253) himself was disappointed in the way in which his mantra was predominately construed to mean: 'get stoned and abandon all constructive activity', since its original conception had distinctly religious undertones. According to Leary (1983), the mantra was concerned with finding the deepest nature of things, through embracing various levels of consciousness and interacting harmoniously with the world (ibid).

Regardless, the court utilised this mantra and the resulting sensationalist discourse from the media, to emphasise the dangerous infiltration of the psychedelic counter-culture (*Leary* v. *US*, 1967). The fact that Leary was originally sentenced to 30 years imprisonment and $30,000 fine for less than half an ounce of cannabis, highlights the substantial threat the state felt by this movement. This threat fostered the political environment necessary to cement the Single Convention, and it paved the way for the two subsequent drug conventions; thus producing domestic legislation across the globe to fully give effect to them (Fortson, 2011).

Although Leary's conviction was eventually overturned on the unrelated argument that the Marijuana Tax Act (1937) was unconstitutional, this ruling paved the way for the formation of the CSA; a piece of US domestic legislation which mirrors much of the international drug control framework and the MDA, 1971. This case and its subsequent appeal were heard at the very precipice of Nixon's 'War on drugs' (Nixon, 1971: n.p.). It therefore demonstrates the partisan approach between the state and the individual at its extreme; which highlights some of the core moral and philosophical issues to their greatest degree. This demarcation is further exacerbated by the secular arguments Leary's legal team put forward since they allude to the notion of cognitive liberty and freedom of thought. If we are to accept that the fulfilment all other rights and freedoms are premised on this idea, then this notion clearly takes the binary between the state and the individual to its zenith; by questioning what it means to be truly free.

Critiquing Hardison

While such arguments were only alluded to in *Leary* v. *US* (1967), the UK case of *R* v. *Hardison* (2005) attempted to thoroughly examine and unpack these concepts. Hardison was charged under the MDA for producing and supplying psychedelic substances, MDMA, DMT, 2C-B, LSD and mescaline. He sought to argue that his right to freedom of thought was infringed by the MDA, and as such it should be read in such a way to make it compatible with the ECHR (s3 HRA), otherwise, a declaration of incompatibility was required (s4 HRA). Hardison relied heavily upon Boire's work when constructing this defence. Hardison argued that the prohibition of these substances was based upon an incomplete understanding of human nature, as humans have consumed a variety of psychoactives since the dawn of time (for more detail, see Chapter 1). Employing Boire's (2000: para 7) reasoning, Hardison sought to assert that drug control laws 'manipulate consciousness at it's very roots', since certain mental landscapes are effectively off limits through our inability to legally use certain psychoactives to access them. Walsh (2014: 218) eloquently surmises this restriction by equating the situation to states: 'inducing a kind of psychopharmacological North Korea'.

By asserting that our brain is no longer ours to control, the cognitive liberty argument and rights to freedom of thought move more powerfully beyond human rights to religious freedom, beliefs or culture, since this notion ultimately seeks to maximise everyone's autonomy; as opposed to offering exemptions for a select few. It is for this reason Walsh (2014) considers the cognitive liberty argument to be one which threatens the very structure of global prohibition. In a similar vein to the broader autonomy arguments relied upon in *Prince and Others* (2018) and *Amparo in Review* 237/2014; 548/2018 (see Chapter 4: 'Beyond the human right to health'), the idea of cognitive liberty moves beyond protecting arbitrary categorisations of therapeutic or religious drug use. In fact, when determining the scope and content of the right to privacy, the Constitutional Court of South Africa in *Prince and Others* (2018) linked the right to privacy to the idea of cognitive liberty, through citing an earlier US case in relation to possessing obscene materials:

> If the First Amendment means anything, it means that a State has no business telling a man, sitting alone in his own house, what books he may read or what films he may watch. Our whole constitutional heritage rebels at the thought of giving government the power to control men's minds. (2018: para 54 citing *Stanley* v. *Georgia*, 1969)

In view of this argument, which seeks to maximise everyone's autonomy, the *Hardison* case and the philosophical and normative matters the case produced, merited a thorough analysis. However, somewhat predictably, Judge Niblett rejected Hardison's logic and his Article 9 claim which incorporates the freedom of thought, as he considered that the court was bound by *Taylor*, despite that fact that the judicial reasoning process was arguably lacking here (see 'Critiquing *Taylor*'). Judge Niblett believed Hardison's arguments went beyond his judicial remit:

> I am the judge of the law. It is no part of my function, or any court's function, to engage in philosophical or political debate, or to make decisions based upon arguments relating to the efficacy, or otherwise, of any

> particular enactment of the legislature. Nor is it my function to make moral judgments one way or the other. (Judge Niblett as cited in *R* v. *Hardison*, Lewes Crown Court, January 2005, unreported)

Although the UK judiciary have no power to strike down primary legislation, and the HRA effectively puts the judicial deference to parliament on a stronger statutory basis, Judge Niblett could have openly spelled out the moral issues and values associated with the freedom of thought argument. He could have contextualised these in line with the arguments put forth by Alder (2006), Beck (2008) and Tsakyrakis (2009), as highlighted throughout Chapters 4 and 5. Even when judges perceive their duty as one limited to finding and applying the law, Waldron (2009: 13) observes that the moral argument still entangles itself with deference to texts and precedents, since 'judges are not machines'. Rather, there are reasons why judges regard themselves as bound by statutes, constitutional texts or otherwise defer to precedent, and these are *moral* reasons:

> [R]easons of concern for established expectations, reasons of deference to democratic institutions, and reasons associated with integrity and the moral value of treating like cases alike. (ibid: 13–14)

Contrary to Judge Niblett's assertions, it could be argued that judges never really leave moral reasoning behind. In engaging with heteronomous reasoning – reasoning that defers to what others think on the matter (i.e. the Court of Appeal in *Taylor*), Judge Niblett is still entangled in moral argumentation, since legal reasoning is a hybrid of moral and legal sensibility; they pervade one another (ibid).

Unfortunately, heteronomous reasoning in the drug policy sphere, as a form of moral argumentation, often leads to judges constructing the 'worst-case scenario' to justify engaging the qualifications specified in Article 9(2) ECHR. For Walsh (2014: 224), this hollows out the protection that Article 9 should afford. The usual argument that all psychoactives are criminogenic, and thus pose public safety and health dangers are especially fallible where psychedelics are concerned. Nutt et al.'s (2007) research reveals the highest discrepancy between the harms posed by psychedelics to the individual and society and their criminal classification. Hence, it is worthwhile suggesting that the judiciary should examine any case where human rights ideals conflict with drug policies according to their own unique merits. The dissenting judgments in *Prince* (2002) and the majority in *Gonzales* (2006), *Prince and Others* (2018) and the Mexican cannabis judgments highlighted in Chapter 4 – *Amparo in Review* 237/2014; 548/2018 – acknowledge this conflict, since the central question posed was how much trouble the state was expected to go to in order to accommodate the human rights of psychoactive users (*Prince*, 2002: para 149).

If Judge Niblett were to likewise address such questions, then the cognitive liberty argument takes this conflict to its zenith. Through limiting our choices, drug prohibition laws close off our capacity to experience certain mind states, which then limits who we can become (Walsh, 2014). The Buddha (translated by Müller and Fausböll, 1881: 3) eloquently confirms: 'All we are is the result of what we have thought. The mind is everything. What we think we become'. Such a profound conviction from a prominent religious figure no doubt introduces an element of circularity to this discussion.

If religion is to truly embrace: 'one's understanding of the world, of one's part in it' (Walsh, 2014: 212 paraphrasing James, 1961), then surely this should encompass the ability to access certain knowledge as is engendered through varying states of consciousness? Though this section ultimately demonstrates it is more pragmatic to argue for the freedom of religion limb in Article 9, many of the cases discussed highlight that the posited divisions between religion, belief, free thought, spirituality, cultural practices and health, do not reflect the complexity of lived experience. Only the notion of cognitive liberty, as a broader autonomy-based argument, gives credence to the complexity of human psychoactive usage here. But, most defendants have been reluctant to place this argument before the court, given the short thrift which is usually afforded to autonomy-based arguments, and the perceived protective power attached to religious or therapeutic use. Yet, this is beginning to change in certain jurisdictions with respect to cannabis (see Chapter 4: 'Moving beyond the human right to health' section).

Conclusion

This chapter demonstrates how religious rights could be used as conceptual starting points to challenge the drug control framework, in relation to the use of psychoactives. While a human rights lens can embrace a broad conception of religion, and related human rights to belief, spirituality, health and well-being, culture and thought; in practice, the definitional tests and the case law demonstrate that human rights are often applied arbitrarily; serving only to protect the religious rights of an isolated few.

Despite the compatibility of both the human rights and the drug control frameworks (excepting the PSA), a hegemonic narrative is found to pervade the drug control sphere, since the legislative texts and the case law conform to a particular cultural, historical, economic and political narrative, with a focus on 'othering' (Hulsether, 2005). Domestically, an even narrower approach is adopted since the UK judiciary has not yet found for an individual's rights to use psychoactives on a religious basis. This state of affairs becomes even more severe when analysing case law which enmeshes human rights to spirituality, the freedom of belief, the freedom of thought and the notion of cognitive liberty. For the most part, the domestic and comparable case law highlighted here fails to consider a broader context for human drug use, though there are a couple of notable autonomy-based exceptions.

Judicial reticence to find in favour of the individual when drug control and human rights laws conflict is also evidenced by deferring to the UN drug conventions (see 'Critiquing *Taylor*'), or otherwise hiding behind a veil of objectivity; superficially engaging in consequentialist reasoning, when justifying limiting a person's human rights (see 'Comparable case law'). Not only are judges clearly constrained by the ideology of prohibition, but this chapter also illustrates the legal constraints placed upon judges as well.

Constitutionally speaking, the UK courts, can at most, interpret drug control legislation in a legally compatible way with the ECHR (s3 HRA), or issue a declaration of incompatibility (s4 HRA), requiring parliament to remedy any legislative defects. This possibly reinforces the UK judiciary's deference to parliament. Although judges in the case law examples outside of the UK do not have to maintain the principle of parliamentary sovereignty, judges often regard themselves as bound by what has been reasoned previously – in statutes, constitutional texts or historical precedents (Waldron, 2009).

Even when judges move away from heteronomous to autonomous reasoning (see the South African *Prince* cases; *People* v. *Woody*, 1964; *Gonzales*, 2006), the UN drug conventions still limit any religious exemptions to ***traditional*** uses by 'small clearly determined groups' (Article 32(4) the 1971 Convention); legally promulgating the hegemonic narrative which predominately makes allowances for the exotic 'other'. Perhaps somewhat ironically, any broader autonomy-based arguments (i.e. the right to privacy), restricts a judge's ruling further. This is because a court can only find for the individual on this basis, in relation to personal consumption (Article 3(2), the 1988 Convention; see also Chapter 4). Therefore, in order to transform drug policy from a human rights-based perspective, the Conclusion chapter will identify a potential approach to policy making that can flow from the human rights analysis, and the conceptual arguments, developed throughout this book.

Conclusion

This book argues that human rights instruments can be used to challenge the legal framework of drug prohibition, to develop drug policy and to change our approach to drug control. While it is important to use human rights in this way, the legal judicial method is limited in its application to specific drugs, jurisdictions and drug-using contexts. Therefore, this book develops a broader human rights perspective, philosophically and politically, as well as legally. It develops a conceptual framework for human rights in the context of drug control and applies this to the domestic (UK) and international drug control system (Chapters 1–3). The case law chapters illustrate the potential and the limitations of successfully applying this unique perspective in practice (Chapters 4 and 5), in order to show how a human rights lens could provide a new perspective on drug control issues. In drawing the conceptual framework together, this final chapter makes the case for broader democratic participation to change our approach to drug policy making, before considering directions for future research.

Developing and applying a human rights perspective

Human rights are contextualised and legitimised as a valid concept in Chapter 1, a feat which most researchers exploring the interplay between the human rights and drug control regimes fail to do. The conclusions drawn that human rights are pluralistically universal and malleable instruments – capable of viewing drug use as rooted in our common humanity and as constituting a culturally diverse, evolving activity – substantiate their application to human drug use. Exploring the origin and value of human drug use provides deeper insights into how social, cultural, political, economic and historical influences affect how and why we consume drugs. When these insights are combined with the commonality of human drug use across time and geographical space, a more convincing argument can be made that a human rights lens can reflect the complexities of lived experience.

This argument is cemented in the 'definitions' of health and religion subsections in Chapters 4 and 5. These chapters illustrate the orthodox way in which health rights and religious rights are defined in the case law, and how they ought to be defined, to better reflect our drug using purposes. Additionally, Chapters 4 and 5 broaden out the type of human rights argument which could be relied upon here, since autonomy-based human rights, such as the right to privacy, the free development of personality and the freedom of thought, give credence to the often enmeshed contexts of human drug use, and they challenge the ideology of prohibition (see the subsection below for more detail on this particular point). Yet, this book recognises that judiciaries, in the main, conform to a hegemonic narrative which pervades the drug control framework. Jurisdictions such as the US, protect narrower conceptions of health and religious rights (if at all), and judges in England and Wales consistently fail to uphold any individual rights-based claims.

Human rights can also embrace normative thinking through addressing a fundamental conflict within the drug policy field: the interests of the state in restricting certain psychoactives, versus the interests of individuals in consuming them. The global model of drug prohibition, still favoured by most states, emphasises the harms individuals can cause to societies through drug-related activities, while the drug policy reform position reverses the emphasis towards the harms prohibitionist policies pose to the individual. Unpacking the moral questions raised when pitting a state's interests against an individual's in Chapter 2 reveals the philosophical positions which shape the drug policy debate. Normative – deontological and consequentialist – arguments all advocate either increases/decreases in individual empowerment or in state control. The correlativity of the rights and duties doctrine, the rise of individualism and the dynamic, malleable nature of human rights show that a human rights lens can reconfigure the conflict to elevate the status of the individual person who uses drugs. This can alter existing power struggles, and point to more innovative bottom-up policy proposals to benefit the individual and broader societal interests. Unpacking *perceived* societal interests, by questioning the interests a state actually represents, also challenges dominant state narratives on the morality of drug use.

To facilitate a more open-minded approach to drug control, this book highlights that the case law in Chapters 4 and 5 should concern itself with consequentialist, empirical measures of benefit/harm, as well as deontological issues regarding the significance an individual accords their drug use. Often the judiciary (predominately in the UK)[1] does not properly engage in either a consequentialist or a deontological reasoning process. Instead, judges defer the issue to parliament or an otherwise prevailing state institution, privileging the *perceived* interests of the state. This happens despite the fact that judicial tests (i.e. balancing and proportionality tests) offer the space to explore the relevant moral,

1 Though it is acknowledged that the UK courts are constrained procedurally by the HRA which puts judicial deference to parliament on a stronger statutory basis.

philosophical and legal issues, to address this conflict between the state and the individual. Nevertheless, this book draws on case law examples outside of the UK which do comprehensively spell out these issues (see *People* v. *Woody*, 1964; *R* v. *Parker*, 2000, *Prince*, 2002; *Conant* v. *Walters*, 2003; *R* v. *Hitzig*, 2003; *Gonzales*, 2006; *Amparo in Review* 237/2014; *Prince and Others*, 2017, 2018; *Amparo in Review* 548/2018). Therefore, this book shows that a human rights perspective is capable of reconfiguring the binary identified to be at the crux of drug policies, in practice as well as in theory, even if all of the domestic case law thus far fails to do so.

The legal architecture behind the drug control and human rights frameworks and the inner workings of both systems at an international and domestic (UK) level is explored in Chapter 3. Both systems are flexible and organic, capable of adapting to most changing circumstances under the existing legislative framework. International human rights instruments have a higher legal and institutional standing than international drug control instruments, but the high political standing afforded to the international human rights regime is beginning to wane. The rise of ideological nationalism could pose a threat to the international and domestic (UK) systems of human rights.

Human rights are facing a legitimacy crisis, one which is especially illuminated within a UK context, given the depreciation of the ECHR as a *foreign* construction and calls for a *distinctly* British Bill of Rights. And yet, Chapter 3 shows that UK judges have a substantial amount of freedom to challenge the drug control system within the existing legal architecture, and it considers what this could look like in the future. While the international and domestic human rights regimes are regulated by flexible, organic instruments, capable of responding to most changing circumstances, Chapters 4 and 5 nevertheless reveal that the domestic system of human rights can be politicised when applied to drug control issues. Though UK judges do not have the power to strike down primary legislation to change drug policies themselves (c.f. the case law examples from jurisdictions outside of the UK), they do not properly engage with relevant human rights questions; deferring instead to the UN drug conventions (*R* v. *Taylor*, 2001) or to parliament (*R* v. *Quayle and Others*, 2005).

Conversely, at an international level, the drug control system is becoming less influential. Human rights and civil society bodies are increasingly confronting the global system of drug prohibition, with the UNGASS 2016 process facilitating a dialogue for states, civil society, NGOs, human rights bodies and other relevant stakeholders to have a legitimate input in drug policy discussions. It is perhaps for this reason that judges in other jurisdictions (i.e. Mexico and South Africa) are becoming more emboldened to challenge the very ideology of prohibition – shifting the balance of power away from the dominant economic and political powers who were behind the formation of the international drug control regime. Of course, economic interests were historically one of the main drivers here and Chapters 4 and 5 highlight the continued judicial deference to this narrative. The religious rights or health rights of cannabis consumers are given a shorter thrift when compared with their ayahuasca or peyote using counterparts. To a certain extent, this drug discrimination is due to the economic ramifications of exempting a highly marketable drug from the global model of prohibition.

While case law in several jurisdictions is drawn on to show how human rights can successfully challenge the status quo, the leading case law in the UK, as this book's focal jurisdiction, reveals that human right arguments can only go so far in the courts. Judges in the UK have been unwilling to engage in relevant human rights questions and adopt dynamic interpretations of drug control law. Courts in England and Wales exemplify the static, default position of assuming that drug control law supersedes human rights considerations. This book not only examines the architectural framework of the human rights and drug control systems to reveal where there is domestic and international legal room for manoeuvre, but it scrutinises the very idea of human rights as applied to drug control. In doing so, this book develops and applies three conceptual arguments to change the way in which we think about drug control issues. In sum, these arguments are:

- Human rights are broad living instruments capable of reflecting and understanding human drug use (Chapter 1);
- Human rights can better address the state/individual binary which is identified to be at the crux of drug policies (Chapter 2); and
- For the most part, human rights and drug control frameworks are legally compatible (Chapter 3).

How can human rights provide a new perspective on drug control?

Applying the three conceptual arguments (see Chapters 1–3) to the case law (see Chapters 4 and 5) can provide a new perspective on drug control issues. A human rights lens can *challenge the ideology of prohibition* if we are to accept human rights as broad instruments capable of understanding and reflecting human drug use. Human rights could also be utilised to help us develop *an alternative moral policy response* to drug prohibition by focussing on the relationship between the state and the individual. Finally, while the human rights and drug control frameworks are 'for the most part' legally compatible, this book also recognises that both systems can be *politicised*. Taken together these significant findings could be used to provide a new perspective on drug control, improve our approach to the drug policy making process and offer a direction for future research.

Challenging the ideology of prohibition

A key failing of the human rights regime, when applied to drug control legislation, is the refusal of most judiciaries and law makers to move beyond arbitrary conceptualisations of human rights to 'health' and 'religion'. Such posited divisions between religion, spirituality, health, free thought and well-being are not reflective of the complexity of lived experience. Research in this area has focused predominately on where legal room for manoeuvre exists, rather than on questioning the impact of these posited divisions (Barrett et al., 2008; Hunt, 2008; Lines, 2017).

Traditionally, the human rights framework has been harnessed in an arbitrary way since religious drug use exemptions have typically been afforded to small 'indigenous' or 'traditional' groups, who pose little threat to the hegemonic order of global drug prohibition. Such exemptions are built into the existing drug control regime (Article 32(4) the 1971 Convention; Article 14(2) the 1988 Convention) so they do not challenge the ideology of prohibition itself. Additionally, the courts in England and Wales and case law examples from several other jurisdictions follow external, state-derived conceptions of 'health' when drug control and human rights regimes conflict. These state-approved definitions do not always reflect an individual's motivations for and experiences of drug use. Fortunately, this book moves beyond the arbitrary categorisations of human rights to 'health' and 'religion'. The 'definitions' subsections in Chapters 4 and 5 show that the international and domestic human rights and drug control frameworks can advance a holistic, social constructionist and internal view of health, and a broader view of religion than is typically accommodated in practice.

The *Prince* (2002, 2017, 2018) cases, the *Gonzales* (2006) ayahuasca decision, and the *People* v. *Woody* (1964) peyote case, also serve as useful examples of case law which moves outside of divisive health and religious categorisations, by more fully appreciating the interconnected significance accorded to various substances. The increasing recognition of shamanic drug-using practices which fully integrate health, religion and spirituality also exemplifies the orthodox way in which health rights and religious rights have typically been defined. Both the drug control and human rights frameworks are rooted in western traditional thought, and this book challenges the narrow conceptions of and the posited divisions between 'health' and 'religion'.

Through recognising the interconnected significance an individual accords their drug use, we are able to challenge the very ideology of prohibition. Acknowledging broader categories of human drug use and the experiences of those who consume psychoactive substances challenges prohibitionist policies which protect reductive, narrow conceptions of health and religion. The broader regulatory implications resulting from this perspective could therefore recognise the potential gains psychoactives could have for individuals and society, as opposed to only focusing on the risks. From an individualist's perspective – which promotes the full capacity of individuals to flourish and develop in societies (see Chapter 2) – human rights can then apply beyond traditional and medical prohibitive paradigms; integrating broader categorisations such as 'human flourishing'.

As highlighted in Chapter 5, the CONAD regulations in Brazil move towards the development and flourishing of individuals, as they constitute moral codes which respect ayahuasca shamanism. These regulations evolved through a participatory process with affected groups. Resultantly, the CONAD regulations emphasise anthropological considerations, to avoid relying solely on a biomedical approach, as this did not reflect the modality of ayahuasca use in Brazil (CONAD Resolution No. 1/2010; also see Labate and Feeney, 2012). I have similarly drawn on the cannabis social club model in Chapter 2 to show the potential benefits that cannabis use within this setting can have for the individual. Since the model was created by cannabis consumers, it has the potential to incorporate a more holistic understanding of health and well-being, as the social aspect could be intertwined with positive health outcomes. By facilitating human flourishing cannabis social clubs also challenge the ideology of prohibition. This bottom-up regulatory approach offers a useful example of how to contest the dominant powers in drug policy design. In theory, the model confers a rare level of control to the people who use cannabis, empowering them to live according to their conception of a good life.

The interconnected significance an individual accords their drug use is clearly relevant to show how human rights could be harnessed in the future to develop regulatory ideas which more accurately reflect individual motivations for and experiences of drug use. The book therefore has broader implications if researchers were to move beyond arbitrary categorisations of human rights. While this book uses human rights to health and religion in Chapters 4 and 5 as primary case studies (or conceptual starting points), the majority of human rights cases challenging drug control laws have historically relied upon these grounds. Indeed, more protective power is perceived to exist here.

When assessing the compatibility of drug control laws with human rights obligations, judicial tests (i.e. balancing tests) determine whether or not the state's drug control laws are justified. If an individual were to take cannabis for health reasons, i.e. to relieve pain, it is likely that the court would engage in a different balancing exercise to someone taking cannabis to enhance pleasure. The notion of 'pleasure' when consuming psychoactives is not typically accommodated within our conceptions of health and well-being, despite my arguments to the contrary (see Bone and Seddon, 2015). Hypothetically then, a court is more likely to be justified in preventing cannabis use for pleasure, if there is no obvious health benefit to be weighed in the balance against whatever other societal harms it perceives to exist.

Contrastingly, autonomy-based human rights such as the right to privacy, the free development of personality, and the right to freedom of thought, remove the need for an individual to justify their drug use in the same way. Rather the onus is reversed and instead the state is required to justify their own prohibitionist drug laws to the court. Crucially then, the autonomy-based arguments developed in Chapters 4 and 5 have the potential to threaten the idea of global drug prohibition to the greatest degree. While human rights cases rooted in health and religion are no doubt legitimate, as they reflect genuine motivations for use, autonomy-based claims take the conflict between the state and the individual to its zenith.

The recent Mexican and South African judgments outlined in Chapters 4 and 5 challenge the constitutionality of their respective states' prohibition of cannabis on broader autonomy grounds. Fundamental normative issues revealed to be at the core of drug policy: the conflict between the interests of the state in restricting certain psychoactives and the individual's freedom to consume can be fully explored on autonomy grounds. Questions such as: 'Can government legitimately dictate what people eat, drink or smoke in the confines of their own homes or in properly designated places?' have the potential to dismantle the prohibitionist paradigm, by conferring upon citizens the freedom to consume psychoactives, without government intervention, in the absence of harm (see *Prince*, 2017: para 20). Broader autonomy-based claims could also reflect our drug-using purposes more accurately, than relying upon narrow conceptions of health and religious rights. While defendants have been reluctant to place such arguments before the court, given the short thrift which has historically been afforded to them, this is beginning to change.

An alternative moral policy response

The success of autonomy-based human rights claims in drug case law is welcome, since addressing the fundamental conflict between the state and the individual, identified to be at the heart of drug policy issues, facilitates normative thinking. Chapter 2 demonstrates how a human rights perspective can challenge dominant state narratives on the 'morality' of drug use, and the importance of embracing normative – deontological and consequentialist reasoning – to develop an alternative moral policy response to prohibition.

Chapters 4 and 5 show how courts, particularly in the UK, engage in a process termed 'active nullification' (Lines, 2017: 154). There is an assumption that drug control law supersedes human rights considerations. Therefore, normative questions – which openly spell out and weigh up the moral questions involved when weighing an individual's human rights against a state's interests in enforcing prohibition – are not readily engaged with. The UK judiciary has revealed itself to be constrained by the criminalising underpinnings of the drug control regime, as they have been unwilling to adopt a braver stance and question this criminogenic ontology. Interestingly, Article 8(2) ECHR (as discussed in relation to health and privacy interests) includes 'the prevention of disorder or crime' as a legitimate aim for interference with an individual's human right. No such limitation applies with respect to Article 9(2) ECHR (as discussed in relation to freedom of religion, belief or freedom of thought). This limitation arguably brings an element of circularity to proceedings – it allows for the UK government to criminalise drug-related conduct and for judges to engage Article 8(2) on this basis alone – since drug-related conduct is considered a crime. While in practice, UK judges are constrained by the criminogenic ontology of drug control in relation to both Articles 8 and 9 rights, on a purely legal basis the judiciary is more constrained under Article 8(2) in relation to preventing crime. Criminalisation could act as a barrier for the UK judiciary here, especially in comparison with other jurisdictions.

The impartiality of the judiciary and its independent or unelected nature is essential for the foundations of democracy to guard against majoritarian rule. Key normative questions that are raised throughout the case law analysis in Chapters 4 and 5 include:

> What are a state's positive and negative obligations in relation to respecting an individual's human right to health? What intrinsic value do individuals attach to their drug use? Why are some individuals afforded human rights to consume psychoactives for religious purposes and not others – particularly if just as much significance is attached to this use? Are the aims pursued by prohibition legitimate and are there any alternatives which could better address these aims? Are the limitations placed on the human rights of individuals proportionate to the legitimate aims pursued by prohibition? To what extent can the government regulate or prohibit drug use considered to be harmful and how much trouble is the state expected to go to in order to accommodate the human rights of psychoactive consumers?

Exploring such questions could help to develop an alternative moral policy response, by showing that the UK judiciary and comparable jurisdictions ought to question dominant prohibitionist narratives. When human rights are at stake the courts should not automatically be hindered by the criminalising underpinnings of the drug control regime.

Even when judges do engage in a normative reasoning process, Chapters 4 and 5 reveal that a human rights adjudication process typically involves consequentialist as opposed to deontological reasoning, which can allow judges to hide behind a legal veil of objectivity. By accepting the criminalising ontology of the drug control regime, judges run the risk of weighing *perceived* notions of 'harm' and 'risk' too heavily in favour of the state, who retain a monopoly on the morality of drug use through implementing the global policy of drug prohibition. The *Taylor* case provides a useful example to reinforce this point (see Chapter 5). When determining whether the limitations on the Rastafari defendant's religious rights to consume cannabis were necessary and proportionate to the aims pursued by prohibition, this decision was made solely by reference to public interest concerns, which were substantiated via the existence of the UN drug conventions. Relying on consequentialist reasoning alone can bolster core value-based convictions; helping judges to construct worst-case scenarios, which fail to reflect the reality of lived experience when consuming psychoactives.

Accordingly, this book highlighted the value of exploring both deontological and consequentialist arguments in a clear transparent manner when critiquing the judicial reasoning process. This allows judges to move beyond the dominant prohibitionist paradigm – focusing solely on the harms and risks caused by psychoactives – towards acknowledging the benefits psychoactives can have for the individual and for society more broadly as well. Case law which questions dominant state narratives on prohibition can help us to develop an alternative moral policy response, by unpacking societal values and questioning the interests a state actually represents.

One of the most interesting findings from the book is the fact that a human rights lens can fundamentally provide a new perspective on drug control, even while operating within the prevailing prohibitionist paradigm. Hence, a human rights lens has a transformative capacity to alter the drug control system as it presently stands. The religious ayahuasca and peyote cases, the medical cannabis case law in Canada and the US, and the reliance upon broader autonomy-based arguments in Mexico and South Africa evidence the potential for human rights to change drug policy and to facilitate more normative ways of thinking about drugs.

While there is little doubt that the judicial limb does have strong potential to influence drug policies in some liberal democracies, the fact remains that drug policy is inherently political and engaging in deontological and consequentialist reasoning to change our moral policy response to drug use can only go so far (for some people using some substances in some jurisdictions). Despite the overwhelming evidence from the reform camp documenting the failings of the prohibitionist regime, for the most part, the status quo still remains. One of the reasons for this is the failure of social scientists, in particular, to take normative thinking – questioning the way the world ought to be – very seriously (Braithwaite, 2000).

It is crucial then to move beyond the judicial remit and to incorporate the normative thinking embraced throughout this book into the drug policy making process – in order to develop an alternative moral policy response to drug control issues. The idea that the policy of drug prohibition is fully representative of a state exemplifying the interests and values of all its citizenry is inevitably a fallacy. Human drug use is a far more common and complex phenomenon than is understood under a prohibitionist paradigm, with benefits as well as risks attached. It is therefore important to unpack any assumptions about the values a society might have, and drug policy reformers ought to shape and elucidate such values, alongside presenting any empirical evidence which favours reform.

Drug policy reformers can then help to develop an alternative moral policy response to drug control issues. This should constitute a key aspect of the reform agenda, since what a society believes to be morally right often overrides any empirical evidence presented to them (Haidt, 2012; Rolles, 2017; Bone and de Hoedt, 2018). By arguing from a position of moral authority, prohibitionists have had an advantage for decades. One way to displace the moralistic approach adopted by the state, to test whether the state is truly representing the interests and values of a society here, is to question the 'evidence-based policy' (EBP) paradigm in drug policy – what constitutes 'evidence' and who gets to speak with any authority? This book reiterates that the medical establishment and law enforcement bodies, who help comprise 'the state' have the most power in drug policy making, legitimising a social control agenda which perceives those who consume drugs to be bad or sick or both (Tupper, 2012; Stevens, 2017).

By focusing on the relationship between the state and the individual, a human rights lens can confront these structures of power and privilege, and challenge the natural order of things (see Goodhart, 2014). Fundamentally, drug policy issues are normative and deeply political. Thus, a more nuanced understanding of the relationship between politics, public engagement and evidence needs to be developed than the typical 'EBP' espoused at present. A human rights lens capable of transcending the 'objective' evidence utilised in drug policy could therefore 'marry the goals of transparency and democratic accountability with respect for logic and evidence' (MacGregor, Singleton and Trautmann, 2014: 934). A more participatory, inclusive approach to drug policy making is needed to shift the balance of power in order to reconcile democracy and inclusiveness with the utilisation of knowledge and expertise (Roberts, 2014). A human rights perspective could reconcile this need for democracy and expertise, by openly addressing the relative weight accorded to different types of benefit and harm within both a consequentialist and a deontological remit to develop an alternative moral policy response to prohibition (see 'The case for broader participation' section for more detail).

The politicisation of the human rights and drug control systems

To deepen our understanding of the role of politics in drug policy making, it is also necessary to acknowledge the politicisation of the human rights and drug control systems. As highlighted throughout Chapters 1–3, the forces of globalisation have led to a waning of national political power. This has led to an increased level of uncertainty around the globe and a retreat to particularistic positions, which ground a sense of identity for people. This rise of ideological nationalism has stoked partisan politics and has led to a growing resistance to transnational forms of governance.

International human rights bodies, for instance, are increasingly perceived as lacking a clear democratic mandate. The UK serves as a particularly useful example here, as there are calls to repeal the HRA and withdraw from the ECHR once the Brexit process is complete. The fantastical promise of national restoration and of 'taking back control' in the Brexit vote leave campaign, complements the idea that the ECHR is a foreign construction and that it should not be incorporated into our domestic legislation via the HRA (see Chapters 1–3 for more detail). At the time of writing, the current UK human rights architecture is thought to undermine democratic accountability to the public, and predominately protect criminals, terrorists and people perceived to be 'not like us' (see Chapters 1 and 3).

Acknowledging the politicisation of the international and domestic human rights regime is essential. Although this book shows that both the human rights and drug control regimes are regulated by flexible, organic instruments which for the most part are legally compatible, the politicisation of the human rights framework demonstrates the limitations in trying to change drug policy, and alter our perspective on drug control issues through human rights case law alone. This is especially the case if the general public are becoming increasingly hostile to the whole idea of human rights.

It is also worth noting that the international and domestic (UK) drug control system can be politicised as well. The prohibitory controls in the early and mid-20th century developed from powerful economic and geopolitical interests, with the US emerging as the dominant political power, bestowing a moral authority over the arbitrary distinction between illicit and licit drugs. For decades, judges have applied international drug control law, via domestic legislation in the courts, more recently acknowledging the racist and irrational origins of these laws (*Prince and Others*, 2017, 2018). Chapters 4 and 5 evidenced how the moralistic, politicised nature of the drug control regime has affected the way in which some judges have weighed competing human rights considerations in the case law.

Closer to home, the UK's Psychoactive Substances Act (2016) (PSA) provided a more recent example of how the politicised, arbitrary distinction between licit/illicit drugs continues to pervade. Imposing a blanket ban on any 'non-exempted' psychoactive substance is inherently moralistic, since the PSA is not even premised on the consequentialist idea of reducing harm; rather the Act bans everything not expressly allowed by the government. There was an abject failure to account for the relationship between politics, public engagement and evidence during this policy making process. The government initially failed to consult their own experts, the ACMD, when drafting the PSA, and the general public were not consulted.

Despite the politicisation of human rights and drug control laws, there is considerable wriggle room to legally interpret the drug control framework in a way that is dynamic and human rights-based. As detailed in Chapter 3, the latitude afforded to state parties to the UN drug conventions allows for all psychoactives to be decriminalised for personal use, an array of harm reduction measures and national wiggle room to legally implement regulatory policies for health purposes given the *telos* and the utilitarian objective and purpose of the three UN conventions. A legal regulatory framework can also be implemented for psychoactives used for 'religious', 'magical' and 'traditional' purposes without contravening the UN conventions (see Article 14(2) the 1988 convention and Article 32(4) the 1971 convention), and Chapters 4 and 5 illustrate the definitional breadth of what can constitute a human right to 'health' and 'religion'. From a purely legal standpoint then, there is considerable legal room for human rights to be used to change the prohibitionist status quo. But of course, in practice, the broad flexibility and the organic nature of the human rights and drug control frameworks can have a limited impact, due to the politicisation of both systems.

Moreover, the UN conventions do not allow state parties to implement legal regulatory frameworks for controlled substances used for non-medical purposes outside of a religious or traditional setting. As explained in Chapters 3–5, it is clear that any regulatory exceptions beyond medical, religious or traditional use can only apply to possession alone. As such, a legal regulatory framework for the recreational use of any psychoactive controlled by the UN conventions does not comply with international law.

For some politicians and drug policy reformers, this does not pose too much of a problem. At the time of writing Canada, Uruguay and several US states have created a legal regulatory framework for the recreational use of cannabis, with more countries expected to follow soon. However, an awareness of the politicisation of the human rights regime, in particular, emphasises the dangers of ignoring international law. If we perceive international law as an ideology, which sustains the structure of the international political order, then it does not matter whether or not the ideology is true. What matters is that the ideology is accepted by states to legitimise the wielding of international power (Scott, 1994; see also Chapter 2). Thus, it is a belief in the *idea* of the international political order which is of paramount importance here. Hence, the international system of human rights which is reciprocally intertwined with domestic systems of rights (see Chapter 3) could be weakened further if states disregard their treaty obligations under international law.

This does not mean that we should allow states to blindly follow and implement the international global system of drug prohibition without critique. On the contrary, this book highlights how drug control laws can be interpreted in a way that is human rights-based, and the potential and limitations of applying human rights law to drug control cases in domestic courts, and in comparable jurisdictions outside of the UK. To prevent weakening the ideology of international law, which includes the protection of human rights, Chapter 3 proposed that states could adopt *inter se* modification. This approach involves two or more countries creating a mini-treaty between themselves to regulate cannabis or any other controlled psychoactive in a way which still adheres to the *telos* of the UN drug conventions; by promoting the health and welfare of humankind (see Jelsma et al., 2018 for a detailed overview).

Ultimately, through exploring the politicisation of both the human rights and drug control systems we can understand that drug policy is inherently political, and that the growing resistance to human rights is due to a perceived lack of democratic accountability to the public. In a UK context, there is also a perception that the rights of the least popular members of society are prioritised, which further entrenches the populist hostility to the idea of human rights (see Chapters 1 and 3). Since human rights are thought to have their strongest appeal when they are understood as benefitting individuals against the exercise of public power, Wicks, Ziegler and Hodson (2015) suggest building a human rights culture of substantive and constructive debate, to develop an educated, informed approach in relation to the concept of human rights.

With that in mind then, I would argue that there is a need to facilitate a more inclusive, democratic approach to drug policy making which could give effect to the 'general will' of the people, thereby responding to the growing resistance to transnational forms of governance. The notion of populism can be freed from its right-wing nationalistic connotations, by giving people the opportunity to contribute to the drug policy making process in order to develop drug policies which are grounded in human rights. This could then challenge the politicisation of the human rights and drug control regimes, from the bottom up.

The case for broader democratic participation

> 'Criminalizing conduct, as we currently do so readily in this area, can only ever be justified if it can be shown to enhance civic freedom in a significant way. The more general point is that rather than making law enforcement one of the centrepieces of policy, we should be building serious normative thinking into our regulatory design right from the start. And this will involve engaging in a proper dialogue with citizens so that policy is the transparent outcome of deep contestation within deliberative democracies'. (Seddon, 2013: 17 paraphrasing Braithwaite, 2008: 199–207)

Since there is a clear disconnect between politics, public engagement and the evidence in the drug policy making process, there exists a growing body of literature within drug policy scholarship which recognises the value of a more participatory, inclusive approach to policy making. This could help to legitimise drug policy outcomes, reflecting 'the general will of the people', by balancing the need for democracy with respect for knowledge and evidence. A democratic participatory approach to drug policy making could also challenge dominant state narratives on the morality of drug use, by elevating the voices of people who use drugs and the voices of other citizens.

While it is tempting to think that the emotional and value-driven aspects of drug policy can be resolved by appealing to 'EBP' alone, this is an illusion. As highlighted, the EBP paradigm is not free from ideology. Some voices thought to comprise the 'state' (i.e. law enforcement bodies and the medical establishment) are privileged over others, and these voices could be constrained by the moralistic, criminal underpinnings of the drug control regime. Integrating democratic participatory approaches within drug policy making could therefore help to develop an alternative moral policy response to prohibition, and respond to the broader social and political context which has led to the increased politicisation of human rights.

Democratic participation and deliberative democracy is a popular and growing field within the political science literature (Bächtiger et al., 2018) and drug policy researchers are beginning to recognise the potential of broader democratic participation (Ritter, Lancaster and Diprose, 2018, Askew and Bone, 2019). According to Ritter, Lancaster and Diprose (ibid: 2), the goal of deliberative democracy is move beyond raw public opinion, by creating an 'inclusive, democratic, deliberative and thoughtful process of political decision-making on drug policy in order to give voice to "the people"'. Deliberative democracy requires rational and reasoned modes of communication, where the force of the better argument wins the day (ibid). Forums for deliberative democracy include deliberative polling, consensus conferences, roundtables, summits, citizen's juries and citizen's assemblies.

A deliberative forum could therefore offer the space for citizens to debate some of the key drug control issues explored throughout this book including (but by no means limited to):

- The availability and accessibility of medicines (especially cannabis);
- psychedelic spirituality and therapy;
- The multiple purposes of drug use;
- The limits and the potential of the law for implementing regulatory alternatives to prohibition;
- The role of the state in protecting us from drug-related harm;
- The social utility and benefits of drug use when balanced against competing notions of 'harm' (balancing competing interests within a deontological and consequentialist remit).

A mock court trial could also provide another interesting forum for citizens (and possibly drug policy specialists, judicial bodies, policy makers and other interested stakeholders) to deliberate specifically on the human rights case law examples highlighted throughout this book, or on other hypothetical scenarios. Judicial balancing tests could ensure that deliberation on case law examples remains rational and reasoned, where state and individual interests are balanced explicitly from a deontological and consequentialist perspective. Indeed, judges, policy makers and drug policy specialists are not uniquely competent to determine the normative value that ought to be accorded to different types of harm and benefit when assessing the goals of drug policy and policy options.

As a deliberative forum, a mock court trial could be government-led, researcher-led, and/or led by drug policy organisations or other interested stakeholders. A mock trial could culminate in recommendations to parliament, it could involve researchers or other interested stakeholders creating a broader dissemination event to share their findings and influence public policy, and/or it could have more localised implications by challenging the participants' views on drug control issues, increasing their confidence in legal institutions and their understanding of human rights law in the UK. Research has also shown that jury deliberations can actually work to promote civic engagement by reinforcing confidence in fellow citizens and in public institutions (Gastil et al., 2008).

An example of a successful government-led deliberative forum is the Irish Citizens' Assembly which encouraged debate, knowledge exchange and political change; the Assembly made recommendations to parliament, based on its deliberations, ahead of Ireland's abortion referendum in 2018 (Suiter, 2018). A deliberative forum could also be led by researchers to better engage people who use drugs in drug policy. Alongside Dr Rebecca Askew, I am carrying out a research project which aims to understand drug consumers' knowledge of drug policy and legislation, and examine how incorporating their perspectives into reform discussions and the evidence base might contribute to more informed and effective drug policies in the UK (Economic and Social Research Council: ES/R007225/1). As part of the project, educational deliberative workshops will be developed with drug policy organisations in the UK – Transform, Release and the Beckley Foundation – since there is a lack of clarity surrounding drug policy terms and alternative policy approaches (Askew and Bone, 2019).

A deliberative forum could also operate at an international level. Building on the more inclusive UNGASS 2016 process, the Independent Civil Society Task Force on Drugs served as the official liaison between the United Nations and civil society for the ministerial segment of the 62nd session of the CND (Commission on Narcotic Drugs, 2019: E/CN.7/2019/CRP.7). This infrastructure could therefore be increasingly used to promote a deliberative dialogue between national publics, civil society organisations and international drug policy and human rights bodies.

The value of rational, reasoned modes of communication, offered within a deliberative forum is particularly important in an age where ignorance – regarding what is considered to be established knowledge in public policy, is increasingly being perceived as an actual virtue (Nichols, 2017). According to Nichols (ibid), rejecting the advice of experts is a way for people to assert their autonomy by challenging nefarious elites. The current populist movement has brought to the fore a counter-politics of expertise, and with that a political elitism that the public do not know what is good for them (Clarke and Newman, 2017). Delegating drug policy to the 'experts' promotes citizen ignorance further and 'provokes a reciprocal disdain of experts on the part of citizens' (Ritter, Lancaster and Diprose, 2018: 2 citing Mansbridge et al., 2010: 14). Inclusive, rational, deliberative approaches promoted by deliberative democracy could therefore serve to mitigate against this impasse.

Nevertheless, there are limitations regarding what deliberative democracy can offer, since the focus on reasoned deliberation within specific deliberative forums could constrain the very participation being sought (ibid). Deliberative forums could engage in practices which seek to control the policy agenda since rational modes of communication can privilege scientific, political and/or legal modes of thinking (e.g. through deductive reasoning, principles of objectivity, legal principles, etc.) (ibid). Deliberative forums could also be funded by organisations to promote a particular agenda. Therefore, other forms of participatory democracy which engage with multiple modes of communication (i.e. through storytelling or protests), and include non-deliberative forms of action such as activism (i.e. through the CSC model), should also be explored, to widen participation in the future.

Lancaster, Ritter and Diprose (2018) also highlight the importance of creating space and opportunity for the *co-production* of knowledge, by focusing on the *process* of participation, and scrambling the divisions between experts and laypersons, in order for new knowledge to emerge to identify drug policy problems and solutions. To avoid a tokenistic consultation, based only on experts advocating preconceived ideas about drug policy, Askew and Bone (2019) suggest addressing specific social representations within participatory approaches rooted in: health and welfare, harm reduction, human rights, the economy and sanctioning – to tease out the key issues and ideological positions – rather than being too prescriptive by asking people to choose a particular policy approach. Indeed, the perspectives of people who use drugs on UK drug policy and the law can be diverse and complex (ibid). While meaningful participation rests on understanding the various philosophical positions which typically underpin drug policy debates (see also Chapter 2), these positions are not mutually exclusive. People who use drugs drew from a combination of consequentialist and deontological perspectives to shape their views on drug policy, which both challenged and internalised prohibitionist ideology (ibid).

Ultimately, a human rights perspective complements the case for broader participatory approaches in drug policy making. The appeal of human rights, as exemplified throughout this book, is that they are normative and political in their character. Human rights are designed to challenge traditional hierarchies and power structures and they are concerned with enhancing freedom and equality for all.

Directions for future research

Future academic research in this area could build on the findings in this book by questioning the narrow conceptions of, and the posited divisions between human rights to 'health' and religion', as applied to drug control. If researchers were to move beyond arbitrary categorisations of human rights, towards more accurately reflecting the motivations and experiences of drug use, and the interconnected significance an individual can accord their drug use, then more nuanced regulatory ideas could result. In a similar vein, future research ought to explore the viability of autonomy-based claims further, since such arguments could be more appropriate when reflecting the genuine motivations for human drug use.

Since autonomy-based arguments threaten prohibitionist ideology to the greatest degree (see 'Challenging the ideology of prohibition' subsection), researchers could contextualise the viability of these arguments in different jurisdictions and for different substances. Though this book reveals the potential of human rights case law to transform and develop drug policies, this only works in relation to some drugs, in some jurisdictions and for some drug-using purposes. A more detailed exploration of a jurisdiction's legal, socio-political, economic and cultural context could perhaps go some way towards highlighting the potential and the limitations of applying more nuanced and evolving human rights arguments to drug control case law. In a UK context, doctrinal researchers could explore the potential of using Article 8(1) ECHR to determine whether the UK has provided an accessible and effective procedure to establish whether a patient can qualify for medical cannabis under UK law.

Correspondingly, future doctrinal research could investigate the extent to which the UK judiciary is constrained by the criminalising underpinnings of the drug control regime, and study whether this situation uniquely applies to the drug control sphere, or whether criminalisation acts as a barrier for the UK judiciary when assessing an individual's human rights claims in other legal areas; especially in comparison with other jurisdictions. Case law which engages in normative reasoning and questions dominant state narratives on prohibition and its criminogenic ontology can be used to unpack societal values and question the interests a state actually represents.

In moving beyond the judicial remit, future research could develop an alternative moral policy response to prohibition, by advocating for broader participatory approaches to drug policy making, and it could consider the ability of such approaches to reconcile the need for democracy and expertise. The politicisation of both the drug control and human rights regimes reveals a disconnect between politics and public engagement, and an increasing populist hostility to the idea of human rights and transnational governance – particularly within a UK context. To shore up a belief in the idea of the international political order (which includes the protection of human rights), future research could investigate ways to prevent states disregarding their treaty obligations under international law, and this could include exploring the applicability of *inter se* modification of the UN drug conventions.

While the courts can potentially play an important role for citizens in the development and reform of drug policy, in practice judges can often be constrained procedurally, legally and politically. Therefore, the broader perspective that I've developed, by contextualising human rights philosophically, politically and legally when applied to drug policy, offers a more nuanced way to think about drug control issues; providing a new perspective on drug control. Through employing a human rights perspective, this book seeks to open a dialogue to rethink drug policies in a more thoroughgoing and potentially radical way, so that we no longer have to be so constricted by the drug prohibition paradigm.

Bibliography

Advisory Council on the Misuse of Drugs, n.d. *About us.* [Online]. Available at: https://www.gov.uk/government/organisations/advisory-council-on-the-misuse-of-drugs/about [Accessed 27th November 2018].

Aguilar, S., Gutiérrez, V., Sánchez, L. and Nougier, M., 2018. *Medicinal cannabis policies and practices around the world (April 2018).* IDPC Briefing Paper. London: International Drug Policy Consortium Publication.

Ahdar, R. and Leigh, I., 2005. *Religious freedom in the liberal state.* Oxford: Oxford University Press.

Alder, J., 2006. The sublime and the beautiful: Incommensurability and human rights. *Public Law*, 4(Winter), 697–721.

Alexander, L. and Moore, M., 2012. Deontological ethics. *The Stanford Encyclopedia of Philosophy.* [Online]. Available at: http://plato.stanford.edu/entries/ethics-deontological/ [Accessed 9th May 2019].

Alexandrescu, L., 2017. Ethnobotanicals' and 'spice zombies': New psychoactive substances in the mainstream media. *Drugs: Education, Prevention and Policy*, 25(4), 356–364.

Alexy, R., 2003. Constitutional rights, balancing and rationality. *Ratio Juris*, 16(2), 131–140.

Arlacchi, P., 1998. *United Nations General Assembly Special Session (UNGASS) on the world drug problem.* [Online]. Available at: http://www.un.org/ga/20special/ [Accessed 2nd November 2018].

Arnao, G., 1990. The semantics of prohibition: The language of the UN. *The International Journal of Drug Policy*, 2(1), 31–33.

Arnott, D., 2017. The impact diverging public opinion on cannabis and tobacco regulation has on constructive engagement between advocates. *Addiction*, 113, 605–606.

Askew, R. and Bone, M., (2019). Deconstructing prohibitionist ideology: A sociocognitive approach to understand opinions on UK drug policy and the law. *International Journal of Drug Policy*, 74, 33–40.

Asthana, A. and Mason, R., 2016. UK must leave European convention on human rights, says Theresa May. *The Guardian.* [Online]. Available at: https://www.theguardian.com/politics/2016/apr/25/uk-must-leave-european-convention-on-human-rights-theresa-may-eu-referendum [Accessed 9th May 2019].

Babor, T.F., Caulkins, J.P., Edwards, G., Fischer, B., Foxcroft, D.R., Humphreys, K., Obot, I.S., Rehm, J., Reuter, P., Room, R., Rossow I. and Strang, J., 2010. *Drug policy and the public good*. New York: Oxford University Press.

Bache, I. and Flinders, M., 2004. Multi-level governance and British politics. *Public Policy and Administration*, 19(1), 31–51.

Bächtiger, A., Dryzek, J.S., Mansbridge, J. and Warren, M.E., 2018. *The Oxford handbook of deliberative democracy*. Oxford: Oxford University Press.

Bakalar, J. and Grinspoon, L., 1984. *Drug control in a free society*. Cambridge: Cambridge University Press.

Ballotta, D., Bergeron, H. and Hughes, B., 2008. Cannabis control in Europe. *In*: S.R. Sznitman, B. Olsson and R. Room, eds. *A cannabis reader: Global issues and local experiences, European Monitoring Centre for Drugs and Drug Addiction*. Lisbon: EMCDDA, 99–117.

Bancroft, A., 2009. *Drugs, intoxication and society*. Cambridge, MA: Polity Press.

Barber, B., 1995. *Jihad vs. McWorld*. New York: Ballantine Books.

Barrett, D., 2008. *'Unique in international relations'? A comparison of the international narcotics control board and the UN human rights treaty bodies*. London: International Harm Reduction Association.

Barrett, D., 2012. When the UN won't condemn torture you know something's very wrong. *Huffpost*. [Online]. Available at: https://www.huffingtonpost.co.uk/damon-barett/when-the-un-wont-condemn-torture_b_1398946.html?guccounter=1 [Accessed 20th June 2019].

Barrett, D., Lines, R., Schleifer, R., Elliot, R. and Bewley-Taylor, D., 2008. *Recalibrating the regime: The need for a human rights-based approach to international drug policy*. Beckley Foundation Drug Policy Programme, International Harm Reduction Association, Human Rights Watch, Canadian HIV/AIDS Legal Network. [Online]. Available at: http://www.hrw.org/sites/default/files/related_material/beckley0308exec.pdf [Accessed 31st October 2018].

Barrett, D. and Nowak, M., 2009. The United Nations and drug policy: Towards a human rights-based approach. *In*: A. Constantinides and N. Zaikos, eds. *The diversity of international law. Essays in honour of Professor Kalliopi K. Koufa*. Leiden: Martinus Nijhoff Publishers, Brill Academic Publishing, 449–477.

Barrett, L., 1977. *The Rastafarians*. Boston, MA: Beacon Press.

Bates, E., 2018. History. *In*: D. Moeckli, S. Shah and S. Sivakumaran, eds. *International human rights law*, 3rd ed. Oxford: Oxford University Press, 3–21.

Bauman, Z., 1988. *Freedom*. Milton Keynes: Open University Press.

BBC, 2012a. *Dolphins deserve the same rights as humans say scientists*. [Online]. Available at: http://www.bbc.co.uk/news/world-17116882 [Accessed 25th April 2019].

BBC, 2012b. *Rights gone wrong*. [Online]. Available at: http://www.bbc.co.uk/programmes/b01dk5s9 [Accessed 24th April 2019].

Beck, G., 2008. Human rights adjudication under the ECHR: Between value pluralism and essential contestability. *European Human Rights Law Review*, 2, 214–244.

Bedi, S., 2007. What is so special about religion? The dilemma of the religious exemption. *Journal of Political Philosophy*, 15(2), 235–249.

Bentham, J., 1843. Anarchical fallacies. *In*: J. Bowring, ed. vol. II. *The works of Jeremy Bentham*. Edinburgh: William Tait, 489–535.

Berlin, I., 1969. Two concepts of liberty. *In*: I. Berlin, ed. *Four essays on liberty*. Oxford: Oxford University Press, 118–172.

Bewley-Taylor, D., 2012. *International drug control: Consensus fractured.* Cambridge: Cambridge University Press.

Bewley-Taylor, D. and Jelsma, M., 2011. *Fifty years of the 1961 single convention on narcotic drugs: A reinterpretation.* Transnational Institute, Series on Legislative Reform of Drug Policies. Number 12, March 2011. [Online]. Available at: https://www.tni.org/files/download/dlr12.pdf [Accessed 21st October 2018].

Bewley-Taylor, D. and Jelsma, M., 2012. *The UN drug control conventions: The limits of latitude.* Transnational Institute, Series on Legislative Reform of Drug Policies. Number 18, March 2012. [Online]. Available at: http://www.druglawreform.info/images/stories/documents/dlr18.pdf [Accessed 21st October 2018].

Bewley-Taylor, D. and Hallam, C., 2019. *The 2019 commission on narcotic drugs and its ministerial segment: Taking stock of the implementation of the commitments made to jointly address and counter the world drug problem, in particular in light of the 2019 target date.* International Drug Policy Consortium, June 2019. [Online]. Available at: http://fileserver.idpc.net/library/CND-Proceedings-Report_2019.pdf [Accessed 20th June 2019].

Bewley-Taylor, D. and Trace, M., 2006. *The International Narcotics Control Board: Watchdog or Guardian of the UN Drug Conventions?* The Beckley Foundation Drug Policy Programme, Report 7th February. [Online]. Available at: http://www.beckleyfoundation.org/pdf/Report_07.pdf [Accessed 27th January 2018].

Bilder, R.B., 2004. An overview of international human rights law. *In*: H. Hannum, ed. *Guide to international human rights practice*, 4th ed. University of Wisconsin Legal Studies Research Paper Series: Transnational Publishers, 3–18. https://papers.ssrn.com/sol3/papers.cfm?abstract_id=1641167

Blainey, M.G., 2013. *A ritual key to mystical solutions: Ayahuasca therapy, secularism and the Santo Daime religion in Belgium.* Ph.D. Department of Anthropology, Tulane University, New Orleans, LA.

Blainey, M.G., 2015. Forbidden therapies: Santo Daime, ayahuasca, and the prohibition of entheogens in Western society. *Journal of Religion & Health*, 54(1), 287–302.

Blickman, T., 2017. Letter in response to John Collins, "Losing UNGASS? Lessons from civil society, past and present", *Drugs and Alcohol Today*, 17(3), 143–144.

Blum, R., 1969. *Society and drugs.* San Francisco, CA: Jossey Bass.

Boire, R.G., 1999/2000. On cognitive liberty (Part I). *Journal of Cognitive Liberties*, 1(1), 7–13.

Boire, R.G., 2000. On cognitive liberty (Part II). *Journal of Cognitive Liberties*, 2(1), 7–20.

Boire, R.G., 2003a. On cognitive liberty (Part IV). *Journal of Cognitive Liberties*, 4(1), 15–24.

Boire, R.G., 2003b. *Medical marijuana and cognitive liberty: First amendment implications of marijuana legislation.* Center for Cognitive Liberty & Ethics. [Online]. Available at: http://www.cognitiveliberty.org/dll/mj2003_rpt.html [Accessed 28th October 2018].

Boister, N., 2001. *Penal aspects of the UN drug conventions.* The Hague: Kluwer.

Boister, N. and Jelsma, M., 2018. *Inter se* modification of the UN drug control conventions: An exploration of its applicability to legitimise the legal regulation of cannabis markets. *International Community Law Review*, 20(5), 456–492.

Boiteux, L., Peluzio, L. and Souza Alves, C., 2014. Human rights and drug conventions: Searching for humanitarian reason in drug laws. *In*: B.C. Labate and C. Cavnar, eds. *Prohibition, religious freedom, and human rights: Regulating traditional drug use*. Berlin, Heidelberg: Springer-Verlag, 1–25.

Bone, M., 2014a. From the sacrilegious to the sacramental: A global review of Rastafari cannabis case law. *In*: B.C. Labate and C. Cavnar, eds. *Prohibition, religious freedom, and human rights: Regulating traditional drug use*. Berlin, Heidelberg: Springer-Verlag, 89–109.

Bone, M., 2014b. Is the medicinal consumption of cannabis effectively regulated from a human rights perspective? *In*: P. Mungroo, Y. Ping and M. Bone, eds. *Cannabis regulation: The world is moving forward what is stopping us?* London: House of Lords, 28–35. [Online]. Available at: http://www.cannabisresearch.co.uk/ [Accessed 1st May 2018].

Bone, M., 2017. *Human rights, politics and power: The case of the UK's cannabis social club movement*. Paper presented at the 11th International Society of Drug Policy (ISSDP) conference, May 2017, Aarhus; Paper presented at Breaking Convention conference, June 2017, Greenwich. [Online]. Available at: https://www.youtube.com/watch?v=YHrXH01AHsU [Accessed 25th January 2019].

Bone, M. and de Hoedt, G., 2018. Being the change: Charting Greg de Hoedt's cannabis journey. *Drugs and Alcohol Today*, 18(2), 126–136.

Bone, M., Potter, G. and Klein, A., 2018. Introduction: Cultivation, medication, activism and cannabis policy. *Drugs and Alcohol Today*, 18(2), 73–79.

Bone, M. and Seddon, T., 2015. Human rights, public health and medicinal cannabis use. *Critical Public Health*, 26(1), 51–61.

Bonello, G., 2005. The European Court of human rights. *In*: R.K.M., Smith and C. van den Anker, eds. *The essentials of human rights*, 1st ed. London: Hodder Arnold, 115–118.

Boorse, C., 1975. On the distinction between disease and illness. *Philosophy and Public Affairs*, 5(1), 49–68.

Braithwaite, J., 2000. Republican theory and crime control. *In*: S. Karstedt and K.D. Bussmann, eds. *Social dynamics of crime and control: New theories for a world in transition*. Oxford: Hart.

Braithwaite, J. and Drahos, P., 2000. *Global business regulation*. Cambridge: Cambridge University Press.

Bremmer, I., 2010. *The end of the free market: Who wins the war between states and corporations?* London: Penguin Books Ltd.

Brems, E., 2009. Human rights: Minimum and maximum perspectives. *Human Rights Law Review*, 9(3), 349–372.

Brenner, N., Jessop, B., Jones, M. and MacLeod, G., 2003. Introduction: State space in question. *In*: N. Brenner, B. Jessop, M. Jones and G. MacLeod, eds. *State/space: A reader*. Oxford: Blackwell, 1–27.

British Paediatric Neurology Association, 2018. *Guidance on the use of cannabis-based products for medicinal use in children and young people with epilepsy (31 October 2018)*. [Online]. Available at: https://www.bpna.org.uk/userfiles/BPNA_CBPM_Guidance_Oct2018.pdf [Accessed 11th June 2019].

Bromley, P.E., 2008. *Human rights and the League of Nations: How ideas about human rights came to be included in the Charter and work of the League of Nations*. Proceedings of the annual meeting of the Western Political Science Association, Manchester Hyatt, San Diego, CA, 20th March 2008. [Online]. Available at: http://citation.allacademic.com/meta/p_mla_apa_research_citation/2/3/7/9/4/p237945_index.html [Accessed 14th April 2018].

Brown, C., 1999. Universal human rights: A critique. *In*: T. Dunne and N.J. Wheeler, eds. *Human rights in global politics*. Cambridge: Cambridge University Press, 103–127.

Buchanan, A., 2008. Human rights and the legitimacy of the international order. *Legal Theory*, 14(1), 39–70.

Bunton, R. and Coveney, J., 2011. Drugs' pleasures. *Critical Public Health*, 21(1), 9–23.

Burgess, N., 2016. The lost symbol: A semiotic analysis of the Psychoactive Substances Act 2016. *Aberdeen Student Law Review*, 7(1), 109–120.

Burke, P., 1990. Rank the reactionary. *In*: G.G. Iggers and J.M. Powell, eds. *Leopold von Ranke and the shaping of the historical discipline*. New York: Syracuse, 36–44.

Burnett, J., 1999. *Liquid pleasures: A social history of drinks in modern Britain*. London: Routledge.

Buxton, J., 2006. *The political economy of narcotics: Production consumption and global markets*. London: Zed Books Ltd.

Buxton, J., 2008. *The historical foundations of the narcotic drug control regime*. Policy research working paper 4553. The World Bank Development Research Group, World Bank Publications. [Online]. Available at: https://play.google.com/books/reader?id=c_5JlcnddHkC&printsec=frontcover&output=reader&hl=en&pg=GBS.PA3.w.0.9.0 [Accessed 3rd May 2019].

Buxton, J., 2011. Introduction. *In*: J. Buxton, ed. *The politics of narcotic drugs: A survey*, 1st ed. London: Routledge, 3–8.

Carter, I., 2012. Positive and negative liberty. *The Stanford Encyclopedia of Philosophy*. [Online]. Available at: http://plato.stanford.edu/entries/liberty-positive-negative/ [Accessed 10th April 2019].

Chapman, A.R., 2017. Can human rights standards help protect children and youth from the detrimental impact of alcohol beverage marketing and promotional activities? *Addiction*, 112(Suppl. 1), 117–121.

Clapham, A., 2015. *Human rights: A very short introduction*, 2nd ed. Oxford: Oxford University Press.

Clarke, J. and Newman, J., 2017. 'People in this country have had enough of experts': Brexit and the paradoxes of populism. *Critical Policy Studies*, 11, 101–116.

Coggon, J., 2012. *What makes health public? A critical evaluation of moral, legal, and political claims in public health*. Cambridge: Cambridge University Press.

Cohen, P., 2003. The drug prohibition church and the adventure of reformation. *International Journal of Drug Policy*, 14(2), 213–215.

Conners, P., 2010. *White hand society: The psychedelic partnership of Timothy Leary and Allen Ginsberg*. San Francisco, CA: City Lights Books.

Conrad, P. and Barker, K.K., 2010. The social construction of illness: Key insights and policy implications. *Journal of Health and Social Behaviour*, 51(S), S67–S79.

Coomber, R., Oliver, M. and Morris, C., 2003. Using cannabis therapeutically in the UK: A qualitative analysis. *Journal of Drug Issues*, 33(2), 325–356.

Courtwright, D.T., 2002. *Forces of habit: Drugs and the making of the modern world*. Cambridge, MA: Harvard University Press.

Courtwright, D.T., 2005. Mr ATOD's wild ride: What do alcohol, tobacco and other drugs have in common? *The Social History of Alcohol and Drugs*, 20(1), 105–140.

Csete, J., 2012. *Overhauling oversight: Human rights at the INCB*. LSE Ideas: Governing the Global Drug Wars, Special Report 2012. [Online]. Available at: http://www2.lse.ac.uk/IDEAS/publications/reports/pdf/SR014/Csete_Joanne.pdf [Accessed 29th January 2019].

Csordas, T. and Kleinman, A., 1996. The therapeutic process. *In*: T. Johnson and C. Sargent, eds. *Medical Anthropology*. New York: Praeger.

Dasgupta, R., 2018. The demise of the nation state. *The Guardian*. [Online]. Available at: https://www.theguardian.com/news/2018/apr/05/demise-of-the-nation-state-rana-dasgupta [Accessed 16th April 2019].

Davidson, B., 2017. Storytelling and evidence-based policy: Lessons from the grey literature. *Palgrave Communications*, 3, 17093.

Decorte, T., Pardal, M., Parés, Ò., Bone, M. and Johansson, J., (forthcoming). Mapping cannabis social clubs in Europe. *European Journal of Criminology*.

Dembour, M.-B., 2005. The European convention on human rights. *In*: R.K.M., Smith and C. van den Anker, eds. *The essentials of human rights*, 1st ed. London: Hodder Arnold, 113–115.

Dennis, F. and Farrugia, A., 2017. Materialising drugged pleasures: Practice, politics, care. *International Journal of Drug Policy*, 49: 86–91.

Denver Psilocybin Initiative, 2019. *Vote YES on I-301 Denver, CO – May 7, 2019*. [Online]. Available at: https://decriminalizedenver.org/ [Accessed 16th June 2019].

Derrida, J., 1995. The rhetoric of drugs. *In*: E. Weber, ed. *Points… Interviews 1974–94*. Stanford, CA: Stanford University Press, 228–254.

Devlin, P., 1959/1965. *The enforcement of morals*. New York: Oxford University Press.

Dicey, A.V., 1885/1959. *Introduction to the study of the law of the constitution*, 1st ed. 1885, 10th ed. 1959. London: Macmillan.

Dickson, B., 2015. Repeal the HRA and rely on the common law? *In*: K.S. Ziegler, E. Wicks and L. Hodson, eds. *The UK and European human rights: A strained relationship?* Portland, OR: Hart Publishing.

Donnelly, J., 1982. Human rights as natural rights. *Human Rights Quarterly*, 4(3), 391–405.

Donnelly, J., 2003. *Universal human rights: In theory and practice*, 2nd ed. New York: Cornell University Press.

Donnelly, J., 2007. The relative universality of human rights. *Human Rights Quarterly*, 29(2), 281–306.

Douzinas, C., 2000. *The end of human rights: Critical thought at the turn of the century*. Portland, OR: Hart Publishing.

Doward, J., 2013. Bolivians demand the right to chew coca leaves. *The Guardian*, 13 January [Online]. Available at: http://www.theguardian.com/world/2013/jan/13/bolivia-drugs-row-chew-coca [Accessed 3rd March 2017].

Dunleavy, P., 2007. The state. *In*: R.E. Goodin, P. Pettit and T. Pogge, eds. *A companion to contemporary political philosophy*, 2nd ed. Oxford: Blackwell Publishing Ltd., 793–803.

Dworkin, R., 2013. *Religion without God*. Cambridge, MA: Harvard University Press.

Dzehtsiarou, K., Lock, T., Johnson, P., de Londras, F., Greene, A. and Bates, E., 2015. *The legal implications of a repeal of the Human Rights Act 1998 and withdrawal from the European convention on human rights (May 12, 2015)*. [Online]. Available at SSRN: https://ssrn.com/abstract=2605487 [Accessed 19th June 2019].

Eastwood, N., Fox, E. and Rosmarin A., 2016. *A quiet revolution: Drug decriminalisation across the globe*. 2nd ed. London: Release.

Economic and Social Research Council, n.d. *Does UK drug policy require reform? Engaging drug takers into the debate*. Funder: Economic and Social Research Council (ESRC), Grant number: ES/R007225/1. [Online]. Available at: https://app.dimensions.ai/details/grant/grant.7611152 [Accessed 25th May 2019].

Edelstein, L., 1943. *The Hippocratic oath: Text, translation, and interpretation*. Baltimore, MD: Johns Hopkins Press.

Edge, P.W., 2006. *Religion and law: An introduction*. Aldershot: Ashgate.

Edmunson, W.A., 2004. *An introduction to rights*. Cambridge: Cambridge University Press.

Eisenberg, L., 1977. Disease and illness: Distinctions between professional and popular ideas of sickness. *Culture, Medicine and Psychiatry*, 1, 9–23.

ENCOD, 2011. *Code of conduct for European cannabis social clubs*. [Online]. Available at: http://www.encod.org/info/CODE-OF-CONDUCT-FOR-EUROPEAN.html [Accessed 25th January 2018].

Engels, F., 1875/1975. The origins of the family, private property, and the state. *In*: K. Marx and F. Engels, eds. *Collected works*, vol. 26. London: Lawrence and Wishart.

Exworthy, M., Mannion, R. and Powell, M., 2016. *Dismantling the NHS? Evaluating the impact of health reforms*. Bristol: Policy Press.

FAAAT, 2018. *Major shift in global drug policies: The human rights council catches up with the commission on narcotic drugs*. [Online]. Available at: http://faaat.net/think-tank-en/cnd61-hrc37/ [Accessed 20th June 2019].

Feeney, K. and Labate, B.C., 2013. Religious freedom and the expansion of ayahuasca ceremonies in Europe. *In*: C. Adams, D. Luke, A. Waldstein, B. Sessa and D. King, eds. *Breaking convention: Essays on psychedelic consciousness*. London: Strange Attractor Press.

Feinberg, J., 1984. *Harm to others*. New York: Oxford University Press.

Fielding, A. and Singleton, N., 2018. Roadmaps to regulation, cannabis, psychedelics, MDMA and NPS. The Beckley Foundation. [Online]. Available at: http://beckleyfoundation.org/wp-content/uploads/2016/04/RoadmapsCPMN-Summary.pdf [Accessed 18th June].

Fitzpatrick, M., 2013. Our society is hooked on harm reduction. *Spiked*. [Online]. Available at: http://www.spiked-online.com/newsite/article/11389#.Ui32NvmyApY [Accessed 1st September 2018].

Fortson, R., 2011. *Misuse of drugs and drug trafficking offences*, 6th ed. London: Sweet & Maxwell.

Fortson, R., 2016. The Psychoactive Substances Act 2016. *Criminal Law Review*, 5, 303–323.

Foucault, M., 1979. *The history of sexuality volume 1: An introduction*. London: Allen Lane.

Foucault, M., 1980. *Power/knowledge*. Brighton: Harvester.

Foucault, M., 1991. Governmentality. *In*: R. Braidotti in G. Burchell, C. Gordon and P. Miller, eds. and Trans. *The Foucault effect: Studies in governmentality*. Chicago, IL: University of Chicago Press, 87–104.

Fraser, N., 1989. *Unruly practices: Power, discourse and gender in contemporary social theory*. Minneapolis, MN: University of Minnesota Press.

Freidson, E., 1970. *Profession of medicine: A study of the sociology of applied knowledge*. New York: Harper and Row.

Gastil, J., Black, L.W., Pierre Deess, E. and Leighter, J., 2008. From group member to democratic citizen: How deliberating with fellow jurors reshapes civic attitudes. *Human Communication Research*, 34(1), 137–169.

Gerards, J. H. and Glas, L.R., 2017. Access to justice in the European convention on human rights system. *Netherlands Quarterly of Human Rights*, 35(1): 11–30.

Gies, L., 2015. Human rights, the British press and the deserving claimant. *In*: E. Wicks, K.S. Ziegler and L. Hodson, eds. *The UK and European human rights, a strained relationship?* Oxford: Hart Publishing, 473–492.

Gilmore, N., 1996. Drug use and human rights: Privacy, vulnerability, disability and human rights infringements. *Journal of Contemporary Health Law and Policy*, 12(2), 335–447.

Gimenez Corte, C., 2010. The forms of international institutional law: An historical analysis of the scheduling decisions of narcotic drugs and psychotropic substances taken by the United Nations' Commission on Narcotic Drugs. *International Organizations Law Review*, 7(1), 171–221.

Girelli, G., 2019. *The death penalty for drug offences: Global overview 2018*. London: Harm Reduction International.

Glazier, S., 2001. *Encyclopedia of African and African-American religions*. New York: Routledge.

Glendon, M.A., 1991. *Rights talk: The impoverishment of political discourse*. New York: The Free Press.

The Global Commission on Drug Policy, 2019. *Drug policy and deprivation of liberty*. Position paper. [Online]. Available at: http://www.globalcommissionondrugs.org/wp-content/uploads/2019/06/ENG-PP2019_DeprivationLiberty_WEB.pdf [Accessed 14th June 2019].

Good, C., 2010. Human rights and relativism. *Macalester Journal of Philosophy*, 19(1), Article 4, 27–52.

Goode, E., 1997. *Between politics and reason: The drug legalization debate*. New York: St. Martin's Press.

Goodhart, M., 2012. The future of human rights. *In*: M. Goodhart, ed. *Human rights: Politics and practice*, 2nd ed. Oxford: Oxford University Press.

Goodhart, M., 2014. Human rights and the politics of contestation. *In*: M. Goodale, ed. *Human Rights at the Crossroads*. Oxford: Oxford University Press.

Goodman, J., Lovejoy, P.E. and Sherratt, A. (eds.), 1995. *Consuming habits: Drugs in history and anthropology*, eds. London: Routledge.

Gregg, B., 2012. *Human rights as social construction*. Cambridge: Cambridge University Press.

Griffin, J., 2008. *On human rights*. Oxford: Oxford University Press.

Groitus, H., 1646/1925. *De jure belli ac pacis libri tres*. Trans. F. W. Kelsey, vol. 2. Oxford: Clarendon Press.

Gunn, T.J., 2003. The complexity of religion and the definition of "religion" in international law. *Harvard Human Rights Journal*, 16, 189–215.

Habermas, J., 1996. *Between facts and norms: Contributions to a discourse theory of law and democracy*. Trans. W. Rehg. Cambridge: MIT.

Haidt, J., 2012. *The righteous mind: Why good people are divided by politics and religion*. London: Penguin Books.

Haidt, J., Koller, S. and Dias, M., 1993. Affect, culture, and morality, or is it wrong to eat your dog? *Journal of Personality and Social Psychology*, 65(4), 613–628.

Hamilton, R., 2010. The concept of health: Beyond normativism and naturalism. *Journal of Evaluation in Clinical Practice*, 16(2), 323–329.

Hannum, H., 2005. The universal declaration of human rights. *In*: R.K.M. Smith and C. van den Anker, eds. *The essentials of human rights*, 1st ed. London: Hodder Arnold, 351–353.

Hardison, C., 2007. We have a problem: Part 1 – A call for a paradigm shift. *Drugs and Alcohol Today*, 7(4), 8–13.

Hardison, C., 2008. Policy forum: We have a problem: Part 2 – A call for a paradigm shift. *Drugs and Alcohol Today*, 8(2), 5–9.

Hari, J., 2015. *Chasing the scream: The first and the last days of the war on drugs*. London: Bloomsbury.

Harris, D.J., O'Boyle, M., Bates, E.P. and Buckley, C.M., 2014. *Law of the European convention on human rights*, 3rd ed. Oxford: Oxford University Press.

Harm Reduction International, 2012. *Commanding general confidence? Human rights, international law and the INCB annual report for 2011*. Harm Reduction International, 12th March 2012. [Online]. Available at: http://www.ihra.net/files/2012/04/05/INCB_Briefing.pdf [Accessed 7th March 2019].

Hart, H.L.A., 1994. *The concept of law*, 2nd ed. Oxford: Oxford University Press.

Hathaway, A.D., 2001. Shortcomings of harm reduction: Toward a morally invested drug reform strategy. *International Journal of Drug Policy*, 12(2), 125–137.

Hay, C. and Lister, M., 2006. Introduction: Theories of the state. *In*: C. Hay, M. Lister and D. Marsh, eds. *The state: Theories and issues (political analysis)*. New York: Palgrave Macmillan.

Hayry, M., 2004. Prescribing cannabis: Freedom, autonomy, and values. *Journal of Medical Ethics*, 30(4), 333–336.

Heywood, A., 1992. *Political ideologies: An introduction*. London: Macmillan Press Ltd.

Hohfeld, W., 1919. *Fundamental legal conceptions as applied in judicial reasoning*. Ed. W. Cook. New Haven, CT: Yale University Press.

Holt, M. and Treloar, C., 2008. Pleasure and drugs. *The International Journal of Drug Policy*, 19(5), 349–424.

Hooghe, L. and Marks, G., 2001. *Multi-level governance and European integration*. Oxford: Rowman and Littlefield Publishers.

Hopgood, S., 2013. *The endtimes of human rights*. New York: Cornell University Press.

Horwitz, P., 2014. A troublesome right: The "law" in Dworkin's treatment of law and religion. *Boston University Law Review*, 94(4), 1225–1240.

Huber, M., André, J., Green, L., van der Horst, H., Jadad, A.R., Kromhout, D., Leonard, B., Lorig, K., Loureiro, M.I., van der Meer, J.W.M., Schnabel, P., Smith, R., van Weel, C. and Smid, H., 2011. How should we define health? *BMJ*, 343, d4163.

Hughes, C.E. and Stevens, A., 2010. What can we learn from the Portuguese decriminalisation of illicit drugs? *British Journal of Criminology*, 50(6), 999–1022.

Hughes, C.E. and Stevens, A., 2012. A resounding success or a disastrous failure: Re-examining the interpretation of evidence on the Portuguese decriminalisation of illicit drugs. *Drug and Alcohol Review*, 31(1), 101–113.

Hulsether, M., 2005. Religion and culture. *In*: J.R. Hinnels, ed. *The Routledge companion to the study of religion*. London: Routledge, 489–508.

Human Rights Watch, 2012. *Letter to the International Narcotics Control Board on capital punishment for drug offences*. [Online]. Available at: https://www.hrw.org/news/2012/03/12/letter-international-narcotics-control-board-capital-punishment-drug-offences [Accessed 20th June 2019].

Hunt, L., 2007. *Inventing human rights: A history*. London: W.W. Norton & Company.

Hunt, P., 2008. *Human rights, health and harm reduction states' amnesia and parallel universes.* London: International Harm Reduction Association. [Online]. Available at: http://www.ihra.net/files/2010/06/16/HumanRightsHealthAndHarmReduction.pdf [Accessed 25th October 2018].

Husak, D., 1992. *Drugs and rights.* New York: Cambridge University Press.

Husak, D. and de Marneffe, P., 2005. *The legalization of drugs (for and against).* New York: Cambridge University Press.

Hutson, J.H., 1991. The bill of rights and the American revolutionary experience. *In*: M.J. Lacey and K. Haakonssen, eds. *A culture of rights.* Cambridge: Cambridge University Press, 62–97.

Iakobishvili, E., 2011. *Inflicting harm: Judicial corporal punishment for drug and alcohol offences in selected countries.* London: International Harm Reduction Association.

Iakobishvili, E., 2012. *Cause for alarm: The incarceration of women for drug offences in Europe and Central Asia, and the need for legislative and sentencing reform.* London: International Harm Reduction Association.

Inglis, B., 1975. *The forbidden game: A social history of drugs.* New York: Scribner.

Ingold, J., 2018. Jeff Sessions' latest memo pushes prosecutors to seek the death penalty against big drug dealers. That could include legal marijuana business owners. *Denver Post.* [Online]. Available at: https://www.denverpost.com/2018/03/22/jeff-sessions-death-penalty-memo-drug-dealers-marijuana/ [Accessed 14th June 2019].

International Center for Ethnobotanical Education, Research and Service, 2019. *World Ayahuasca Conference 2019.* [Online]. Available at: https://www.ayaconference.com/ [Accessed 24th June 2019].

International Drug Policy Consortium, 2019. *Drug policy guide*, 3rd ed. [Online]. Available at: http://fileserver.idpc.net/library/IDPC-drug-policy-guide_3-edition_FINAL.pdf [Accessed 24th June 2019].

International Narcotics Control Board, n.d. *The International Narcotics Control Board.* [Online]. Available at: http://www.incb.org/incb/en/about.html [Accessed 1st April 2018].

Ishay, M., 2004. *The history of human rights: From ancient times to the globalization era.* London: University of California Press.

Jacobson, S., 2019. *Britain's first medicinal cannabis clinic opens in Greater Manchester.* [Online]. Available at: https://www.theguardian.com/society/2019/mar/09/britains-first-medicinal-cannabis-clinic-opens [Accessed 19th June 2019].

James, R.R., (ed.), 1974. *Winston S Churchill: His complete speeches 1897–1963.* New York: Chelsea House/Bowker.

James, W., 1961. *The varieties of religious experience.* New York: Collier Books.

Jay, Z., 2017. Keeping rights at home: British conceptions of rights and compliance with the European court of human rights. *The British Journal of Politics and International Relations,* 19(4), 842–860.

Jelsma, M., Boister, N., Bewley-Taylor, D., Walsh, J. and Fitzmaurice, M., 2018. *Balancing treaty stability and change: Inter se modification of the UN drug control conventions to facilitate cannabis regulation.* WOLA, TNI, GDPO. Policy Report 7, March 2018. [Online]. Available at: https://www.tni.org/files/publicationdownloads/balancing_treaty_stability_and_change.pdf [Accessed 21st June 2019].

Jessop, B., 2008. The state and state building. *In*: R.A.W. Rhodes, S.A. Binder and B.A. Rockman, eds. *The Oxford handbook of political institutions.* Oxford: Oxford University Press, 111–130.

Johansen, P.Ø. and Krebs, T.S., 2015. Psychedelics not linked to mental health problems or suicidal behavior: A population study. *Journal of Psychopharmacology*, 29(3), 270–279.

Jones, C., 2006. Cannabis as an alternative medicine. *Queens Health Sciences Journal*, 8(1), 29–33.

Kant, I., 1798/1978. *Anthropology from a pragmatic point of view*. Trans. V.L. Dowdell. Carbondale: Southern Illinois University Press.

Kerrigan, K., 2005. The council of Europe. *In*: R.K.M. Smith and C. van den Anker, eds. *The essentials of human rights*, 1st ed. London: Hodder Arnold, 69–72.

Klein, A. and Potter, G.R., 2018. The three betrayals of the medical cannabis growing activist: From multiple victimhood to reconstruction, redemption and activism. *International Journal of Drug Policy*, 53, 65–72.

Klein, A. and Stothard, B., 2016. Special issue: The regulation of pleasure. *Drugs and Alcohol Today*, 16(3), 181–184.

Labate, B.C., Cavnar, C. and Gearin, A.K., 2017. *The world ayahuasca diaspora: Reinventions and controversies*, 1st ed. London and New York: Routledge.

Labate, B.C. and Feeney, K., 2012. Ayahuasca and the process of regulation in Brazil and internationally. *International Journal of Drug Policy*, 23(2), 154–161.

Labate, B.C. and Jungaberle, H., 2011. *The internationalization of ayahuasca*. Berlin: Lit Verlag.

Labate, B.C. and MacRae, E., 2010. *Ayahuasca, ritual and religion in Brazil*. London: Equinox.

Lancaster K., 2014. Social construction and the evidence-based drug policy endeavour. *International Journal of Drug Policy*, 25(5), 948–951.

Lancaster, K., Ritter, A. and Diprose, R., 2018. Recasting participation in drug policy. *Contemporary Drug Problems*, 45(4), 351–365.

Lancaster, K., Seear, K., Treloar, C. and Ritter, A., 2017. The productive techniques and constitutive effects of 'evidence-based policy' and 'consumer participation' discourses in health policy processes. *Social Science & Medicine*, 176, 60–68.

Lander, D.R., 2014. Legalize spiritual discovery: The trials of Dr. Timothy Leary. *In*: B.C. Labate and C. Cavnar, eds. *Prohibition, religious freedom, and human rights: Regulating traditional drug use*. Berlin, Heidelberg: Springer-Verlag, 165–189.

Landman, T., 2013. Social magic and the temple of human rights: Critical reflections on Stephen Hopgood's endtimes of human rights. *In*: D. Lettinga and L. van Troost, eds. *Debating the endtimes of human rights activism and institutions in a neo-Westphalian world*. The Strategic Studies Project. Amnesty International Netherlands, 25–31. [Online]. Available at: https://eprints.soas.ac.uk/21546/1/debating_the_endtimes_of_human_rights.pdf [Accessed 19th June 2019].

Langlois, A.J., 2013. Normative and theoretical foundations of human rights. *In*: M. Goodhart, ed. *Human rights: Politics and practice*, 2nd ed. Oxford: Oxford University Press, 11–26.

Leary, T., 1983. Flashbacks: An autobiography. Los Angeles, CA: J.P. Tarcher, Inc.

Leary, T., 1990. *Flashbacks: A personal and cultural history of an era*. New York: G.P. Putman's Sons.

Lenton, S., 2014. New regulated markets for recreational cannabis: Public health or private profit? *Addiction*, 109, 354–355.

Levine, H.G., 2003. Global drug prohibition: Its uses and crises. *The International Journal of Drug Policy*, 14: 145–153.

Lines, R., 2017. *Drug control and human rights in international law*. Cambridge: Cambridge University Press.

Lister, M. and Marsh, D., 2006. Conclusion. *In*: C. Hay, M. Lister and D. Marsh, eds. *The state: Theories and issues (political analysis)*. New York: Palgrave Macmillan.

Locke, J., 1690/1952. *The second treatise of government*. Ed. T.P. Peardon. Indianapolis, IN: Bobbs-Merrill.

Lyness, S.M. and McCambridge, J., 2014. The alcohol industry, charities and policy influence in the UK. *European Journal of Public Health*, 24(4), 557–561.

Lyons, D., 1970. The correlativity of rights and duties. *Nous*, 4(1), 45–55.

MacCoun, R.J. and Reuter, P., 2001. *Drug war heresies: Learning from other vices, times and places*. Cambridge: Cambridge University Press.

MacCoun, R.J. and Reuter, P., 2011. Assessing drug prohibition: A guide for agnostics. *Annual Review for Law and Social Science*, 7, 61–78.

MacGregor, S., Singleton, N. and Trautmann, F., 2014. Towards good governance in drug policy: Evidence, stakeholders and politics. *International Journal of Drug Policy*, 25(5), 931–934.

MacKinnon, C., 1989. *Towards a feminist theory of the state*. Cambridge, MA: Harvard University Press.

Manderson, D., 1993. *From Mr Sin to Mr Big*. Melbourne: Oxford University Press.

Marks, A., 2019. Defining personal consumption in drug legislation and Spanish cannabis clubs. *International and Comparative Law Quarterly*, 68(1), 193–223.

Marks, S.P., 2013. The past and future of the separation of human rights into categories. *Maryland Journal of International Law*, 24(1), 209–243.

Martin, L.H., 2005. Religion and cognition. *In*: J.R. Hinnels, ed. *The Routledge companion to the study of religion*. London: Routledge, 473–488.

McAllister, W.B., 2000. *Drug diplomacy in the twentieth century: An international history*. London: Routledge.

McAllister, W.B., 2012. *Reflections on a century of international drug control*. LSE Ideas: Governing the Global Drug Wars (Special Report). [Online]. Available at: http://www2.lse.ac.uk/IDEAS/publications/reports/pdf/SR014/McAllister_William.pdf [Accessed 27th January 2017].

McCambridge, J., 2012. Dealing responsibly with the alcohol industry in London. *Alcohol and Alcoholism*, 47(6), 635–637.

McCoy, A.W., 1980. *Drug traffic: Narcotics and organized crime in Australia*. Sydney: Harper and Row.

McGarry, J., 2011. Effecting legal certainty under the Human Rights Act. *Judicial Review*, 16(1), 66–71.

McKenna, T., 1992. *Food of the gods: A radical history of plants drugs and human evolution*. New York: Bantam Books.

Mhango, M.O., 2008. The constitutional protection of minority religious rights in Malawi: The case of Rastafari students. *Journal of African Law*, 52(2), 218–244.

Mialon, M. and McCambridge, J., 2018 Alcohol industry corporate social responsibility initiatives and harmful drinking: A systematic review. *European Journal of Public Health*, 28(4), 664–673.

Mill, J.S., 1859/2001. *On liberty*. Kitchener: Batoche Books.

Miller, D. and Harkins, C., 2010. Corporate strategy, corporate capture: Food and alcohol industry lobbying and public health. *Critical Social Policy*, 30(4), 564–589.

Moore, D., 2007. Erasing pleasure from public discourse on illicit drugs: On the creation and reproduction of an absence. *International Journal of Drug Policy*, 19(5), 353–358.

Morris, C.W., 2011. The state. *In*: G. Klosko, ed. *The Oxford handbook of the history of political philosophy*. Oxford: Oxford University Press, 544–561.

Moyn, S., 2012. The last utopia: Human rights in history. Cambridge, MA: Harvard University Press.

Műller, M. and Fausböll, V., 1881. *The dhammapada and sutta nipata*. Sacred Books of the East, vol. 10 [Online]. Available at: http://www.sacred-texts.com/bud/sbe10/sbe1003.htm (Accessed 4th January 2018).

Mungroo, P., Ping, Y. and Bone, M., 2014. *Cannabis regulation: The world is moving forward, what is stopping us?* London Cannabis Conference. London: The House of Lords [Online]. Available at:http://www.cannabisresearch.co.uk/sites/default/files/Cannabis%20conference%20report%202014%20London.pdf [Accessed 3rd May 2018].

National Health Service, 2018. *Medical cannabis (and cannabis oils)*. [Online]. Available at: https://www.nhs.uk/conditions/medical-cannabis/ [Accessed 19th June 2019].

Newdick, C., 2005. *Who should we treat? Rights, rationing and resources in the NHS*, 2nd ed. Oxford: Oxford University Press.

Nichols, T., 2017. *The death of expertise: The campaign against established knowledge and why it matters*. Oxford: Oxford University Press.

Nickel, J., 2010. Human rights. *The Stanford Encyclopedia of Philosophy*. Available at: http://plato.stanford.edu/archives/spr2012/entries/rights-human/ [Accessed 1st April 2019].

Nikogosian, H. and Kickbusch, I., 2016. The legal strength of international health instruments: What it brings to global health governance? *International Journal of Health Policy and Management*, 5(12), 683–685.

Nixon, R., 1971. *President Nixon declares drug abuse "public enemy number one"*. Richard Nixon Foundation. [Online]. Available at: https://www.nixonfoundation.org/2016/06/26404/ [Accessed 24th May 2019].

Nonhuman Rights Project, 2019. *Our objectives*. [Online]. Available at: https://www.nonhumanrights.org/who-we-are/ [Accessed 14th April 2019].

Nowak, M., 2005. The international covenants on civil and political rights and on economic, social and cultural rights. *In*: R.K.M. Smith and C. van den Anker, eds. *The essentials of human rights*, 1st ed. London: Hodder Arnold, 193–195.

Nutt, D., 2009. *Estimating drug harms: A risky business?* Centre for Crime and Justice Studies. Briefing 10th October 2009. [Online]. Available at: http://www.crimeandjustice.org.uk/opus1714/Estimating_drug_harms.pdf [Accessed 15th April 2017).

Nutt, D., 2012. *Drugs without the hot air: Minimising the harms of legal and illegal drugs*. Cambridge: UIT Cambridge.

Nutt, D., King, L., Saulsbury, W. and Blakemore, C., 2007. Development of a rational scale to assess the harm of drugs of potential misuse. *The Lancet*, 369(9566): 1047–1053.

O'Brien, D., 2001. Rastafarianism and the law. *New Law Journal*, 151, 509–510.

O'Brien, D. and Carter, V., 2002–2003. Chant down Babylon: Freedom of religion and the Rastafarian challenge to majoritarianism. *Journal of Law and Religion*, 18(1), 219–248.

O'Cinneide, C., 2017. Rights under pressure. *European Human Rights Law Review*, 1, 43–48. [Online]. Available at: http://discovery.ucl.ac.uk/1542510/1/O%27Cinneide_final%20draft%20Rights%20Under%20Pressure.pdf [Accessed 18th June 2019].

Office of National Drug Control Policy, 1989. *National Drug Control Strategy*. [Online]. Available at: https://www.ncjrs.gov/pdffiles1/ondcp/119466.pdf [Accessed 28th March 2019].

Office of the United Nations High Commissioner for Human Rights (OHCHR), n.d.a. *Human Rights Committee: Membership*. [Online] Available at: https://www.ohchr.org/EN/HRBodies/CCPR/Pages/Membership.aspx [Accessed 18th June 2019].

Office of the United Nations High Commissioner for Human Rights (OHCHR), n.d.b. *Universal human rights instruments*. [Online] Available at: https://www.ohchr.org/EN/ProfessionalInterest/Pages/UniversalHumanRightsInstruments.aspx [Accessed 18th June 2019].

O'Neill, O., 1996. *Toward justice and virtue: A constructive account of practical reasoning*. Cambridge: Cambridge University Press.

Oxford Dictionaries, 2019. *Entheogen*. [Online]. Available at: https://www.lexico.com/en/definition/entheogen [Accessed 23rd June 2019].

Parekh, B., 2005. Pluralist universalism and human rights. *In*: R.K.M. Smith and C. van den Anker, eds. *The essentials of human rights*. London: Hodder Arnold.

Parekh, B., 2006. *Rethinking multiculturalism: Cultural diversity and political theory*, 2nd ed. Hampshire: Macmillan Publishers.

Patients4NHS, 2018. *Turning the NHS into a market*. [Online]. Available at: http://www.patients4nhs.org.uk/marketisation-of-the-nhs/ [Accessed 22nd May 2019].

Peplow, A., 2017. *Withdrawal from the ECHR after Miller – A matter of prerogative?* UK Constitutional Law Association. [Online]. Available at: https://ukconstitutionallaw.org/2017/02/28/alex-peplow-withdrawal-from-the-echr-after-miller-a-matter-of-prerogative/ [Accessed 19th June 2019].

Perry, M.J., 1998. *The idea of human rights: Four inquiries*. New York: Oxford University Press.

Pogge, T., 2000. The international significance of human rights. *Journal of Ethics*, 4(1–2), 45–69.

Police Foundation, 2000. *Drugs and the law: Report of the inquiry into the Misuse of Drugs Act 1971*. London: Police Foundation.

Potter, G. and Chatwin, C., 2018. Not particularly special: Critiquing 'NPS' as a category of drugs. *Drugs: Education, Prevention and Policy*, 29(4), 329–336.

Poulter, S., 1998. *Ethnicity, law and human rights*. Oxford: Oxford University Press.

Public Health England, n.d. *Campaign Resource Centre*. [Online]. Available at: https://campaignresources.phe.gov.uk/resources/campaigns [Accessed 22nd May 2019].

Purfendorf, S., 1673/1991. *On the duty of man and citizen* [*De Officio Hominis et Civis*]. Ed. J. Tully and Trans. M. Silverthorne. Cambridge: Cambridge University Press.

Puska, P., 2018. WHO FCTC as a pioneering and learning instrument comment on "The legal strength of international health instruments: What it brings to global health governance?" *International Journal of Health Policy and Management*, 7(1), 75–77.

Raz, J., 2010. Human rights without foundations. *In*: S. Besson and J. Tasioulas, eds. *The philosophy of international law*. Oxford: Oxford University Press.

Rehman, J., 2010. *International human rights law*, 2nd ed. Dorset: Pearson Education Ltd.

Release and Transform, 2015. *Parliamentary briefing: Psychoactive Substances Bill*, 2nd reading House of Lords. 9th June 2015. [Online]. Available at: https://www.release.org.uk/sites/default/files/pdf/publications/Psychoactive%20Substances%20Bill%20Lords%20Briefing%202nd%20Reading%20%28new%29.pdf [Accessed 22nd March 2019].

Reuter, P. and Pardo, B., 2017. New psychoactive substances: Are there any good options for regulating new psychoactive substances? *International Journal of Drug Policy*, 40(1), 117–122.

Richards, D., 1986. *Sex, drugs, death and the law: An essay on over-criminalisation*. Lanham, MD: Rowman and Littlefield Publishers.

Ritter, A., Lancaster, K. and Diprose, R., 2018. Improving drug policy: The potential of broader democratic participation. *International Journal of Drug Policy*, 55(1), 1–7.

Roberts, M., 2014. Making drug policy together: Reflections on evidence, engagement and participation. *International Journal of Drug Policy*, 25(5), 952–958.

Robinson, E.H., 2013. The distinction between state and government. *Geography Compass*, 7(8), 556–566.

Rolles, S., 2009a. *After the war on drugs: Blueprint for regulation*. Bristol: Transform Drug Policy Foundation.

Rolles, S., 2009b. *A comparison of the cost-effectiveness of prohibition and regulation of drugs*. Transform Drug Policy Foundation. [Online]. Available at: https://transformdrugs.org/wp-content/uploads/2018/10/Cost-Effectiveness.pdf [Accessed 14th June 2019].

Rolles, S., 2017. *NoNonsense legalizing drugs: The key to ending the war*. Oxford: New Internationalist Publications.

Rolles, S., Murkin, G., Powell, M., Kushlick, D., Saunter, N. and Slater, J., 2016. *The Alternative World Drug Report*, 2nd ed. Transform Drug Policy Foundation. Count the Costs. [Online]. Available at: https://transformdrugs.org/wp-content/uploads/2018/10/AWDR-2nd-edition.pdf [Accessed 24th June 2019].

Room, R., 2006. International control of alcohol: Alternative paths forward. *Drug and Alcohol Review*, 25(6), 581–595.

Room, R., 2013. Healthy is as healthy does: Where will a voluntary code get us on international alcohol control? *Addiction*, 108(3), 456–457.

Rorty, R., 1999. Human rights, rationality and sentimentality. *In*: The Belgrade Circle, ed. *The politics of human rights*. London: Verso, 67–83.

Rose, N., 2003. Neurochemical selves. *Society*, 41(1), 46–59.

Rose, N. and Miller, P., 1992. Political power beyond the state: Problematics of government. *The British Journal of Sociology*, 43(2), 173–205.

The Royal College of Physicians, 2018. *Recommendations on cannabis-based products for medicinal use (31 October 2018)*. [Online]. Available at: https://www.rcplondon.ac.uk/projects/outputs/recommendations-cannabis-based-products-medicinal-use [Accessed 13th May 2019].

Ruggiero, V., 1999. Drugs as a password and the law as a drug: Discussing the legalisation of illicit substances. *In*: N. South, ed. *Drugs: Cultures, controls and everyday life*. London: SAGE Publications, 123–129.

Sandberg, R., 2011. Judging religious drug use: The misuse of the definition of religion. *In*: B.C. Labate and H. Jungaberle, eds. *The internationalization of ayahuasca*. Zurich: LIT VERLAG, 389–401.

Sangiuliano, A.R., 2014. Towards a natural law foundationalist theory of universal human rights. *Transnational Legal Theory*, 5(2), 218–240.

Saunders, (2007) Narcotic. Dorland's Medical Dictionary for Health Consumers. *The Free Dictionary*. [Online]. Available at: http://medical-dictionary.thefreedictionary.com/narcotic [Accessed 10 April 2018].

Scott, S.V., 1994. International law as ideology: Theorizing the relationship between international law and international politics. *European Journal of International Law*, 5(3), 313–325.

Seddon, T., 2010. Let's not talk about drugs. *Drugs and Alcohol Today*, 10(3), 21–23.

Seddon, T., 2013. Regulating global drug problems. RegNet Research Paper No. 2013/6: 1–30.

Seddon, T., 2016. Inventing drugs: A genealogy of a regulatory concept. *Journal of Law and Society*, 43(3), 393–415.

Sen, A., 2004. Health achievement and equity: External and internal perspectives. *In*: S. Anand, F. Peter and A. Sen, eds. *Public health, ethics and equity*. Oxford: Oxford University Press.

Sessa, B., 2017. *The psychedelic renaissance: Reassessing the role of psychedelic drugs in 21st century psychiatry and society*, 2nd ed. London: Muswell Hill Press.

Sessa, B., 2018. The 21st century psychedelic renaissance: Heroic steps forward on the back of an elephant. *Psychopharmacology*, 235(2), 551–560.

Shiner, M., 2009. *Drug use and social change: The distortion of history*. Basingstoke: Palgrave Macmillan.

Shweder, R.A., 1990. In defense of moral realism: Reply to Gabennesch. *Child Development*, 61(6), 2060–2067.

Shweder, R.A., Much, N.C., Mahapatra, M. and Park, L., 1997. The "big three" of morality (autonomy, community, and divinity), and the "big three" explanations of suffering. *In*: A. Brandt and P. Rozin, eds. *Morality and health*. New York: Routledge, 119–169.

Siegel, R.K., 2005. *Intoxication: The universal drive for mind-altering substances*. Rochester, VT: Park Street Press.

Slack, J., 2015. *It's your human right to take drugs: Junkies could use privacy law to avoid jail say MPs*. [Online]. The Daily Mail. Available at: http://www.dailymail.co.uk/news/article-3202864/It-s-human-right-drugs-Junkies-use-privacy-law-avoid-jail-say-MPs.html [Accessed 18th August 2017 and 29th April 2019].

Smail, D.L., 2008. *On deep history and the brain*. London: University of California Press.

Steiner, H., 1994. *An essay on rights*. Oxford: Blackwell.

Steiner, H.J., Alston, P. and Goodman, R., 2008. *International human rights in context: Law politics and morals*, 3rd ed. Oxford: Oxford University Press.

Stevens, A., 2017. Principles, pragmatism and prohibition: Explaining continuity and change in British drug policy. *In*: A. Liebling, S. Maruna and L. McAra, eds. *The Oxford handbook of criminology*, 6th ed. Oxford: Oxford University Press, 825–846.

Stevens, A. and Zampini, G.F., 2018. Drug policy constellations: A Habermasian approach for understanding English drug policy. *International Journal of Drug Policy*, 57, 61–71.

Stewart, H., 2010. The limits of the harm principle. *Criminal Law and Philosophy*, 4(1), 17–35.

Suiter, J., 2018. Deliberation in action – Ireland's abortion referendum. *Political Insight*, 9(3), 30–32.

Supiot, A., 2007. *Homo juridicus: On the anthropological function of the law*. London: Verso.

Sumnall, H., 2017. *The laughing gas verdicts represent a failure of Britain's drug policy*. The Guardian, 1st September 2017. [Online]. Available at: https://www.theguardian.com/commentisfree/2017/sep/01/laughing-gas-verdicts-britain-drug-policy-nitrous-oxide-harmful-drugs [Accessed 20th June 2019].

Szasz, T., 1987. *Insanity: The idea and its consequences.* New York: Riley.

Szasz, T., 1992. *Our right to drugs: The case for a free market.* New York: Praeger.

Szasz, T., 2003. *Ceremonial chemistry: The ritual persecution of drugs, addicts and pushers.* New York: Syracuse University Press.

Takahashi, S., 2016. *Human rights and drug control: The false dichotomy.* Portland, OR: Hart Publishing.

Taylor, A.L. and Dhillon, I.S., 2013. An international legal strategy for alcohol control: Not a framework convention – At least not yet. *Addiction*, 108(3), 450–455.

Taylor, S., Buchanan, J. and Ayres, T., 2016. Prohibition, privilege and the drug apartheid: The failure of drug policy reform to address the underlying fallacies of drug prohibition. *Criminology and Criminal Justice*, 16(4), 452–469.

Tobin, J., 2012. *The right to health in international law.* Oxford: Oxford University Press.

Toebes, B., 1999. *The right to health as a human right in international law.* Oxford: Intersentia.

Tomlinson, J., 1991. *Cultural imperialism: A critical introduction.* Baltimore, MD: Johns Hopkins Press.

Transform Drug Policy Foundation, 2012. *The war on drugs: Undermining human rights. Count the costs: 50 years of the war on drugs.* [Online]. Available at: http://www.countthecosts.org/sites/default/files/Human_rights_briefing.pdf (Accessed 15th October 2018).

Transform Drug Policy Foundation, 2013. *Drug legalisation omnibus survey for Transform Drug Policy Foundation.* IPOS MORI. [Online]. Available at: https://www.ipsos.com/sites/default/files/migrations/enuk/files/Assets/Docs/Polls/SRI_Transform_poll_drugs.pdf [Accessed 21st June 2019].

Tsakyrakis, S., 2009. Proportionality: An assault on human rights? *International Journal of Constitutional Law*, 7(3), 468–493.

Tupper, K.W., 2002. Entheogens and existential intelligence: The use of plant teachers as cognitive tools. *Canadian Journal of Education*, 27(4), 499–516.

Tupper, K.W., 2008. The globalization of ayahuasca: Harm reduction or benefit maximisation? *International Journal of Drug Policy*, 19(4), 297–303.

Tupper, K.W., 2012. Psychoactive substances and the English language: "drugs," discourses, and public policy (beyond the buzzword: Problematising "drugs"). *Contemporary Drug Problems*, 39(3), 461.

Tupper, K.W. and Labate, B.C., 2012. Plants, psychoactive substances and the international narcotics control board: The control of nature and the nature of control. *International Centre on Human Rights and Drug Policy*, 2(1), 17–28.

United Nations Aids, 2014. *The gap report 2014: People who inject drugs.* [Online]. Available at: https://www.unaids.org/sites/default/files/media_asset/05_Peoplewhoinjectdrugs.pdf [Accessed 20th May 2019].

United Nations Office on Drugs and Crime, 2019a. *Commission on narcotic drugs.* [Online]. Available at: https://www.unodc.org/unodc/en/commissions/CND/index.html [Accessed 20th June 2019].

United Nations Office on Drugs and Crime, 2019b. *About UNODC.* [Online]. Available at: https://www.unodc.org/unodc/en/about-unodc/index.html?ref=menutop [Accessed 20th June 2019].

United Nations Treaty Collection, 2015a. *International covenant on civil and political rights.* [Online]. Available at: http://treaties.un.org/Pages/ViewDetails.aspx?src=TREATY&mtdsg_no=IV-4&chapter=4&lang=en [Accessed 18th June 2019].

United Nations Treaty Collection, 2015b. *Optional protocol to the international covenant on civil and political rights.* [Online]. Available at: http://treaties.un.org/Pages/ViewDetails.aspx?src=TREATY&mtdsg_no=IV-5&chapter=4&lang=en [Accessed 18th June 2019].

United Nations Treaty Collection, 2015c. *Optional protocol to the international covenant on economic, social and cultural rights*. [Online]. Available at: https://treaties.un.org/pages/viewdetails.aspx?src=ind&mtdsg_no=iv-3-a&chapter=4&lang=en> [Accessed 18th June 2019].

United Nations Treaty Collection, 2015d. *International covenant on economic, social and cultural rights*. [Online]. Available at: http://treaties.un.org/Pages/ViewDetails.aspx?src=TREATY&mtdsg_no=IV-3&chapter=4&lang=en [Accessed 18th June 2019].

United Nations Treaty Collection, 2015e. *Chapter IV: Human rights*. [Online]. Available at: http://treaties.un.org/Pages/Treaties.aspx?id=4&subid=A&lang=en> [Accessed 18th June 2019].

United Nations Treaty Collection, 2015f. *Single convention on narcotic drugs*. [Online]. Available at: http://treaties.un.org/Pages/ViewDetails.aspx?src=IND&mtdsg_no=VI-15&chapter=6&lang=en [Accessed 18th June 2019].

United Nations Treaty Collection, 2015g. *Convention on psychotropic substances*. [Online]. Available at: http://treaties.un.org/Pages/ViewDetails.aspx?src=TREATY&mtdsg_no=VI-16&chapter=6&lang=en [Accessed 18th June 2019].

United Nations Treaty Collection, 2015h. *United Nations convention against illicit traffic in narcotic drugs and psychotropic substances*. [Online]. Available at: https://treaties.un.org/Pages/ViewDetails.aspx?src=TREATY&mtdsg_no=VI-19&chapter=6&clang=_en [Accessed 18th June 2019].

Van Ree, E., 1999. Drugs as a human right. *The International Journal of Drug Policy*, 10(2), 89–98.

Waldron, J., 1996. *Law and disagreement*. Oxford: Oxford University Press.

Waldron, J., 2009. Judges as moral reasoners. *International Journal of Constitutional Law*, 7(1), 2–24.

Waldstein, A., 2010. Menace or Medicine? Anthropological perspectives on the self-administration of high potency cannabis in the UK. *Drugs and Alcohol Today*, 10(3), 37–43.

Walsh, C., 2010. Drugs and human rights: Private palliatives, sacramental freedoms and cognitive liberty. *The International Journal of Human Rights*, 14(3), 425–441.

Walsh, C., 2011. Drugs, the internet and change. *Journal of Psychoactive Drugs*, 43(1), 55–63.

Walsh, C., 2014. Beyond religious freedom: Psychedelics and cognitive liberty. *In*: B.C. Labate and C. Cavnar, eds. *Prohibition, religious freedom, and human rights: Regulating traditional drug use*. Berlin, Heidelberg: Springer-Verlag, 211–235.

Walsh, C., 2015. Plant psychedelics in the English courts: Legal uncertainty, guinea pigs and 'dog law'. *In*: H. Ellens and T.B. Roberts, eds. *The psychedelic policy quagmire: Health, law, freedom, and society*, Santa Barbara, CA: Praeger, 299–316.

Walsh, C., 2017a. Caught in the crossfire: Plant medicines and the Psychoactive Substances Act 2016. *Journal of Psychedelic Studies*, 1(2), 41–49.

Walsh, C., 2017b. Ayahuasca in the English courts: Legal entanglements with the jungle vine. *In*: B. Labate, C. Cavnar and A.K. Gearin, eds. *The world ayahuasca diaspora: Reinventions and controversies*. London, New York: Routledge.

Weber, M., 1946. Politics as a vocation. *In*: H.H. Gerth and C. Wright Mills, Trans. and eds. *From Max Weber: Essays in sociology*. Oxford: Oxford University Press, 77–128.

Weil, A., 1983. No bad drugs: The Newservice interview with Andrew Weil. *In*: J. Parker and C. Dye, eds. *Newservice (May–June 1983: 22–31)*. [Online]. Available at: http://www.doitnow.org/pages/weil.html [Accessed 14 January 2018].

Weil, A. and Rosen, W., 1983. *Chocolate to morphine: Understanding mind active drugs.* New York: Houghton-Mifflin Company.

Wenar, L., 2011. Rights. *The Stanford Encyclopedia of Philosophy.* [Online]. Available at: http://plato.stanford.edu/archives/spr2012/entries/rights/ [Accessed 23rd May 2019].

Werb, D., Kerr, T., Bohdan, N., Strathdee, S., Montaner, J. and Wood, E., 2013. The temporal relationship between drug supply indicators: An audit of international government surveillance systems. *BMJ Open*, 3(9), e003077.

Wicks, E., 2007. *Human rights and healthcare.* Portland, OR: Hart Publishing.

Wicks, E., 2014. *Dying with conscience: The potential application of Article 9 ECHR to assisted dying (November 7, 2014).* University of Leicester School of Law Research Paper No. 14-26. [Online]. Available at SSRN: https://ssrn.com/abstract=2520485 [Accessed 14th May 2019].

Wicks, E., Ziegler, K.S. and Hodson, L., 2015. *The UK and European human rights: A strained relationship?* Oxford: Hart Publishing.

Wilson, J.Q., 1995. *On character: Essays by James Q. Wilson.* Washington, DC: American Enterprise Institute.

Wright, A.M., 2007. Dude, which religion do I have to join to get some drugs? How the Supreme Court got it wrong in *Gonzales v. O Centro Espirita Beneficiente Uniao Do Vegetal*, 546 U.S. 418 (2006). *Nebraska Law Review*, 86(4), 987–1006.

Zeigler, D., 2013. On delaying a framework convention on alcohol control: Regrettably agreeing but calling for strategic action to accelerate the process. *Addiction*, 108(3), 457–459.

Index

www.ingramcontent.com/pod-product-compliance
Ingram Content Group UK Ltd.
Pitfield, Milton Keynes, MK11 3LW, UK
UKHW011004180926
475701UK00004B/553

9781032087177